DISREMEMBERING THE DICTATORSHIP

The Politics of Memory in the Spanish Transition to Democracy

J Lubani P65 et seq

P67   oppressive silence

P52   Unamuno

P71   Fugitive / apparition

P72   Fugitive — no articulated past

P77   Renuscitate — Frankenstein

Portada Hispánica

8

Rodopi

Amsterdam - Atlanta, GA 2000

DISREMEMBERING THE DICTATORSHIP

The Politics of Memory in the Spanish Transition to Democracy

Edited by

Joan Ramon Resina

Cover illustration: 'El 14 de abril en las Ramblas' by Julio Borrell

Cover design: Peggy Vogel

The paper on which this book is printed meets the requirements of "ISO 9706:1994, Information and documentation - Paper for documents - Requirements for permanence".

ISBN: 90-420-1352-4
Transferred to digital printing 2003
Printed in The Netherlands

To Christina Dupláa
in memoriam

Contents

Introduction

Joan Ramon Resina

It is often said that the current interest in memory goes back to the nineteen-eighties, a decade that saw an increased attention to national identities and the disappearance of the generation that had experienced the dramatic mid-century events, most notably the survivors of extermination camps (Ginzburg 353). Since that decade, concern with memories of all kinds has been mounting: with places of memory, monuments, landscape, traumatic experiences, holocaust revisonism and counter-revisionism, museum politics, and even the emergence of a new "social science," Hauntology, whose theoretical foundation has been bolstered by as illustrious a philosophical contribution as Derrida's *Specters of Marx*. It may be worth noting, however, that the appeal of memory was already strong in the seventies. That decade saw renewed interest in Maurice Halbwachs's important work, *Les Cadres sociaux de la mémoire* (1925), a book which, as Carlo Ginzburg noticed, started to claim attention only after its author had died at Auschwitz in 1944 (Ginzburg 353). Under the impact of the events of May '68 and, more decisively, of the anti-colonial struggles and the resurfacing of supressed national concerns among subjugated European peoples on both sides of the Iron Curtain, social thinkers and literary authors busied themselves with the present's relation to the past—a past that was then beginning to look problematic after the sea change of the Cold War and the full blast of consummerist capitalism.

Theoretical stirrings of a preoccupation with the past can be found in the poststructuralist phase of Roland Barthes, in essays like "Le discours de l'histoire" (1967), which anticipates a finer, subtler work like *Camera Lucida* (1980), an essay devoted to the visible yet immaterial traces of that which has been and to the effects of those traces on the contemplator's emotions. Implicitly, Barthes was writing about the phantasm (Greek for image or appearance). The language he employs in this essay is deliberately suited to the relation between a body's technological epiphany and the unnatural atmosphere in which it appears, an atmosphere in which live bodies cannot breathe. Speaking of Avedon's photograph of Philip Randolph, he writes:

> Thus the air is the luminous shadow which accompanies the body; and if the photograph fails to show this air, then the body moves without a shadow, and once this shadow is severed, as in the myth of the Woman without a Shadow, there remains no more than a sterile body. (110)

Barthes trenchantly defined the viewer's relation to photography as one might describe the subject's relation to memory: as intentionality without a clearly defined object; perhaps without any object at all. "One might say that the Photograph separates attention from perception, and yields up only the former, even if it is impossible without the latter; this is the aberrant thing, *noesis* without *noeme*, an action of thought without thought, an aim without a target" (111). "Aberrant" is the right word. The ghost is deviant, for it is devious; it "errs" or strays because it disorients others. What is the sense of its mute interpellation, that looking without seeing about which Barthes would wax so eloquent? How is one to catch this pure appearance and hold it down, like Odysseus held Protheus, in order to extract the truth? Can it know *for us* then, if its gaze is turned towards that which is not us? This is for Barthes the photograph's paradoxical effect:

> It accomplishes the unheard-of identification of reality ("*that-has-been*") with truth ("there-she-is"); it becomes at once evidential and exclamative; it bears the effigy to that crazy point where affect (love, compassion, grief, enthusiasm, desire) is a guarantee of Being. (113)

Characteristically, Barthes put his finger on sensitive areas of intelligence. Is not the current concern with memory, whether in relation to traumatic experience or to the subject's potential identifications—ethnic, cultural, national, gender, or sexual—, largely a concern with rescuing Being from the ocean of fluctuating abstractions in which late modernity submerged it? Does not the concern with the trace verge on that hallucinating craziness which a critic of the national imaginary as unsympathetic as Jon Juaristi denounces as a political pathology? At the same time, is not the ghost, that residue of the past in the emotions of the living, the only guarantee, in a world of simulacra and media-powered discourses, that something has actually been and that it is still soldered to Being, *our* being? There is no evading this evidence: whether dreamed or suffered, the past is the stuff we are made of. History, for Marx, was a nightmare weighing heavily upon the living. And he too knew about specters. He could announce a new specter haunting Europe, the specter of Communism, only insofar as Communism was visited by the nightmare of millennial exploitation and suffering. Marxism is not a serenely contemplative philosophy of history but one haunted by the cries and whispers of bloodless and nameless figures. Resonating in the rarefied medium of the past, those voices clamor for a justice that will always come too late for them—too late and yet also too soon, for the end of history is expected to lay all the ghosts to rest. In that way history will twice make casualties of its uncelebrated agents, first as victims and then as definitively disremembered anachronisms. Until that second coming, though, specters will not let up. They will continue to importune the remorseful memory of the living, asking for the arrears of an ever-outstanding debt.

If the endurance of the grief of history as lived in each agent's particularity—social class, ethnic or racial others, women, oppressed national groups—is evidence of a melancholy disposition, of incapacity to renounce a bygone world, it is also clear proof that affect has survived the strictures of bourgeois abstraction and has returned to haunt the ruined spaces of our technologized postmodern fantasy. Specters can radicalize the present, whose roots they are. It was their demands on an affect-blind and sense-blocking modernity that Foucault, at the beginning of the seventies, sought to incorporate into critical discourse. He asked for a "philosophy of the phantasm" to facilitate the reappearance of realities that called into question the cozy categories of modern thought: body, state, reason, image, inside and outside, the imaginary. He urged that "Phantasms must be allowed to function at the limit of bodies; against bodies, because they stick to bodies and protrude from them, but also because they touch them, cut them, break them into sections, regionalize them, and multiply their surfaces" (169). Furthermore: "Phantasms do not extend organisms into an imaginary domain; they topologize the materiality of the body. They should consequently be freed from the dilemmas of truth and falsehood and of being and non-being" (170).

3

A hypostatization of memory, the phantasm is an imageless presence (one recognizes ghosts by their lack of reflection in a mirror) and in that sense the opposite of Barthes's photographic icon, with its identification of the "*has-been*" with truth ("there-it-is"). Ghosts, like the memories they stand for, are beyond the ontological realm and, in that respect, beyond empirical skirmishes, beyond proof or disproof outside their own affect-effect. To say that they are unreal, in the sense that they are not or were not, is irrelevant; to predicate anything about them is already to avow their aporetic presence. What seems fundamental, however, and I would hazard that this alone is the reason so much attention is vested in them, is their action on bodies, what Foucault calls their topologization. By this he means that the phantasm calls into question the organicist notion of body, the ideology of its unitary nature, its ontology. It is not so much that the body has contributed to metaphorize the structures of power, giving rise to organicist conceptions of the polity, but that the opposite seems more likely: the most extreme form of weakness—and it is above all in its weakness that the body is experienced and known intimately—received its unitary seal from power's perennial passion for unification and subordination. Power—whose metaphysics Foucault obstinately denied—, not the body, constitutes the primary and most fertile source of totalizations. A body totalized is a subjected body, the body as subject. Conversely, a body topologized, regionalized, deconstructed into surfaces and competing factions/functions is a body left to itself: incomprehensible, experience-driven, autonomous. Such a body has no imaginary counterpart, not even Plato's black stallion, for that emblem of passion is already harnessed to a political symbolism. Its brisk lunge is part of a unitary conception governed by the classic paraphernalia of statesmanship: the chariot and its self-possessed charioteer.

Platonism was in fact uppermost in Foucault's mind when he proposed a theory of ghosts; and rightly so, for Platonism is itself a theory of simulacra embedded in a theory of anamnesia. The idea, let us recall, was the *real* phantasmatized and forgotten. To know was to remember, and this meant that reality was heuristically, not empirically demonstrable. Reality is a vapor of memories, but in an ironical turn (the famous Socratic irony) those memories are everything but undecidable. In the shady world of phenomena, they are the only things endowed with certainty. Even if Foucault was interested in the incorporeal, in that which advances between surfaces and cannot be "incorporated" in the image, he turned away from the metaphysical foundation of mimesis, spurning the theory of representation. The question follows automatically: In the absence of aura, of originality, can memory still be the cognitive warrant of truth? Not for Foucault. He calls for the severance of the classic connection between primordial memory (or appearance) and essence, between image and ontology, seeking to reentitle the event and to divest singularity of the transparency of the universals, those idols of the mind. "To pervert Platonism," he says,

> is to search out the smallest details, to descend [...] as far as its crop of hair or the dirt under its fingernails—those things that were never hallowed by an idea; it is to discover its initial decentering in order to recenter itself around the Model, the Identical, and the Same; it is the decentering of oneself with respect to Platonism so as to give rise to the play (as with every perversion) of surfaces at its border. (168)

Self-decentering with respect to a cognitive model that yields recognition of the perennially same; identifying the model's original bias by which it centered itself and gave rise to the illusion of universality; descending to the neglected detail, the trifling, and the parochial, as excluded surfaces jarring the model's smooth border: these are necessary conditions for a critical theory of ghosts. They are equally requirements for a critical approach to the politics of memory, and not least that of the Spanish Transition. There is scarcely a story more mythologized by the intellectual clerisy than the story of the Transition. Francoist myths pale by comparison with this story's success not only among those most interested in its viability—the national and international political and economic elites—but also among the literatti, scholars, and large segments of the media-consuming population. To question this myth, to pervert its tidy Platonic paradigm, is to place oneself at an odd angle with respect to its axis; to become ex-centric with respect to its truth. It is not sufficient to discover in it a simulacrum, for simulacra refer to ideas; they imply a model and thus a center reconstructed around an ever more abstract principle, like those master narratives allegedly fallen into disrepute in the postmodern era. A simulacrum cannot be merely denounced, for that implies that one is in possession of a sounder paradigm of truth, of a more irreducible ontology. Nor can it be debunked by reference to its model: how is one to tell between the two? How, for example, can one decide between the "false" idea of Spain promoted by Francoism and the "true" (or at any rate, legitimate) idea of it reestablished by the Transition? The answer to this question, some may suggest, is quite easy: by calling upon certain privileged witnesses: documents, the historical record, living survivors of the pre-Francoist era; in short, by appealing to memory. Yet memory is precisely what is in question. This most brittle, unstable, undemonstrable reality possible: the very opposite of Platonic certainty.

The problem of a world invaded by simulacra of human manufacture is the subject of a postmodern cult film, *Blade Runner*. In an unrecognizable Los Angeles of the twenty-first century, somewhat reminiscent of Fritz Lang's Metropolis—itself inspired by New York's 1920s skyline—, one of the last representatives of the Anglo-American Lone Ranger breed of the previous century takes on the task of killing, or in the new police jargon, "retiring," Earth-invading creatures. No longer mechanical, like Rotwang's robot, Maria, in Lang's classic, but a mixture of genetic engineering and technological design, these humanoids are much improved generations of synthetic life. Like Maria, they have been designed to solve the eternal problem of labor; but unlike the workers of Metropolis, they are not consigned to the lower city: they are simply expelled from the Earth, placed in an off-planet labor colony and forbidden to reenter the earthly paradise, just as the workers of Metropolis could not enter Fredersen's pleasure garden. Labor problems, however, are never resolved to everyone's satisfaction. Humanoid creatures that they are, the replicants curse their fate and rebel against their maker. They grasp the meaning of death and, in consequence, they strive to live on. Those who disobey and come back to earth are hunted down and exterminated. The problem is: they look exactly like humans; they think, have emotions, cling to life exactly as humans do. How is one to tell between genuinely human bodies and their threatening simulacra, the "replicants," as they are called by those in the know?

As is usual in futuristic films, technology delivers the means. An emotion sensor, resembling an ophthalmoscope, registers pupil contractions when a replicant reacts in perplexity to an examiner's prodding questions. In the end, the difference, aside from the physical vigor and much shorter life span of these creatures, boils

6

down to the presence or absence of experiential traces. Humans, by virtue of their natural origin and slow maturation, have memories. But even this can be misleading, as the film's sentimental edge quickly shows. Lovely female replicants also have endearing memories of childhood, even documentary proof of them in the form of photographs (so much for Barthes's assertion that truth and reality converge in the evidential "trace" left by a memory). But as the twenty-first century's whisky-drinking replica of Philip Marlowe explains to the infatuated replicant, memories can also be implanted, just like any other part of her lovely body. Beyond her fond memories of Mom, can she remember the day when a boy showed her "his" and she chickened out when it was her turn to show him "hers"? The replicant is clearly at a loss, probably trying to figure out what this prattle about "his" and "hers" is all about. This moment is interesting, though, not only for the sex-ridden and sexist assumption of what constitutes authentically American experience—what distinguishes, that is, an original from an alien; but even more so for the unexpected turn towards what Foucault calls the descent to the model's "crop of hair or the dirt under its fingernails—those things that were never hallowed by an idea."

Much could be made of the puerile recourse to this "shared vestige" of American sexual education in introducing the audience to the erotic scene that clinches the replicant's humanization and the film's capitulation to hackneyed formulas. One may note the man's presumption in teasing out a woman's sexual connivance on the basis of a reputedly national rite of passage, or the coy boldness with which the child in him confesses to knowing the adults' dirty little secrets. It is the lingering idea of transgression, of a memory smuggled by every child into seemly adulthood, that makes the confession of the "dirty little secret" significant at the moment of mis-recognition between the sexes. The importance of that little incident back then, when she chickened out and did not show him "hers," underscores the alienation of sex, turns sex into the ultimate alien in a gendered universe where sexuality has become the construct par excellence. But leaving aside this sentimental gimmick, "smuggled" in as if it were dirt under the fingernails of American puritanism, one thing deserves to be retained from it, namely the role of the phantasmatic trace left by a remote experience that centered the body sexually, by default as it were. This moment redeems an otherwise boyish and largely citational

7

film: the stirring moment of recall of a "dirty" little story that did not enter the grand social narrative and consequently could not be implanted in the simulacrum.

This American film can serve as an allegory for the recent clash of memories in Spain. Several questions can be diverted from this film to political reality. For example: Who has been redefined as alien in this tale, and by whom? Whose memories are genuine and whose implanted? How can someone whose memory is called fictitious face down the sycophants of the Transition story, those Platonic storytellers who take for granted the endurance, nay the existence of an entity that comes of age (reaches "political maturity") through a democratic rite of passage? Can this alienated someone not protest that, in a different rendering of the tale, the ritual passage establishes the identity of the (political) body; that in a profound social sense baptism stands for creation, not rehabilitation? And is forgiveness of the original sin of Fascism the same as rehabilitation? Forgiveness implies forgetting and starting anew; whereas to rehabilitate is to bring forth prostrate memories of good character and intrinsic worth. In either case, a change of consciousness is involved, not so much of the subject but of those who forget or else reconstruct the master narrative by building upon the subject's alleged prelapsarian and even postlapsarian loftiness of aim.

More untimely inquiries could be made about the legend of the natural transition of a political construct, let us say a nation, to its triumphant democratic maturity. Doubtless, the most disturbing one, for the storytellers, would be to question their evolutionary tale of the organic, linear growth of a unitary, self-same being called Spain. Is not that protagonist a function, in Propp's formulaic sense? Is it anything more than a political bottomline, the dog that barked in the dark, in short a necessary because mandatory construct? Was not the Transition, as well as the thing in transit, the result of tinkering, not only with the state's political and economic structures but also with the official memories of that very process? Were they not contrived, these memories of consensus forming the bulwark of today's political identities? Was not a massive memory implantation required to naturalize the political "body in transit" that came out of the constitutional workshop in 1978? Presumably, the protagonists of that arrangement also have their dirty little secrets, and their model has lots of dirt under its manicured fingernails. Yet *these* unseemly things are deeply buried, marked ever so faintly by a tale-telling ooze. Although that ooze still looks just like perspiration, it signals nonetheless the presence of the crop of hair. In time the odor may turn into stench, but not before it is all too remote to strike anyone as relevant or even memorable. Who cares today about the rot and reek under the scaffold on which the throne is raised? Or, what amounts to the same thing, who is willing to pose questions about the seat and scope of sovereignty? Only aliens. And they can be detected precisely because they raise such untoward questions.

"All profound changes in consciousness," remarks Benedict Anderson, "by their very nature, bring with them characteristic amnesias. Out of such oblivions, in specific historical circumstances, spring narratives" (Anderson 204). And narratives have indeed sprung from and about Spain's recent past. It is a curious fact: cultural anti-francoism was primarily lyric, and dramatic to some extent, whereas the Transition has been overwhelmingly a matter of narrative, both in novel and film. Even when narratives have stressed the theme of memory, there has been something consoling in their rendering of subjective loss and disorientation, as if there were something biologically positive and life-enhancing in letting go of the past and living in a perpetual dawn-announcing dusk. Many such narratives have composed the metaphysical underside of political transformations. However, it would not be accurate to say that in these narratives the "poetic" confronts the political; much less that it conceals it. On the contrary, politics is never far from them, for at bottom they *are* political tales. They are that not, or not primarily, on account of their sometimes crude ideological or pseudo-ideological content but above all by virtue of their self-conscious vocation as alternative private worlds. In those necessarily schematic worlds, the reader, as previously the author, lives off a truth-effect to which she or he inevitably contributes by deploying certain memories and to the extent that other memories are simultaneously consigned to oblivion.

A stimulating approach to the literature of the Transition would be to study it in reference to what it leaves out, what it substracts from what we know from experience or what can be learned from less popular and more inaccessible sources. There has been a great deal of cultural activity around the Transition, and no less so around the culture of the Transition, to the point that this expression, initially coined to designate a political interval, soon became a periodizing category in cultural history. Seldom, however, has the significance of culture *for* the Transition been an object of critical attention. The prophesied cultural renascence after the end of the dictatorship was slow in coming, and then it needed vigorous help, with the state performing as obstetrician. The reason for this intervention was not only that the new regime, like the old one, needed to dress itself in cultural finery, which it did, but above all that it sought to govern by hegemony—something the dictatorship had been unable to do.

Like classic bourgeois liberal states, the new democratic regime, especially under socialist stewardship, enlisted the help of the aesthetic in inducing its subjects to introject political rule as a harmonious, imaginative, even critical projection of their own creative acquiescence. As Terry Eagleton observes, the aesthetic formally harmonizes the conflict between the particular and the universal, subjecting their tensions to a totalizing law that appears to accord with the autonomous condition of the parts that make up the art work (32). The conflict between particular and universal is the most profound, durable, and entrenched conflict in Spain, as it is for any colonial or semi-colonial state. One need only glance back at the cultural promotion and symbolic concentration in the heady years of reestablished electoralism to realize that the resolution of the conflict was fictitious even at the ideal level of culture. Culture then, as often in the past, became a powerful ideological tool. There were, of course, large cultural areas whose particularism could not be harmonized with the universalizing state model. That no attempt was ever made to resolve them suggests two not incompatible possibilities: one, that the state did not wish to risk exposing the particularity of its law by refracting it through stubbornly specific media, such as the peripheral languages; two, that in conditions of marginality and semi-colonization, still prevalent for Spain's peripheral nationalities, the aesthetic failed to resolve the conflict between the particular and the universal, because, as Eagleton says in reference to the Irish, there the aesthetic is engaged in recording "the lived specificity of a unique people in the teeth of that abstract universalism that is taken to be the very mark of modernity" (33).

From the early days of Spain's modernity, when Juan Luis Cebrián, chief editor of *El País*, described the reemerging Catalan culture as a sinking Titanic, the arguments used to talk away the aesthetics of particular cultures became an eloquent sign that the state's brand of culture—culture *tout court*—was being constituted to eliminate any competing claims to collective expression. No cultural practices would be sanctioned that might question the state's relentless drive to subject under its universalizing law each and every one of the individuals and groups falling within its jurisdiction. A new master narrative appeared about the time when Lyotard described the postmodern condition as bereft of the universalizing narratives of modernity. Unaware of committing an anachronism, the culture *of* the Transition appropriated the old values of bourgeois liberalism, imagination, and enlightened reason, pitting them against the "sectarianism" of particular aesthetics. From then on, whatever was not universal in the state's sense became ideological, partial, and—the suggestion was ever present— fanatic.

The dominant narrative strategy has been to simulate a temporal division in what is patently a political one. Adjoining the boundary on the wrong side are the particular cultures, on which diminishing and demeaning descriptions of folklorism, provincialism, and self-absorption are heaped to justify their expulsion from the bounds of universal (i.e. state sponsored) culture. Irrespectively of their function, contents, or significance, particular cultures are consigned to an inert temporality whose effect upon them is to liquidate any claims to viability and relevance. Atavism, relapse, non-contemporaneity are common descriptors. But if these tags are taken at face value, so must their obverse: return of the repressed, for theirs is the time of ghosts, of revenants and specters. A specter is haunting Spain, the specter of difference. In response, the spooked majority strikes out in panic, emits exorcisms, abjures the wraith with threats and incantations, taking the name of reason in vain. On the politically correct side we find a dazzling tale of modernity, creativity, and rationality: an ugly duckling tale of marvellous transmogrification. There is no need or space for illustrations. Merely an example of the rhetoric: the swift consensus with which every conservative politician (conservatism is here understood regardless of political self-definition, for the principle of the state's immutability overrules the internal dissension resulting from its bipartisan ownership) and every media hack have naturalized the perverse division of political forces into "constitutionalist" (referring to state mononationalists) and "nationalist" (advocates of

11

Spain's plurinationality). This terminology, borrowed from Jürgen Habermas's never implemented proposition for a purely civic and political organization of the German Federal Republic, is perverse because it ignores Habermas's fundamental condition: the state's effective disentanglement from national identity and its cultural ground (256-57). This condition for a purely civic polity pointed precisely in the opposite direction from the one followed by the post-Francoist Spanish state. For one of the state's success stories has been the promotion of a renewed Spanish identity, one, furthermore, that is presented as *evolving* from its national kernel, from historical seeds firmly planted in Spain's traditional culture and language and in the soil or asphalt of its authentic geography. Even more perverse than the spurious terminology is the innuendo attached to the terms, for the difference between conservatives who wish to prevent constitutional ammendments at alls costs and reformers who wish to modify the Constitution's more restrictive aspects is presented as a conflict between the partisans of legal guarantees and seditious zealots operating on the fringes of the law.

If the rhetoric employed in much of Transition culture—that of Enlightenment reason and modern bourgeois values—is surprisingly out of touch with recent world developments, its mechanism and purpose are not. For what media hacks and literary writers have been doing over the last two decades is to strengthen, if not actually give birth to, a newfangled state nationalism, one that seeks to unify political subjects around the theme of the democratic, enlightened, modernized, and finally influential Spanish nation (for a recent version of this euphoric view, see Fusi). Through such a strategy, the dominant political class relentlessly forwards its nationalizing work without drawing attention to its game, because it can advance more effectively through the negative work of combating alternative national aspirations by relocating them on the fringes of democracy and even of legality. The key to this double game is very simple: on no account will the Spanish state allow an equation between the different national projects. As a consequence, these projects cannot be expected to balance on the same ideological plane. Again, there is nothing surprising in this. Is this not a time-hallowed strategy of aggressive nationalism? "The law of political power always works best when it is invisible," says Eagleton (33), and so does that of nationalism. It prospers best when it sinks to the roots and stops being aware of its colors, for it pervades the whole plant. This much can be learned from Michael Billig's eloquent and profusely illustrated *Banal Nationalism*.

Besides, if nationalism has become once more a master narrative, what about the loose, fragmentary discourses associated with the peripheral nationalities, the "nationalisms," as hegemonic discourse calls those ghostly formations? Properly speaking, particularistic discourse that seeks to inflect a specific group as a nation is not nationalistic, precisely to the extent that it must labor to legitimate the nation. Discourse cannot be nationalistic without presupposing that which it aims to foster and enhance, and so it cannot both presuppose it and endeavor to bring it about without begging the question. It is possible, of course, that radical discourse mimics the hegemonic narrative against which it struggles for dear life. In this sense, and in this sense only, emancipatory discourse is anachronistic, as its foes insist; and it is so not just for one but for two reasons. First, it is anachronistic in the already stated sense that such discourse inverts the order of memory and remembers the future, as radical thought has always done. It must recall a future of difference, of particularity exercised in the freedom of equal dignity and access. Then it is anachronistic all over again in its dependence on the Platonic model it both mimics and fights, to the extent that *that* model is anachronistic. To quote Eagleton once more: "as political radicals our identity stands and falls with those we oppose. It is in this sense, above all, that they have the upper hand" (27). This is true not just in the sense of the master-slave dialectic, but also, in this case, because the game must be played in the oppressor's territory and by his rules. To embody the nation politically means to legitimate its existence in the realm of the universal; it means, in other words, not only to reorganize collective life in freedom *de facto* but also to obtain *de jure* international recognition and representation, which in practice are conditions of that freedom. The rules of national legitimation, however, cannot refer to a transcendent authority—history, for example, or that fictitious entity called "the international community"—, for they are established within the nationalistic discourse of already accredited nations.

Much has been purposefully forgotten and much more has become increasingly difficult to remember since the Spanish Transition, for a successful master narrative not only contains its own subplots as a mushroom houses its spores, but also establishes the rules of plausibility for each retelling. Still, it is important to distinguish carefully between history and public memory, although the two can obviously merge. That happens when the historian takes on the role of opinion fabricator, or when history becomes the pretext for narrative effects (rather than the other way around), as in the vogue of historical novels in the decade and a half after the dictatorship. None of this has much to do with historical memory but has everything to do with heritage, an indispensable constituent for national consolidation. For a nation, especially one that emerges from self-imposed ostracism and international disrepute, does not need historical memories—above all, it does not need an accurate representation of its past—but resonant ones, and those are accrued through heritage building. "Heritage," explains David Lowenthal, "diverges from history not in being biased but in its view of bias. Historians aim to reduce bias; heritage sanctions and strengthens it" (Lowenthal 8). Lowenthal's approach to heritage is nonchalant, or perhaps just realistic. He does not denounce heritage for cultivating error, for he thinks that error is the inevitable stuff of collective organization and solidarity; but he clearly assumes that an austere line ought to be drawn between heritage and historical knowledge. He posits, in effect, two kinds of memories or relations to the past. It is evident, therefore, that the dissipation of historical memory can refer only to the second kind, since this dissipation is a precondition for the articulation of an effectual heritage.

Thus, heritage and a people's self-consciousness are intertwined. Heritage is, to resort to Barthes's eloquent description of the "air" in the photograph, "the luminous shadow which accompanies the body." Of course, in this case the body involved is the body politic, one which, like the Woman without a Shadow, must remain infertile when deprived of this thin air of myth. But to look at this shadow alone is not to look at an object; it is to perform an aberrant act of attention at the cost of perception, which is nonetheless presumed. When all is told, in post-Franco Spain historical memory has been not so much diffuse or inaccessible as cumbersome and inconvenient, for it threatens with infertility an elderly body that wills itself youthful and, like old ladies, dare not tell its age.

Works Cited

Anderson, Benedict. *Imagined Communities*. 2nd. ed. London: Verso, 1991.

Barthes, Roland. *Camera Lucida: Reflections on Photography*. Trans. Richard Howard. New York: The Noonday Press, 1981.

———. "Le discours de l'histoire." *Social Science Information* 6.4 (1967): 65-75.

Billig, Michael. *Banal Nationalism*. London: Sage, 1995.

Eagleton, Terry. "Nationalism: Irony and Commitment." In Terry Eagleton, Fredric Jameson, Edward W. Said, with an Introduction by Seamus Deane, *Nationalism, Colonialism, and Literature*. Minneapolis: University of Minnesota Press, 1990: 23-39.

Foucault, Michel. *Language, Counter-Memory, Practice: Selected Essays and Interviews*. Ed. Donald F. Bouchard. Trans. Donald F. Bouchard and Sherry Simon. Ithaca: Cornell University Press, 1977.

Fusi, Juan Pablo. "España: El fin del siglo XX." *Visiones de fin de siglo*. Ed. Raymond Carr. Madrid: Taurus, 1999: 161-88.

Ginzburg, Carlo. "Shared Memories, Private Recollections." *History and Memory* 9. 1/2 (1997): 353-63.

Habermas, Jürgen. "Historical Consciousness and Post-Traditional Identity: The Federal Republic's Orientation to the West." *The New Conservatism. Cultural Criticism and the Historians' Debate*. Trans. Shierry Weber Nicholsen. Cambridge: The MIT Press, 1989: 249-67.

Lowenthal, David. "Fabricating Heritage." *History and Memory* 10.1 (1998): 5-24.

Lyotard, Jean-François. *The Postmodern Condition: A Report on Knowledge*. Trans. Geoff Bennington and Brian Massumi. Minneapolis: University of Minnesota Press, 1984.

Scott, Ridley. *Blade Runner*. Los Angeles: Embassy Home Entertainment, 1987.

1

Politics and the Invention of Memory.
For a Sociology of the Transition to Democracy in Spain

Salvador Cardús i Ros

Preamble

The sociology of the Transition to democracy in Spain is still incomplete. Only very recently, on the occasion of the twentieth anniversary of the acceptance of the 1978 Spanish Constitution, and after many years of prudent and discreet silence, has it become possible to raise the odd *ripple* of criticism against the social and political influences and conditioning generated by the whole process. Yet this development has fallen short of being a critical review or even a properly historical approximation. Instead, it is something in the service of an idealised conception of the Constitution rather than something expressing the wish to sociologically reassess the changes undergone in the balance of power from the time that the Franco regime bequeathed its political heritage to the Spanish people up to the point at which the current model of democracy became possible.

It is certainly the case that there are a good number of biographies and memoirs that help us, in certain ways, to get close to that era. But we should not confuse the subjective memory of those involved in a given occurrence with an (accurate or unreliable) account of factual events, and less still with a critical analysis of those events. Memory, whether of the kind developed at an individual level, or of the sort that is constructed socially and internalised by the group, is in all cases an *invention*, in the sense used by E.J. Hobsbawm when he talks about the *invention of tradition* (Hobsbawm, 1983). It is an invention that wishes to account for a specific conception of the individual or the group. That is to say, it is an interpretation of a reality that, essentially, aims to justify the intervention of the main actors involved, and to rationalise the experience of those who create or impose memory itself. There are magnificent and well-documented analyses of the Transition coming from the field of the journalistic essay, such as the one offered by Gregorio Morán in *El precio de la transición* (The Price of the Transition, 1991). However, although such works allow us to know the key elements in the process, in the final analysis they are incomplete, in part because of insufficient information, and in part because the perspective from which the phenomenon is observed is too short. Above all, this kind of work is incomplete because the genre in which it is conceived imposes a synthesis that is necessary to the transmission of information and ideas but is inevitably limited from the sociological point of view. There are also numerous studies that have been undertaken within the areas of political science, constitutional law, or state theory, which contain a juridical reflection on—and a formal analysis of— the model that came about in the Transition, but which do not expose the complex social processes involved in the construction of a new political culture. Finally, those who have come closest to what we understand by the term "sociology of the Transition" are historians working along the same lines as Pedro Carlos González Cuevas ("La invenció d'una tradició," 1994).

In short, then, we cannot say that there is a *sociology* of the Transition. And things stand as they do because the difficulties of this sociology have been—and still are—both political and methodological. Political, first of all, because we are dealing here with a process that took place under conditions that, had they been explicit, would have weakened the Transition's legitimacy and even, perhaps, the possibility of its success. For this reason, up to the present, all Transition sociology has had to bear in mind the political and moral consequences of disguising a process that was, on the other hand, receiving the uncritical enthusiasm and acclaim of a broad range of national and international bodies. Any critical analysis of the Transition to democracy has been suspected of being a criticism of democracy itself, or at the very least, of creating obstacles to its consolidation.

In the second place, we also need to refer to methodological or even epistemological difficulties, since the Transition is, basically, a process of historical and social amnesia, and the invention of a *new* political tradition (the contradiction is valid). As such, the object of study, the prime material of analysis, are not principally visible and objective facts but rather complex strategies of "invisibilization" that include both intentional *forgetting* and the production of false records of events. The object that this sociology needs to come to terms with is, in effect, the manufacturing of a great lie—and I use the word in a sense that is free from any moral connotation—that had the politically *laudable* intention of turning the page from an authoritarian to a democratic regime without bringing about a political breakdown and, in the process, achieving the unheard of situation in which the dictatorship's juridico-political framework became the source of legitimacy for the new democratic model.

It is not the intention of this article to carry out a *politological* (and far less a political) evaluation of Spanish democracy's impure "genesis," among other reasons because it is far from clear that any democratic system has ever had what we might call an immaculate conception, or that any democratic regime has ever been able to sustain itself through impeccable juridical procedures. Therefore, if we speak about the *impure* character of the Spanish democratic foundations, we do not do so in reference to considerations of a juridical nature, which determine that, in the case of Spain, we cannot strictly speak of a *constituent process* because there never was a break between the old and the new regimes, and above all because the minimum requirements considered essential by Constitutional Law or by the Theory of State were not met (Fossas and Pérez Francesc 73-74; Bastida, Varela, and Requejo 180, and Aranguren 30, qtd. in Mateu). If reference is made to this *impure nature*, it is to recall, without any trace of analytical resentment (I have already said that this discussion leaves politics aside), that the Transition to democracy was made possible by the active erasure of the social memory that had been hegemonic up to 1975. By this means the old regime became rapidly invisible and the democratic deficit of the new political edifice was disguised (Mateu, op. cit.). Above all, we speak about impurity in order to underscore that this *impure nature* of the democratic groundwork is the necessary starting point for an understanding of the characteristics of the Transition itself.

The reasons for the erasure of memory

There are many reasons why the Transition depended on the erasure of memory and the reinvention of a *new* political tradition. But the main reason is that a process of change built on the strength of the previous memory would never have facilitated a broad social consensus in favor of democracy at a time, let us not forget it, when Spain had allowed the dictator to die in his bed rather than ejecting him from power. This circumstance exposed the fact that the 1939 military triumph, on which the dictatorship rested, had dilated its legitimating force through several decades down to 1975. For this reason, a transition to democracy carried out *against* the dictatorship would have reactivated the memory—or rather, the diverse and counterposed memories—of the dramatic division of Spanish society in the Civil War, visions that had never been fused into a single common memory. And not only this, but also the fact that, having developed for nearly forty years under a dictatorship, the larger part of Spanish society had internalised a political culture that trivialized the authoritarian character of Franco's regime. In turn, this nonchalance was helped along by the contemporizing attitude of the international community. Compromise with the regime had gone much too far for a break with it to be staged at this late date. It would have been considered unnecessary and socially unjustified.

Other reasons—more particular, though no less decisive—explain the need to erase the collective memories (somewhat confused, in fact) that were still vivid in 1975. For example, the fact that the main actors in the Transition had to take decisions not only without being unaware of the strength of the adversary but also without having been able to assess their own abilities. And, naturally, no one wished to recall exactly *who* had been *what* during the previous regime, and even less to do it while facing the prospect of having to adapt very quickly to different political coordinates, mainly through the turncoat activity that came to be known as "changing [the colour of one's] shirt," a reference to the emblematic uniforms of various ideological currents.

It should be noted that we are talking here about a process that did not take place within a framework of democratic liberties, but rather under the shadow of all that has been said about *the rattling of swords*. That is, in a situation in which the heirs of the regime and those with whom democratic aspirations are usually associated were forced to negotiate without knowing exactly *what* each side represented, and to do it under the attentive vigilance of an Army that also was uncertain of its limits.

Nor should we ignore the especially relevant fact, pertinent to this entire process, of the *construction* of the monarchic figure, a figure that, maintaining an extraordinary—and extremely useful—ambiguity during the Transition, became a symbol both of renovation and of political continuity. The king, who had kept a complicitous silence during the last executions carried out by Franco's regime, who had sworn loyalty to Franco's laws upon the dictator's death, and whose first monarchical reception was held, emblematically, for a representation of fascist ex-combatants, ended up, five years down the line, representing the highest guarantee of the Transition to democracy, thanks to the opportunity offered him by the frustrated coup d'état on February 23, 1981.

We also need to bear in mind that the Transition to democracy was possible to a large extent because it guaranteed the continuity of the fundamental institutions and apparatuses of the state, particularly the Civil Service, and especially those that had played a central role in the previous regime, as was the case with the state police force, the *Guardia Civil*. But continuity was also ensured in other areas of administration and service, from state teachers or university professors to the administration of the judicial system, to give only a couple of examples of institutions that had, at different times and to different degrees, been accomplices to Franco's regime, which explains their enthusiastic collaboration in the task of hiding the footprints of compromising facts.

Continuity of people matched that of institutions. The most emblematic example is that of Adolfo Suárez, who had been General Secretary of the [National] Movement, with the rank of minister and Director General of Radio and Television under Franco. Against all predictions, he was chosen as the public figure to direct the Transition. Other characters from the Franco era kept themselves more in the shadows, though perhaps performing more relevant political roles, while others preferred to distance themselves from the political frontlines, as was the case with Antonio Samaranch.

That on which almost all analysts agree, however, is the question of who or what played a central and exceptional role throughout the process: the media, and particularly the press, are widely recognized as having had an extraordinary importance. The media became an essential part in erasing the memory not only of Franco's regime but also of the "Francoists"—and their corresponding images—a practice that would become basic to political reconstruction. It was a process that required a considerable dose of collective amnesia in order to manufacture a sufficient consensus. The media managed to recreate Franco's regime free from Franco's supporters and to promote the imaginary of a Transition that left an entire era behind, yet took along with it all those who had lived there.

Certain conceptual clarifications regarding memory, prior to further discussion

Before moving ahead with the analysis of the erasure of memory in the Spanish Transition to democracy, we need to make a few conceptual clarifications that will allow a better understanding of how the new political culture of that period was constructed. To begin with, it should be observed that reference is often made to *historical memory* and to *memory erasure* from a naive and almost essentialist perspective, in which there is a confusion of issues as diverse as the *recollection* (reliable or not) of events, the *scientific knowledge* of History, and *memory* in an individual or social sense. In this discussion, however, we propose a clear distinction between these three concepts, which refer to very different things. First, we will call *recollection* that function which involves the psychic capacity to record, with varying degrees of precision, past experiences that have been personally undergone. The precision of a given recollection is related to the social context that preserves, erases or attributes meaning to it, but it depends also on the conditions of the experience itself. Two basic limitations of recollection are its fragmentary character and the lack of social context, all of which renders it vulnerable to subjectivity. Recollection may well be a relatively important part in the construction of *memory*, but these two concepts should not be interpreted as being one and the same.

Secondly, the scientific knowledge of History is the result of a critical and provisional speculation that results from taking into account documents and verified information that the scientist then converts into *data*. The aim of this knowledge is to propose models that will facilitate an understanding of the complexity of the period under study. For this reason we should observe that the scientific

22

knowledge of History is also largely unrelated to *historical memory*, unless the latter is included as an object of the historian's research.

Finally, memory, both the individual kind and the sort that is imprecisely referred to as *collective*, is a set of narratives resulting from the social interpretation of reality. In the case of personal memory, this refers to narratives that attribute sense and order to one's personal biography, in relation to a general social framework into which the individual wants or needs to be integrated. Social or collective memory designates the set of narratives that are hegemonic in a specific group and that refer to and deal with the present as experienced by a differentiated community. *Memory* understood in this way does not strive for precision of recollection—there are times in fact when recollection may even be a great obstacle to producing an efficient memory, as Nietzsche suggests—nor is it constructed according to the canons of scientific knowledge. On the contrary, all memory follows the logic of oral, written or audio-visual narrative, depending on the paradigm of knowledge that prevails within the social space in which it is deployed.

All things considered, we can say that the construction of memory has recourse to four principles found in all narrative: anachronism, anthropomorphism, polarisation and integration (Platinga, 1992). These four principles, respectively, make it evident, first, that a simple chronicle of events (though exhaustive and ordered) would be incomprehensible and incoherent; second, that all memory is interpretation from the point of view of the individual or the community narrating it; third, that memory is constructed in dialectical terms, invoking or even creating a conflict without which there would be no history, and finally, that memory is an open narrative that incorporates personal and external recollection, but also includes fiction, things forgotten and errors that are *necessary* in order to make memory coherent and significant.

Lastly, from a sociological perspective we need to make three further observations regarding the construction or fabrication of memory. First, that memory always has a time or period in which it is useful, but which expires as it becomes necessary to include new elements that require a reinterpretation of the present. That is, memory (as we use the term here) is not necessarily and fundamentally accumulative but is instead a permanent reconstruction. The second observation is that memory is not so much the interpretation of the past as a justification of the present in terms of certain expectations about the future. In a strict sense, then, it is above all the change of expectations that makes it necessary to revise and re-memorize the past. And a third observation: it is important not to lose sight of the fact that the possibility of fabricating social memory is the genuine jurisdiction of all forms of power. It is therefore unimaginable, sociologically speaking, to have a collective memory of the subjugated or the losers unless this memory is merely a project of a minority or an organized group that opposes the established power precisely by means of a resistant memory.

Seen in this way, when complaints are heard about the dearth of historical memory (in our case, for example, of the Franco regime, or of certain episodes of political side-switching that typified the Transition), it should be made clear that such complaints are terribly naive, if they refer to a hypothetically *scientific* and objective memory of events. In reality, such complaints come from academic or intellectual sectors who, as the guardians of objective knowledge of the past, mourn the loss of the centrality of History over the last twenty-five years (and throughout the Western world) as a discipline in the service of power through the construction of legitimate or official memory. In other cases similar protest entails legitimate criticism and rejection of an imposed hegemonic memory that sustains a particular balance of power that some would like to change. But it should also be said that, to the extent that memory, whether individual or social, is interpreted as we do in these pages, it is not licit to speak simplistically of a battle between truth and untruth, but rather one must speak of a battle between the various truths—or untruths—that each political project invents in order to justify itself even to itself, and to justify its past, present and, above all, its future.

This sociological definition of *historical memory* may be accused of relativism, in the sense that it might seem to be questioning the possibility of the scientific knowledge of History, or in the sense that it renders individual recollection useless. But that would not be true. Our definition recognizes, precisely, the specificity of an established space for the knowledge of History without reference to political objectives, showing that, in contrast, the social function of memory is not to be truthful but to simulate the creation of solid foundations for all those things that are as contingent and precarious as the exercise of power.

Oblivion and memory in Spain's democratization

If we view things in this way, a sociology of the Transition turns into an analysis of the processes of erasure and reinvention of the collective memory in which, as we have already observed, the media participated with particular enthusiasm. We might say that, in some ways, the media played the role that in a different age would have been fulfilled by historians. That is, they took over the function of constructing a collective national mythology.

It is, however, very much the case that, in the absence of a political rupture that would have firmly established who were the winners and who the losers, the invention of a new political memory was an extraordinarily complex and fragile task. We could even say that the Transition lasted as long as it took to overcome the fragility of the newly invented memory. And while it is not my purpose to list all the causes of this fragility—something I could not hope to do in a systematic way—, it is still necessary to outline some of its characteristics.

A memory without an adversary. The new democratic memory had no clearly defined adversary. It is true that Franco represented all that the new regime should not be, but although it was evident that the new model would be constructed against the Franco regime, this could not be done against the *Francoists*, since they were part of the process. Otherwise neither the consensus of the powers that be nor a comfortable popular support would have been achieved. It was therefore necessary to invent new enemies of democracy, yet without pointing the finger at those who had played an important role under Franco. It would be very interesting to follow the line of demarcation for the supposedly *true* adversaries of democracy, who, logically, could not be the members of Franco's regime, but rather the "radicals." By demanding a break with the past, this sector endangered the negotiations between those in power and the legitimating opposition. Or else danger came from the sector of the old regime that resisted change. No one knew precisely the extent of this constituency, and it would have been enormously difficult to reveal the identity of those involved without infringing the conditions under which the Transition took place.

A memory without a past. In addition to these problems, temporal references for the new memory became something of a minefield. A new model against the past was constructed, but it was also constructed *from* the past. For certain participants, having been on the frontlines of the anti-Franco movement (for example, having spent time in prison) was a source of political legitimacy. But at the same time, having been in jail was a poor endorsement when it came to negotiating with the heirs of the former regime, who had been the jailers. The most comfortable approach was to keep talk about the past to a minimum, try to forget it, turn over a new page, or, up to a certain point, allow the veil of confusion to drop down over the question of responsibility. Yet, if the past was uncomfortable, it was also the case that the future, upon which certain commonly held expectations must be built, was far from bright. Perhaps for this reason, even before the Transition reached its conclusion, some spoke of *political disenchantment*. This was the way in which the more radically democratic sectors expressed frustration both with the forgetting of the past and with the inability to mark clear horizons. It is from this point of view that the failed coup d'état of February 23, 1981 turned out to be such effective theatrics. The bursting of a unit of the *Guardia Civil* into the Spanish Parliament, with Lieutenant Colonel Tejero at the head, provided a visual focal point, a clear enemy and, as a consequence, the enemy was now perfectly delimited. During the assault in Parliament, former Francoists faced up to Tejero's antics in a defiant attitude that was magnificently exemplified by the Minister of Defence, General Gutiérrez Mellado in an intervention that freed the Minister definitively from all suspicions of anti-democratic bias. The king, too, passed his baptism of fire, and the monarchy materialized as a symbolic guarantee of the stability of the new constitutional model.

An uncomfortably autonomy-oriented memory. Inventing a political model that would represent the plurinational and pluricultural nature of the state was not particularly difficult. The strategy of diluting the demands of historically legitimate nation-territories through the fabrication of fifteen new and unsolicited autonomous regions was an astute way of getting over a thorny issue. The weather maps in the newspapers no longer divided the state into the factitious regions invented by the old regime to break up the territories with strong cultural and political identities: the Ebro depression, the Cantabrian coast, etc. Now these were replaced by maps of the autonomous regions. In time though, it became clear that of all the changes effected by the Transition this autonomous model was perhaps the most poorly resolved. Having invented this new "autonomous-memory" and established the administrative frontiers, those responsible for the new map forgot to add to it the pluricultural reality with all its consequences. Failure to incorporate a pluricultural memory into the Transition has meant that the expression of cultural and linguistic demands is often articulated as a criticism of the constitutional model. If, on the contrary, cultural plurality had been assumed and accepted by the state-owned media, it is likely that the demands of the so-called *peripheral* nationalisms would have been less significant than they are today.

If we have outlined part of the complex territory of the new memory and memory erasure, a sociological analysis of this process still needs to bring to light the role played by the various institutions that made it possible. We have already suggested the importance of the media, and particularly the press, about which some interesting monographic studies have been done (Pérez Vilariño, 1982; Gifreu, 1983; Moragas, 1984 and Cardús, 1995 and 1998, among others). It would also be essential to know more in detail the role of the school system and of new school programs in the invention of this new political landscape. Also of interest would be the role of cinema and literature in creating new national and anti-national myths. And the same can be said for the role of sport and the rhetoric of rivalry in creating, maintaining, or undermining political spaces.

Conclusion

It has already been said that one of the main difficulties for a sociology of the Transition, conceived as a sociology of power, is that it needs to take into consideration not those things that are or have become visible but rather that which has become invisible. The difficulties lie in explaining not only the new mythical accounts of democratic Spain and how they have been imposed, but also what alternative accounts have been censored or delegitimized by the instruments of the new legitimate symbolic violence (Strubell,

27

1997) and now are placed under suspicion, or have been demonized by pitting them against everything that is *politically correct.*

The undertaking of a sociology of the Transition, which would require the participation of all kinds of experts in the study of culture and power, is of such a scope that currently it can be tackled only in a partial and fragmentary way. We hope, however, that in time someone will gather all the necessary strands and, with a more panoramic vision but without any loss of rigor, will be able to explain this spectacular work of History's "invisibilization."

Works Cited

Aranguren, José Luis. *España: una meditación política.* Barcelona: Ariel, 1983.

Bastida, F. J., J. Varela and J.L. Requejo. *Derecho constitucional. Cuestionario comentado.* Barcelona: Ariel, 1992.

Cardús, Salvador. *Política de paper. Premsa i poder a Catalunya 1981-1992.* Barcelona: La Campana, 1995.

Cardús, Salvador. *La premsa diària a les Illes Balears, el País Valencià i Catalunya (1976-1996).* Barcelona: Fundació Jaume Bofill, 1998.

Fossas, Enric and Josep Lluís Pérez Francesc. *Lliçons de Dret Constitucional.* Barcelona: Enciclopèdia Catalana, 1994.

Gifreu, Josep. *Sistemes i polítiques de la comunicació a Catalunya (Premsa, ràdio, televisió i cinema, 1970-1980).* Barcelona: L'Avenç, 1983.

González Cuevas, Pedro Carlos. "La invenció d'una tradició: visió històrica de la monarquia durant la transició democràtica." *Avenç* 182 (1994): 8-13

Hobsbawm, E., and T. Ranger, eds. *The Invention of Tradition.* Cambridge: Cambridge University Press, 1983.

Mateu, Marcel. "Dèficits democràtics en el procés d'elaboració de la Constitució." *Diàlegs* 2.4 (1999): 49-69.

Moragas i Spa, Miquel de. "Els mitjans de comunicació i el canvi polític a Catalunya." *Papers. Revista de Sociologia* 21 (1984): 93-116.

Morán, Gregorio. *El precio de la transición.* Barcelona: Planeta, 1991.

Pérez Vilariño, José. *Los periódicos ante las autonomías.* Madrid: Akal, 1982.

Plantinga, Theodore. *How Memories Shape Narratives: A Philosophical Essay on Redeeming the Past.* Queenston: The Edwin Mellen Press, 1992.

Strubell, Toni. *El cansament del catalanisme.* Barcelona: La Campana, 1997.

2

Memoria Colectiva y *Lieux de Mémoire* en la España de la Transición

Christina Dupláa

"Venganza no, pero memoria sí" (75) exige Gabriela, la protagonista de la novela de Josefina R. Aldecoa, *La fuerza del destino* (1997), a quienes lideran la España de la transición en la segunda mitad de los años setenta. La ley de la Reforma aprobada por referendum en 1976 —con la abstención recomendada por los partidos de izquierda, defensores en aquel momento de una ruptura política con el régimen franquista— posibilitará el paso de una dictadura a una democracia sin trauma social aparente. La Constitución de 1978 es el resultado de un pacto entre las fuerzas políticas más representativas tras las elecciones generales de 1977. Como señala el historiador Juan Pablo Fusi:

> La Constitución tuvo un mérito indiscutido respecto a todas las Constituciones anteriores: no ser ni la imposición unilateral de un partido ni la expresión de una sola ideología, sino la síntesis y conciliación de posiciones ideológicas divergentes y potencialmente antagónicas. (379)

Sin embargo, este acierto histórico esconde una realidad política y social de grupos de ciudadanos, vinculados a opciones progresistas, que sienten la necesidad y el derecho de releer la historia y de reivindicar su memoria colectiva. A esta unión entre una relectura de los hechos históricos de la España de los últimos cincuenta años y la experiencia del recuerdo colectivo de quienes los vivieron se le domina "memoria histórica".

Antes de analizar el texto de Tomasa Cuevas publicado en 1985 y titulado *Cárcel de mujeres (1939-1945)*,[1] en el cual, a través de voces de mujeres que lucharon contra el fascismo, se reivindica una visión de la guerra civil y de sus inmediatas consecuencias completamente opuesta a la del discurso oficial, considero necesario presentar las fuentes teóricas sobre las que se sustenta mi análisis en lo que afecta a la relación existente entre la memoria y la historia, entre la memoria entendida como una construcción social y la memoria colectiva.

Memoria e historia: una relación problemática

En "Between Memory and History: *Les Lieux de Mémoire*", el historiador de las mentalidades Pierre Nora polemiza la relación existente entre memoria e historia, subrayando que la memoria es algo vivo, que permanece en constante evolución: "open to the dialectic of remembering and forgetting, unconscious of its successive deformations, vulnerable to manipulation and appropriation, susceptible to being long dormant and periodically revived". Sin embargo, la historia es la reconstrucción "always problematic and incomplete, of what is no longer" (8). La memoria es, pues, un proceso que arranca del pasado pero que se vive desde el presente, mientras que la historia es una representación intelectual y secular del pasado, que resulta atractiva al análisis y a la crítica. Esta especie de elitismo que trasluce esta definición de la historia, se enfrenta al carácter "popular" de la memoria, la cual parte y se nutre de la tradición (el ejemplo que él utiliza es el del pueblo judío) y, para muchos grupos, de la oralidad como única vía de comunicación. La memoria es, pues, colectiva, plural y, a la vez, individual; mientras que la historia pertenece a todos y a nadie, y reivindica una autoridad universal. "Memory —añade Nora— attaches itself to sites, whereas history attaches itself to events" (22). Y estos lugares en los que se sitúa la memoria son lo que él denomina *les lieux de mémoire* que, en función del sentido que se le dé a la palabra *lieux*, pueden ser materiales, simbólicos y/o funcionales (por ejemplo: un archivo, una bandera, un testamento).

Pero estos lugares de memoria son para el historiador francés espacios donde cohabitan la memoria y la historia. Por tanto, y aún definiendo ambos términos a partir de lo que les separa, Nora construye este puente intelectual porque sabe que ambas materias están condenadas a complementarse, a pactar entre ellas como se pacta la redacción de una constitución —texto que es para Nora un *lieu de mémoire* (21). Y, de nuevo, hay que recordar que este pacto se conmemora para fortalecer unos hábitos mentales que celebran acciones del pasado. Ni que decir tiene que estas prácticas simbólicas tienen un gran significado y poder político. Como dice en otras palabras el historiador Michel Vovelle: "Las mentalidades remiten de manera privilegiada al recuerdo, a la memoria, a formas de resistencia" (15). Si la mentalidad remite a la memoria y los lugares de memoria proporcionan el marco, vocabulario e intencionalidad a un hecho histórico o a una tradición cultural, es fácil aceptar que la conmemoración es un acto de memoria colectiva, con el cual el grupo social en cuestión refuerza su identidad nacional. En el siglo XX —siglo de los grandes movimientos de masas— se celebran y conmemoran acciones bélicas representadas por medio de construcciones monumentales que recuerdan victorias o pérdidas, como por ejemplo: los memoriales a la guerra del Vietnam, a la guerra civil española (El Valle de los Caídos), a los crímenes del nazismo a través de los museos-memoriales del Holocausto, etc.

La memoria como construcción social

Maurice Halbwachs (1877-1945) fue uno de los más brillantes representantes de la escuela francesa de sociología fundada por Emile Durkheim. Sus textos sobre memoria más importantes son *Les Cadres sociaux de la mémoire* (1925), *La Topographie légendaire des évangiles en Terre Sainte* (1941) y *La mémoire collective* (1950). Este último trabajo se publicó cinco años después de su muerte en el campo de concentración nazi de Buchenwald.[2]

Entre las interpretaciones y críticas más recientes al trabajo intelectual del sociólogo francés se encuentra la de Ramón Ramos, el cual indica que la teoría de la memoria colectiva de Halbwachs se basa, fundamentalmente, en tres ideas cruciales: 1) *ser* es perseverar; 2) la memoria es el medio para perseverar; y 3) la memoria se construye socialmente. Dicho de otra manera: los seres humanos para *ser* tienen que recordar dentro de un grupo (64-65). Estas tres ideas son la síntesis entre la tesis del pensamiento clásico griego, que defiende que el pasado es lo firme y estable y el presente lo cambiante y precario, y la posición contraria del filósofo Henri Bergson, que entiende que el pasado es el conjunto de presentes pasados (67). Para Halbwachs, el pasado que la memoria reactualiza, es decir, el pasado que el recuerdo convierte en presente, es una construcción social. La siguiente cita de Ramos aclara su interpretación del pensamiento del sociólogo francés:

31

La memoria informa sobre un pasado del presente, es decir, un pasado que cambia y se reescribe en función del presente (de los sucesivos presentes). Esta redescripción o reconstrucción se opera socialmente. La razón fundamental radica, en que al no ser la experiencia la de un ser práctica y comunicativamente aislado, sino la de alguien que comparte el mundo con otros, esos otros participan también en la memoria de lo ocurrido. No sólo aparecen en sus recuerdos en forma de sujetos socialmente significativos, sino que también recuerdan: han sido copartícipes o testigos. Resulta de ello que mis recuerdos coexisten con los recuerdos de los demás y que esa coexistencia lleva a una tupida interpretación comunicativa de la que resulta un pasado reconstruido que es producto de todos y de ninguno en particular. (71)

Y este pasado enmarcado, en un lenguaje, un espacio, un tiempo y una conciencia de grupo, es lo que nos permitirá hablar de "memoria colectiva".

Memoria colectiva y olvido

En un sugerente artículo titulado "Los afluentes del recuerdo: la memoria colectiva", Amalio Blanco afirma que la memoria "es un caudal que discurre internamente [...]; se sostiene por procesos neurobiológicos [...], pero se nutre necesariamente de afluentes externos" (86). De ahí se desprende que para Blanco la memoria pertenece al individuo pero también al grupo. "Cada una de nuestras sociedades —sigue Blanco— reserva de manera perfectamente organizada, regulada e institucionalizada determinados espacios para recordar colectivamente acontecimientos del pasado [...], que suelen ir acompañados de rituales y simbologías" (86). Y añade Blanco:

Hay, pues, una memoria individual y una memoria colectiva, idénticas en la dinámica de sus relaciones a la conciencia individual y a la conciencia colectiva. Ambas se complementan, se apoyan y se penetran mutuamente, pero es la memoria colectiva la que sirve de envoltura a la individual [...], la que acabará por institucionarse y regularse transitando a lo largo de generaciones como signo de identidad de grupos, comunidades y sociedades. (89)

Habiendo establecido la relación entre la memoria, la historia, la relación entre ambas y la memoria colectiva, es preciso sintetizar los elementos que definen el recuerdo en una determinada sociedad. Creo que el propósito de Amalio Blanco es el mismo cuando escribe:

> La memoria colectiva es uno de los emergentes de la dinámica *grupal*, de esa dinámica *histórica* en la que los individuos han ido creando de manera conjunta *marcos de referencia* para orientarse en el mundo que les rodea. La memoria colectiva es uno de los productos de la *intersubjetividad*, es una de las consecuencias de la capacidad que el hombre tiene para la interacción y la comunicación y, desde ahí, para la construcción de lo *social*. (97)[3]

Si la memoria colectiva afecta a un grupo en un determinado momento histórico y además dispone de un elemento intersubjetivo que hace que los seres humanos se sientan comprometidos en una dinámica social, podemos afirmar que cuando esta dinámica se resquebraja por una acción violenta, la memoria colectiva se convierte, en términos simbólicos, en un arma de resistencia: en un lenguaje de denuncia.

Éste sería el caso de quienes, habiendo sufrido una experiencia traumática, ven en el ejercicio de la memoria una acción que permite impregnar esa experiencia personal dentro del recuerdo colectivo de una sociedad. Para Jorge Semprún, por ejemplo, sus vivencias de deportado al campo de concentración nazi de Buchenwald pertenecen a su propia memoria y a la de una colectividad que vivió la misma experiencia. Cada vez que Semprún escribe[4] o habla de este periodo de su vida, lo hace sabiendo que sus palabras van más allá del mero hecho de una exposición autobiográfica. Su relato como ex-deportado tiene connotaciones emblemáticas porque son la construcción de unos sucesos calificados de crímenes contra la humanidad. No es sólo su experiencia personal la que acongoja a lectores u oyentes, sino el valor colectivo de esa experiencia. Y para quienes no forman parte de esta colectividad afectada, esos hechos son hechos históricos que se añaden a la memoria histórica de la Europa de la segunda mitad del siglo XX.

La reacción contraria a esa necesidad constante de denuncia es la del olvido, o mejor dicho, la del silencio. En un trabajo titulado "Halbwachs y la memoria colectiva: la imagen histórica de Europa como un problema psicológicosocial", Páez, Insúa y Vergara consideran que en el caso de los hechos traumáticos hay elementos que sugieren que se dé una dinámica colectiva de silencio y olvido. "Esto ocurre", añaden, "tanto entre los 'vencedores' como entre los 'vencidos'" (121). Este sería el caso del silencio que han mantenido a lo largo de más de cincuenta años hijos de judíos sobrevivientes de campos de exterminio e hijos de nazis que dirigieron estos campos. Los motivos que tenían para guardar silencio se debía a que querían olvidar, a que temían que no se les entendiera y porque no querían alterar a sus familiares (121). Otro factor que provoca el silencio de un individuo o un grupo sobre un hecho concreto es el tabú que la misma sociedad crea alrededor de un acontecimiento negativo. "Este tabú influye en cómo se codifican o archivan en la memoria los hechos negativos y positivos" (122).

Por último, quiero destacar lo que denomino "recuerdo y olvido institucional" porque son producto de una manipulación y una imposición ideológica en la que se cuestiona la ortodoxia del pasado para justificar el presente y orientar el futuro (así lo indican Middleton y Edwards [25]). La represión sistemática sobre la que se fundamenta cualquier régimen dictatorial afecta al recuerdo y al olvido colectivos, seleccionando aquello que hay que olvidar — generalmente el periodo político anterior— para enfatizar lo que hay que recordar —la cronología de las hazañas bélicas que legitiman el discurso nacionalista impuesto desde el poder. El ejemplo más inmediato que tenemos los españoles en nuestra memoria colectiva es la experiencia vivida y compartida de la dictadura franquista. Prohibiciones, silencios, tabús, miedos... eran realidades cotidianas que cimentaron el control del pasado para controlar el futuro. En definitiva: para controlar quiénes éramos o, mejor dicho, quiénes debíamos ser.

Voces de mujeres: *lieux de mémoire* sexuados

En la España de la transición se publicaron textos memorialísticos de mujeres que padecieron las cárceles franquistas o el exilio y/o la deportación a campos de exterminio nazi. La constante ideológica de estos textos es la de enfrentarse con el "olvido pactado" sobre el que se construyó la actual democracia. La presencia cotidiana de la barbarie política en la vida de quienes habían defendido la legalidad republicana hasta los últimos momentos de la guerra civil no podía ignorarse en la etapa de libertades políticas que se iniciaba tras la muerte de Franco. Había que *recordar* a quienes escribieron una constitución "a la medida de todos" que muchos españoles habían muerto o sufrido demasiado para poder aceptar el reto del "silencio democrático". Pero dentro de este sufrimiento físico y moral de los derrotados, en general, había el de las mujeres, en particular. Las voces de esas mujeres[5] recuerdan que por el mero hecho de tener un cuerpo femenino, la humillación, la tortura, la vejación era doble: como perdedoras y como mujeres. Las violaciones físicas las llevaron a cabo hombres que, además de ser los ganadores de la guerra, conocían el poder que les otorgaba el patriarcado. Nunca les perdonaron "que hubiesen antepuesto su política y su placer a su deber sagrado como guardianas de la familia" (Cavallo, 94).

En este artículo presento el texto *Cárcel de mujeres (1939-1945)* como un *lieu de mémoire*[6] —siguiendo la acertada terminología de Nora— donde cohabitan narrativas autobiográficas[7] que deben enfrentarse a la "desviación" propia de cualquier esfuerzo recordatorio. A esa desviación, en relación al propósito de fiabilidad con el pasado real, lo podemos denominar "memoria creadora". Es decir, la memoria y la historia compiten en el espacio textual dentro de las limitaciones que ambas tienen en cuanto a la "veracidad" del mensaje. La memoria acepta estas limitaciones —según Nora de manera inconsciente— porque reconoce la vulnerabilidad del recuerdo individual y del grupo en cuestión, pero la historia se resiste más porque su estudio se basa, precisamente, en la distancia entre el investigador/a y el documento archivado, presumiblemente no contagiado. Aun reconociendo la distorsión del recuerdo en el presente, recurrimos a él para "construir" la historia de esas mujeres, ya que el franquismo "ignoró" su existencia en los archivos de los centros penitenciarios (Romeu 18). Todos los presos eran catalogados bajo la categoría de presos comunes. Este ejemplo y otros muchos demuestran que siempre hay que cuestionar ese carácter "objetivo" de que presume la historia, olvidando que su propia existencia es el resultado de una re/construcción de hechos cronológicos enumerados desde el prisma de la hegemonía —especialmente en los periodos de regímenes autoritarios.

Tomasa Cuevas recorrió toda España buscando esas voces silenciadas, entrevistándolas y grabándolas para, posteriormente, transcribirlas. La tarea no fue fácil porque muchas de estas mujeres todavía tenían miedo a relatar su experiencia o bien sus esposos se lo prohibían por los mismos motivos (vemos, de nuevo, cómo esas voces son doblemente "colonizadas", como diría Sidonie Smith y Julia Watson). Otras accedieron a hablar pero usando un nombre falso. A todas ellas el pánico aún las invadía.

Otra característica del texto, además del componente sexuado, es la relacionada con la clase social de las entrevistadas. La mayoría de esas mujeres, incluida la propia Tomasa Cuevas, pertenecían y pertenecen a la clase obrera. Tuvieron que empezar a trabajar antes de los diez años en el sector agrícola o en alguna pequeña fábrica. Y muchas de ellas coinciden en señalar que las duras condiciones bajo las que tenían que realizar el trabajo fueron lo que les despertó la conciencia de clase oprimida y las acercó —como le sucede a Cuevas— a la militancia en la Juventud Comunista y, luego, en el Partido Comunista.

El texto de Cuevas consta de 241 páginas divididas en veintidós capítulos, cada uno de ellos dedicado a la vivencia carcelaria de una mujer, un prólogo de Teresa Pàmies —militante comunista como Cuevas— y una introducción que es la autobiografía de la autora del texto desde su infancia hasta su detención al terminar la guerra. Empezaré por analizar el prólogo de Pàmies.

Todos los prólogos en este tipo de textos testimoniales o memorialísticos —que en definitiva son, junto con fotografías (que también las hay en este texto), datos documentales, apéndices, etc. elementos estéticos e ideológicos que ejercen una función de intertextualidad— son presentaciones didácticas con gran influencia sobre la recepción. Es decir, su función es la de presentar el texto indicando a los lectores y lectoras cómo hay que leerlo.[8] Y aún más: les invitan a que participen en el proyecto ideológico de la autora del libro, la cual transmite la experiencia carcelaria de estas mujeres. La siguiente cita del escrito de Pàmies es ilustrativa al respecto:

> Es la odisea de unas mujeres, que por serlo en toda la dimensión, asumieron una doble carga en aquella derrota: la de defender sus ideales si los tenían o su dignidad de mujeres y madres de revolucionarios perseguidos o asesinados. (11)

Pero, ¿cuál es la mecánica utilizada por Cuevas para la obtención de la información deseada? También nos lo dice la autora del prólogo:

> Ha reunido con ayuda de un magnetófono, libretas y bolígrafos, los testimonios más estremecedores para elaborar, junto con su propia experiencia, el libro que me honro en prologar. [...] Kilómetros y kilómetros de cinta magnetofónica; centenares de cuartillas mecanografiadas por jóvenes compañeras que la ayudaron a copiar lo grabado, dejándole a ella —pues sólo ella podía hacerlo— la engorrosa tarea de ordenar, coordinar, verificar materiales valiosos pero a veces reiterativos. (11)

Nos enfrentamos, pues, a un texto que no sólo tiene la mediación de la memoria "desviada" o "contagiada" de la narrativa autobiográfica, sino también la manipulación consciente o inconsciente de todas aquellas personas que han participado en la creación del texto que leerá el público. Es evidente que esta labor es necesaria porque, de lo contrario, la narración sería ilegible y perdería toda su capacidad estética e, incluso, ideológica. Por tanto, hay que asumir —y esto no quita ningún mérito al trabajo de Tomasa Cuevas— que la escritura que al final leemos no es un fiel reflejo de lo que ocurrió, sino el resultado de un gran esfuerzo estilístico por parte de la autora del libro.

En lo que respecta a las voces e historias de la vida de la propia Cuevas (introducción del texto) y de las otras veintidós mujeres (que cuentan con una pequeña narración de Cuevas donde se ofrecen los datos necesarios para legitimar y dar autoridad a la información autobiográfica), tendremos que tener presente lo apuntado con anterioridad: el factor creador de la memoria. Recordar es una acción que se realiza desde el presente y que cada vez que ejercitamos la memoria enfatizamos unos aspectos en detrimento de otros. Desde que ocurrieron los hechos en la realidad hasta la práctica de recordarlos desde infinitos presentes, hemos ido sumando y restando partes de nuestra vida de manera consciente o inconsciente, como acción lógica que se desarrolla a lo largo de nuestro proceso de madurez. Como dice Celia Fernández Prieto en un excelente trabajo sobre la memoria y la autobiografía:

> Los recuerdos se transforman con el paso del tiempo y la evolución del

sujeto, se mezclan, se desdibujan, se revisan se reajustan y lo que realmente sucedió queda definitivamente perdido, cada vez más rodeado de sombras o de emociones que a menudo escapan a todo control racional. (71)

En el caso de estas autobiografías, el juego que se establece entre el pasado y el presente desde el cual se recuerda, inclina la balanza hacia aquellos aspectos que vinculan una acción personal con las necesidades de una colectividad que ha sufrido, en mayor o menor grado, experiencias similares. Este sería el aspecto que refuerza la definición de Halbwachs, cuando éste afirma que la memoria se construye socialmente porque se comparte, con conciencia de grupo, una experiencia, un lenguaje, un espacio y un tiempo ante unos hechos vividos. Hay que sumar, pues, estas experiencias y "olvidar" otros datos autobiográficos que resultan innecesarios para el recuerdo colectivo. Prima el valor testimonial de la memoria frente al "yo" individual característico en la tradición autobiográfica.

Sobre la recepción del relato de estas vidas, es preciso señalar un dato que me parece muy importante: en general los lectores y lectoras de este tipo de autobiografías testimoniales se solidarizan *a priori* con los hechos narrados. Es decir, antes de leer el texto en cuestión simpatizan con su contenido;[9] y si además leen el prólogo, miran las fotografías y el resto de los materiales introducidos en el libro para dar mayor veracidad a lo narrado, pocos serán los que no se sientan conmocionados ante el sufrimiento y la dureza de lo leído. Es más, la difusión de estos textos no sigue las pautas comerciales del resto de la literatura. Las pocas editoriales que se atreven a publicarlos son escasamente conocidas por el público en general y distribuyen los pocos ejemplares que editan —en comparación con otros géneros literarios— en espacios proclives a la venta de este tipo de productos (librerías de mujeres, fundaciones o asociaciones de grupos vinculados con la defensa de los derechos humanos, etc.). Algunos de estos textos, como el de la historiadora Fernanda Romeu Alfaro, *El silencio roto. Mujeres contra el Franquismo*, no encontró apoyo económico privado ni público. La propia autora acabó siendo la editora de su libro.

Al cabo de estos veintitrés años,[10] en los que se aprobó la reforma política, se pactó la transición, se llegó al desencanto y se regularizó un sistema democrático en el que no se rindió ni pidió cuentas a nadie,[11] ¿a quién puede extrañarle este pacto con el olvido? A lo mejor sólo es intolerable desde esos sectores que siguen construyendo lugares de memoria para estimular su memoria colectiva y la memoria histórica de todos los españoles. Nadie busca ninguna venganza, sólo el deseo de ser parte de un proceso histórico. Así lo dice Tomasa Cuevas al final de su libro:

> Espero y deseo que el lector comprenda a estos testimonios vivos [...] No dan a conocer su vida en las cárceles, en las comisarías, en la clandestinidad queriendo pasar cuentas a los culpables [...], pero sí queremos que nuestras vidas sean parte de la Historia de nuestra España. (241)

Notas

1. Tomasa Cuevas escribió dos volúmenes. El primero se titula *Cárcel de mujeres (1939-1945)* y el segundo *Cárcel de mujeres*; ambos se publicaron en 1985. Otro texto testimonial de la autora es *Mujeres de la resistencia*, 1986. En inglés ha aparecido la edición y traducción de Mary E. Giles, titulada *Prison of Women: Testimonies of War and Resistance in Spain, 1939-1975*.
2. Jorge Semprún lo acompañó los últimos días de su vida, según recuerda en *La escritura o la vida*.
3. La cursiva es mía.
4. Uno de sus discursos más conocidos sobre su experiencia concentratoria es "Memoria del ex deportado 44.904".
5. No todas las mujeres encarceladas habían sido activistas políticas. Algunas fueron detenidas por el mero hecho de ser la esposa, la madre o la hermana de un defensor de la causa republicana.
6. En otros trabajos he analizado este tipo de textos desde el marco teórico del testimonio como género literario desarrollado en Latinoamérica: "Testimony and Cultural Memory in Hispanic Narratives: the Case of Montserrat Roig's *Els catalans als camps nazis*", "Testimonio de la exdeportada de Ravensbrück, Neus Català", *La voz testimonial en Montserrat Roig. Estudio cultural de los textos* y "Mujeres, escritura de resistencia, y testimonios anti-franquistas".

7. La literatura peninsular prefiere incluir estos textos dentro de lo que se conoce por el género de las memorias (autobiografía, biografía, autorretrato, diarios). Pero son casi inexistentes los estudios realizados, ya que lo que en realidad se entiende por memorias son autobiografías de intelectuales estudiados/as en la historiografía: Rosa Chacel, María Zambrano, María Teresa León, etc. Anna Caballé, que conoce la existencia de textos de voces de mujeres marginales, señala que en el siglo XX se ha generado un microgénero autobiográfico, como es el de la literatura de los campos de concentración. Así lo indica en "Memorias y autobiografías escritas por mujeres (siglos XIX y XX)"; de la misma autora recomiendo *Narcisos de tinta. Ensayo sobre la literatura autobiográfica en lengua castellana (siglo XIX y XX)*. Sobre testimonios de presas políticas analizadas también desde el espacio autobiográfico, sugiero los estudios de Shirley Mangini, *Memories of Resistance. Women's Voices from the Spanish Civil War* y "Resistencia a la memoria y memorias de resistencia".

8. Los prólogos son para las lationamericanistas especialistas en el género testimonio, Eliana Rivero y Elzbieta Sklodowska, "artefactos discursivos" o "lecturas dirigidas".

9. La mayor parte de la recepción de estos textos se siente ideológicamente comprometida con su contenido. En menor grado, se encuentran los lectores profesionales de la crítica literaria de la literatura testimonial.

10. La redacción de este artículo se lleva a cabo en marzo de 1999.

11. El Partido Comunista de España no tuvo inconveniente en aceptar y pactar la transición política a costa de los sufrimientos de muchos de sus militantes en el largo periodo de la clandestinidad.

Obras Citadas

Aldecoa, Josefina. *La fuerza del destino*. Barcelona: Anagrama, 1997.

Blanco, Amalio. "Los afluentes del recuerdo: la memoria colectiva." *Claves de la memoria*. Ed. José María Ruiz-Vargas. Madrid: Trotta, 1997: 83-105.

Caballé, Anna. "Memorias y autobiografías escritas por mujeres (siglos XIX y XX)." *Breve historia feminista de la literatura española (en lengua castellana)*. Ed. Iris Zavala. Barcelona: Anthropos, 1998. V: 123.

——. *Narcisos de tinta. Ensayo sobre la literatura autobiográfica en lengua castellana (siglo XIX y XX)*. Madrid: Megaluz, 1995.

Català, Neus. *De la resistencia y la deportación. 50 Testimonios de mujeres españolas*. Barcelona: Adgena, 1984.

Cavallo, Susana. "Autobiografía, testimonio y ficción en la literatura carcelaria: Lidia Falcón, Tomasa Cuevas y Eva Forest." *Duoda. Revista d'Estudis Feministes/Revista de Estudios Feministas* 10 (1996): 87-100.

Cuevas, Tomasa. *Cárcel de mujeres*. Barcelona: Siroco, 1985.

——. *Cárcel de mujeres (1939-1945)*. Barcelona: Siroco, 1985.

——. *Mujeres de la resistencia*. Barcelona: Siroco, 1986.

——. *Prison of Women.Testimonies of War and Resistance in Spain, 1939-1975*. Ed. and trans. Mary E. Giles. Albany: State University of New York Press, 1998.

Dupláa, Christina. "Mujeres, escritura de resistencia, y testimonios antifranquistas." *Monographic Review/Revista Monográfica* 11 (1995): 137-45.

——. "Testimonio de la ex-deportada de Ravensbrück, Neus Català." *Letras Peninsulares* 11.1 (1998): 167-79.

——. "Testimony and Cultural Memory in Hispanic Narratives: the Case of Montserrat Roig's *Els catalans als camps nazis. Bulletin of Hispanic Studies* 76.2 (1999): 235-43.

——. *La voz testimonial en Montserrat Roig. Estudio cultural de los textos*. Barcelona: Icaria, 1996.

Fernández Prieto, Celia. "Figuraciones de la memoria en la autobiografía." *Claves de la memoria*. Ed. José María Ruiz-Vargas. Madrid: Trotta, 1997: 67-82.

Fusi, Juan Pablo y Jordi Palafox. *España: 1808-1996. El desafío de la modernidad*. Madrid: Espasa Calpe, 1997.

Halbwachs, Maurice. *Les Cadres sociaux de la mémoire*. Paris: Presses Universitaires de France, 1925.

——. *La Mémoire collective*. Paris: Presses Universitaires de France, 1968 (1ª edición: 1950). (*On Collective Memory*. Ed. Lewis A. Coser. Chicago: The University of Chicago Press, 1992).

——. *La Topographie légendaire des évangiles en Terre Sainte*. París: Presses Universitaires de France, 1971 (1ª edición: 1941).

Mangini, Shirley. *Memories of Resistance. Women's Voices from the Spanish Civil War*. New Haven & London: Yale University Press, 1995. (*Recuerdos de la resistencia. La voz de las mujeres de la guerra civil española*. Trad. Teresa Kennedy. Barcelona: Península, 1997.)

——. "Resistencia a la memoria y memorias de resistencia." *Duoda. Revista d'estudis feministes/Revista de estudios feministas* 10 (1996): 101-14.

Middleton, David y Derek Edwards. *Memoria compartida. La naturaleza social del recuerdo y del olvido.* Trad. Luis Botella García del Cid. Barcelona: Paidós, 1992.

Nora, Pierre. "Between Memory and History: *Les Lieux de mémoire.*" Trad. Marc Roudebush. *Representations* 26 (1989): 7-25.

Páez, D., et al. "Halbwachs y la memoria colectiva: la imagen histórica de Europa como un problema psicológicosocial." *Interacción Social* 2 (1992): 109-25.

Ramos, Ramón. "Maurice Halbwachs y la memoria colectiva." *Revista de Occidente* 100 (1989): 63-81.

Rivero, Eliana. "Acerca del género 'Testimonio': Textos, narradores y 'artefactos'." *Hispamérica. Revista de Literatura* 16. 46-47 (1987): 41-56.

Romeu Alfaro, Fernanda. *El silencio roto. Mujeres contra el Franquismo.* Madrid: Fernanda Romeu Alfaro, 1994.

Semprún, Jorge. *La escritura o la vida.* Barcelona: Tusquets, 1995.

——. "Memoria del ex deportado 44.904." *El País,* 10 de abril, 1995, sec. Internacional: 4-5.

Sklodowska, Elzbieta. *Testimonio hispanoamericano.* New York: Peter Lang, 1992.

Smith, Sidonie y Julia Watson, eds. *De/Colonizing the Subject: The Politics of Gender in Women's Autobiography.* Minneapolis: University of Minnesota Press, 1992.

Vovelle, Michel. *Ideologías y mentalidades.* Trad. Juana Bignozzi. Barcelona: Ariel, 1985.

3

"¡Malditos pueblos!": Apuntes sobre los vascos al final del siglo XX[1]

Philip W. Silver

Para Dr. Carlos Calderón

"El hombre sin patria es como un cadáver sin tumba".
—Arquíloco.

Cuando Virginia Woolf publicó *Mrs. Dalloway*[2] en 1925, gracias a su peculiar condición de "maníaco-depresiva" y gracias a los conocimientos psiquiátricos de su marido, Leonard Woolf, se reveló como uno/a de lo/as escritores/as más lúcidas respecto al hoy denominado *Post-Traumatic Stress Disorder* (PTSD) [Estrés Post-Traumático] [EPT].

Nadie podrá olvidar la escena de esta novela en la que Septimus Warren Smith —alter-ego de la autora— re-vive la muerte de su amigo Evans en la primera guerra mundial, pero esta vez en un parque londinense. Ni podrá ningún lector dejar de sentir un *frisson* al leer que justo antes de la fiesta de Clarissa Dalloway Septimus Smith se suicida. Aquellos trozos de la novela de Woolf rezuman todo el pavor de la primera pesadilla de la literatura occidental, esa escena hacia el final de *La Ilíada* en la que Héctor corre alrededor de la murallas de Troya para distanciarse de Aquiles, cuando aquel evadirse es y será siempre imposible.

I

Hasta mediada la primera guerra mundial —véase la espléndida novela de Pat Barker, *Regeneration* (1992)— se había entendido la palabra "trauma" como significando un golpe fuerte, en cualquier parte del cuerpo, pero luego se empezó a aplicarla al efecto psicológico de un choque físico cuyo resultado se hubiera transferido a la mente de la víctima. Ahora bien, para imprimir claridad a este asunto del estrés post-traumático, he aquí una descripción relativamente completa de los resultados "subjetivos" de ese trauma —tal como fueron deducidos primero por psiquiatras en los soldados hospitalizados durante la primera guerra mundial. Según explica Kai Erikson, para la víctima es como si

> something alien breaks in on you, smashing through whatever barriers your mind has set up as a line of defence. (...) The classic symptoms of trauma range from feelings of restlessness and agitation at one end of the emotional scale to feelings of numbness and bleakness at the other. Traumatized people often scan the surrounding world anxiously for signs of danger, breaking into explosive rages and reacting with a start to ordinary sights and sounds, but at the same time, all that nervous activity takes place against a numbed gray background of *depression*, feelings of helplessness, and a general closing off of the spirit, as the mind tries to insulate itself from further harm. Above all, trauma involves *a continual reliving of some wounding experience in daydreams and nightmares, flashbacks and hallucinations, and in a compulsive seeking out of similar circumstances.* (Erikson 183-84)[3]

Según explica Cathy Caruth, la memoria de una víctima como Smith se empeñaría en repetir, en contra de su voluntad, esa experiencia fuera del alcance de la misma, y que no se ha podido o querido asimilar, y esa experiencia cuasi-inapresable sigue rondándola como un demonio familiar. Sin embargo, dice Cathy Caruth:

> [T]he pathology cannot be defined either by the event itself—which may or may not be catastrophic, and may not traumatize everyone equally—nor can it be defined in terms of a *distortion* of the event, achieving its haunting power as a result of distorting personal significances attached to it. The pathology consists, rather, solely in the *structure of its experience* or reception: the event is not assimilated or experienced fully at the time, but only belatedly, in its repeated *possession* of the one who experiences it. (4)

De manera que en absoluto puede controlarse su reincidencia, y de ahí la sensación de impotencia, la confusión, el estrés y la depresión resultante.

De ahí también el actual interés entre críticos deconstructivistas por este fenómeno del estrés post-traumático, dado que sus pautas de crítica literaria estrictamente intratextuales les habían condenado a un temerario distanciamiento de los acontecimientos históricos. De la misma manera que el discurso crítico-literario de la narratividad invadió la antropología, los deconstructivistas de golpe fueron seducidos por este fenómeno del trauma. Arrimando el ascua a su sardina, descubrieron en el paciente o ex-combatiente, víctima del EPT, el prototipo de un verdadero "agente histórico" que, a pesar de descender al infierno de la historia, y morar en él, no lograba poseer *sino que era poseído por* la historia en la que había tomado parte. Por tanto este agente les serviría a los deconstructivistas de coartada en cuanto que no guardaba ningún recuerdo voluntario a pesar de haber sufrido en carne propia una vivisección a manos de la historia. Por tanto si a estos mismos agentes históricos no les constaba haber participado en la historia, entonces ¿cómo podría echarse en cara a los críticos deconstructivistas que problematizan la historia? ¿Por qué no problematizar aquel "texto" de la historia, si ni siquiera el testigo presencial ejercía control racional sobre ello?

II

Puesto que queremos acercarnos al País Vasco desde esta perspectiva del EPT, sería interesante examinar algunos libros que parecen fiel reflejo de la tremenda situación que se vive ahí a finales del siglo XX. Quisiera examinar el primer libro por lo que tiene de proyección interior del aludido EPT. Y esto con el fin de subrayar cómo miembros muy integrados en ese ambiente social se esfuerzan por apresar una experiencia traumática colectiva de violencia pseudo-indiscriminada, experiencia que por su misma naturaleza se resiste a la captación.

Además me parece urgente corregir una idea respecto a los vascos que está a punto de extenderse entre cierta progresía española —una progresía de mentalidad subconscientemente autoritaria. Me refiero a una idea sesgada que sirve de idea motriz a

El bucle melancólico: historias de nacionalistas vascos, libro galardonado en 1997 con el Premio Espasa Hoy, del poeta, profesor y ensayista Jon Juaristi.

Y digo idea motriz porque su libro *El bucle melancólico* organiza sus nueve ensayos de diversa procedencia alrededor de la extravagante —en este contexto— noción de que la melancolía es una enfermedad congénita de los, o por lo menos de muchos, nacionalistas vascos. Para documentar su aserto Juaristi se apoya en una referencia a Freud que parece haber recogido de un libro de Giorgio Agamben sobre la melancolía. Una idea que le ayuda a dictaminar que la raíz de este peculiar desorden mental reside en una reacción *melancólica* (léase, depresiva) frente a la pérdida de un objeto u Otro/a poseído/a anteriormente o no. Porque, según Juaristi se trataría en realidad de una pérdida "desconocida"; es decir, en el caso de melancólicos vascos de un objeto —la Patria— no sólo nunca poseído sino que ni siquiera existió. De hecho, con su arte de birlibirloque el profesor Juaristi pretende hacernos ver que los nacionalistas vascos sufren ataques de melancolía y/o depresión porque añoran recuperar un estado-nación que nunca tuvieron pero que profesan haber tenido. Y además se hacen víctimas *a priori* de la supuesta pérdida, y así se adelantan a la amenaza (por tanto imaginaria) de que se esté a punto de quitarles aquello que nunca tuvieron.

Pero resulta que esta explicación de la melancolía tomada de Freud se refería a una verdadera pérdida objetual —como posible causa de la melancolía— que se produce sin que se sepa *con precisión la naturaleza exacta* del objeto perdido. Mientras que en el uso de este epígrafe de Agamben que hace Juaristi leemos que paradójicamente sí se produciría la pérdida, pero sin que existiera *nunca ningún objeto perdido*. O sea, para Juaristi el nacionalista vasco desea recuperar algo que nunca tuvo de hecho en sus manos. Ahora bien, por una parte Juaristi tiene razón: el nacionalista vasco nunca tuvo un estado-nación que comprendiese tanto la actual Comunidad Autónoma Vasca como Navarra —ni los territorios vasco-franceses. Sería más bien al revés: que el antiguo reino de Navarra llegó a incorporar provincias vascas actuales. Pero Juaristi causa perplejidad cuando mantiene que no han existido nunca ni estado ni nación vascos.

Ahora bien, sólo he querido situar este libro vasco extraordinariamente (y hasta extrañamente) divertido —pero que no deja de rezumar ambigüedad e inseguridad autobiográfica— dentro de la corriente de los estudios recientes acerca del trauma, porque es evidente que el concepto melancolía-depresión que maneja Juaristi tan hábilmente en su causa no pasa de ser —en cuanto depresión— mera subcategoría del desorden global que hoy conocemos como EPT.

Evidentemente, en cuestiones de trauma ha llovido mucho —la segunda guerra mundial, las de Corea y Vietnam— desde que Freud escribió su última palabra sobre la melancolía. Es más, ha llovido tanto que la metáfora organizadora de *El bucle* no se tiene en pie, y por tanto resulta inservible para fundamentar conceptualmente su libro. Queda más bien haciendo servicio de guardia a la entrada del libro como inamovible soldadito de plomo.

Por tanto un problema básico de *El bucle* sería querer confundir una "maladie" de filósofos que Juaristi y Agamben llaman "melancolía" con el EPT, que es una de las enfermedades colectivas más extendidas y graves del siglo XX. He aquí por qué conviene tomar la medida de los efectos del EPT en el presente libro de Juaristi. Como vimos al comienzo, tanto en la persona de Virginia Woolf como de su alter-ego de ficción, Mr. Septimus Smith, el estrés post-traumático acarrea consecuencias mortales, tanto o más que la "melancolía". Y esto precisamente porque en el caso real de EPT los objetos perdidos *sí existieron alguna vez*, y no son quasi-objetos imaginarios como quiere dar a entender Juaristi con su desafortunado encuadre metafórico de esta "enfermedad" para los nacionalistas vascos.[4]

Después del epígrafe de Freud-Agamben, en orden de importancia estructural, otro eje de *El bucle* podría ser el capítulo "La vieja que pasó llorando", cuyo título proviene de una traducción-adaptación (¿1933?) de Manuel de la Sota y Aburto del drama *Cathleen ni Houlihan* (1902) de William Butler Yeats. Esta obra, según Juaristi, es "el dramón nacionalista [vasco] que más éxito de público cosechó bajo la República" (Juaristi 207). Si no he entendido mal la función de este capítulo en el libro —centra la obra en la alegoría yeatsiana de la "Vieja" o *Patria*— Juaristi quiere que entendamos que la Vieja-nación de Yeats, también en la adaptación vasca, es un perfecto cuento de hadas, pero peligroso, una obvia fantasía nacionalista. Por tanto, el "éxito de público" subrayado por Juaristi significaría otro brote colectivo incontrolable de esa falsa —¿pero real en cuanto a su causa?— melancolía de parte de nacionalistas vascos en plena guerra civil española.

Porque fue precisamente en plena guerra civil, cuando por el derrumbe del frente republicano del Norte (Navarra, Gipuzkoa), debido a los avances hacia el oeste del General Mola y los Requetés, que Euskadi (o Euzkadi) fue diezmada —de hecho y de jure— y por tanto tenía que haber existido a la fuerza. Entonces Euskadi sí luchó por su cuenta y riesgo contra Mola, Franco —y un ala de la Luftwaffe— y al final pactó una rendición ("vergonzosa", según Juaristi) con las fuerzas italianas en Biarritz en agosto de 1937. Sin embargo, esto no es una ficción, porque el mismo Juarisiti da fe de estos hechos en su libro. Entonces, es un tanto desorientador que Juaristi se contradiga aquí respecto a su propio diagnóstico de la causa de la "melancolía" nacionalista en la medida en que insiste constantemente en la *no* existencia, la imaginariedad, de la entidad Euzkadi-Euskadi.

Como vemos en la metáfora-soldado de plomo antes aludida, el discurso de Juaristi tira la piedra pero luego se le olvida esconder la mano. Vuelve una y otra vez a la historia "vergonzosa" del Padre —de los Padres nacionalistas—, pero como un imantado sonámbulo que vuelve a un fatídico lugar. En otras palabras, el nacionalismo, que de joven él mismo llegó a compartir, le parece peligroso pero le fascina; él mismo, arrastrado por "la vieja que pasó llorando", hasta llegó a militar en ETA. Pero, claro, según la versión de *El bucle* él y su quinta eran buenos chicos, terroristas-intelectuales con conciencia de clase que nunca mataron sino sólo conspiraron. Y ahora uno de ellos —hijo nacionalista de nacionalistas— quiere hacernos creer que entonces ETA era distinta.

Por cierto, esta perplejidad no es sólo mía. He aquí otra reacción de la historiadora Idoia Estornés a *El bucle*. Ella opina que "la torpeza y el frentismo de determinada intelectualidad antinacionalista han acarreado el *Santiago y cierra Euskadi* del nacionalismo vasco en las [pen]últimas elecciones. Sin dejar de exponer argumentos cargados de razón en muchas ocasiones, se halla presa de *un histerismo inédito*: este "país" [Euskadi] no existe, no ha existido nunca ni Vasconia, ni Euskadi, ni Euskal Herria, ni el Pays Basque. Como si las urdimbres políticas fueran las únicas que contaran" (Estornés 14). Según parece, "la vieja que pasó llorando" también tiene cualidades de *revenante* para los vascos de *todas* las edades. Como si se tratara del efecto de ese extraño fenómeno de

EPT —pero en toda una colectividad. Recordemos que "Above all trauma involves *a continual reliving of some wounding experience in daydreams and nightmares, flashbacks and hallucinations*, and in a *compulsive* seeking out of *similar circumstances*."

Y como colofón podemos subrayar respecto a *El bucle* que, mientras en sus artículos de prensa —Juaristi es un polemista y miembro activo a favor del Foro de Ermua— no se harta de señalar que los casos irlandés y vasco no se parecen en absoluto, gran parte de *El bucle* se articula sobre citas e ideas del profesor irlandés Connor Cruise O'Brien, precisamente de su libro *Ancestral Voices. Religion and Nationalism in Ireland*. (N.B.: El profesor O'Brien es un conocidísimo anti-nacionalista y acerbo comentarista sobre Irlanda —desde el autoexilio en USA.)

Según parece, el profesor O'Brien es uno de los modelos vitales de Juaristi; salvo que, con admirable coherencia, el crítico vasco se sitúa por lo menos una vez entre los "melancólicos" resurrectos. Hablando de la tradición de *Aberri* y *Jagi-Jagi* y del nacionalista Gallastegui (alias *Gudari*), Juaristi dice que él [mismo] es también un producto de "la Bilbao popular y proletaria de las siete calles y aledaños, donde nacieron Unamuno, *Gudari*, José Antonio Aguirre, y donde yo también vi la luz" (Juaristi 267). Por cierto, este O'Brien vasco termina "La vieja que pasó llorando" con una última y peculiar referencia. Cuando se reúnen los antiguos *gudaris* o ex-combatientes vascos, dice, en su "melancolía" cantan en coro esta canción de los *mendigoxales*: 'Vayamos de monte en monte, jóvenes vascos...' A lo que, metiendo morcilla, Juaristi agrega: "Y entonces siento en el pecho la punzada de una dolorosa y conocida melancolía, que llega acompañada del eco de mis (¿sus?) voces ancestrales" (...) Y luego remata: "me hablan de toda la belleza y la ternura de la vida, pero oigo también entre ellas ["sus" voces ancestrales] *una voz imperiosa*, la de la vieja que pasó llorando, *que clama por el pago de una irresarcible deuda de sangre*" (Juaristi, 268). Pero precisamente de deudas de sangre no hay mención —que se sepa— ni en la obra original de Yeats ni en la adaptación de Manuel de la Sota. ¿De dónde, pues, brotaría esta sangre que parece que viene de fuera, sino del acervo imaginario, del subconsciente del mismo Juaristi?

Sería largo de considerar los muchos libros sobre el nacionalismo vasco de los últimos veinticinco años —es decir, en lo que va de Transición democrática en España— y que rezuman este mismo trauma. Pero hay otro reciente en particular que impresiona por su rigor y seriedad. Me refiero a *La herida patriótica: la cultura del nacionalismo vasco* (1998) del antropólogo —vasco— y también profesor de la Universidad del País Vasco, Mikel Azurmendi. En contraste con el libro de Jon Juaristi, con su gran don de fabulador, el de Azurmendi transparenta con creces la especialidad de su autor conforme repasa las cuestiones de etnia, identidad grupal, violencia, lengua y cultura, y otras fronterizas entre la ética, la antropología, la política y la socio-lingüística, todas referidas naturalmente al entorno vasco actual.

La herida patriótica de Azurmendi representa un avance importante porque no sólo diseca la presente identidad vasca, propuesta y sostenida por la fuerza y cultura de las pistolas por ETA y los jóvenes de la *kale borroka*, sino que este segundo autor se esfuerza por enseñar cómo reconstruir una nueva identidad vasca verdaderamente plural (liberal), en contra de los exclusivismos que rigen en Euskadi hoy. Sin embargo, la metáfora "visceral" de la *herida patriótica* también demoniza —aunque menos— el dogmatismo nacionalista y exclusivista que encontramos en el libro de Juaristi. Pero el segundo autor ve como *literalmente mortal* tanto el golpe como el trauma que resulta de él. Visto lo cual habría que contestar que, si la situación presenta tal gravedad y abandono, entonces es tarde ya para cualquier reconstrucción, porque estaría de más una nueva construcción identitaria. Según el profesor Azurmendi, "el nacionalismo vasco es una herida patriótica, una permanente llaga que hace daño en lo más hondo de la identidad..." (177).

Como vemos, el tono de estos últimos ensayos es más sombrío y patético en contraste con el talante jocoso de Juaristi, cuya risa sardónica ya no le es posible a Azurmendi. Quizás este cambio de tono tenga una explicación mucho más compleja, pero podríamos sintetizarla en el trágico evento histórico del secuestro y asesinato por ETA de Miguel Angel Blanco, joven concejal del Partido Popular de Ermua (Vizcaya) en julio de 1997. No se había dado un asesinato por ETA que tanto conmocionara el País Vasco (y gran parte de España) desde el de María Dolores Catarain, *Yoyes*, ex-militante importante de la misma ETA en 1986. Pero en 1997 una paulatina concienciación del pueblo a favor de la paz negociada hizo que en toda España los ciudadanos se echaran a la calle en una masiva petición del cese de la violencia etarra. Sólo la casta de los políticos, como de costumbre durante la Transición, no supo estar a la altura de sus votantes.

En consecuencia, en los dos años desde que Miguel Angel Blanco fue asesinado, el partido nacionalista vasco se ha dado cuenta de que si ellos no frenan los estragos sociales causados por ETA y sus seguidores, no sólo el ala radical sino de rebote el nacionalismo conservador corre el riesgo de ser borrado del mapa electoral. Porque desde la escisión de Eusko Alkartasuna en 1985 el PNV no es ni siquiera el partido mayoritario, ni ha sabido renunciar a un independentismo en patente contradicción con el Estatuto de Gernika que rige la autonomía de la Comunidad Autónoma Vasca En parte se lo impide su competición ideológica con el nacionalismo radical de ETA-HB.

Dada esta y otras contradicciones del nacionalismo, el Partido Popular está en alza en la Comunidad Atonónoma Vasca, y no sólo por sus notables éxitos en la lucha contra ETA y su entorno social. En contraste con el terrorismo blanco y la corrupción anexa a la lucha anti-terrorista del PSOE, los Populares no sólo han ganado "policialmente" la lucha contra ETA, sino que la Justicia, a través de la Audiencia Nacional —con los jueces Baltasar Garzón, Bueren y Gómez de Liaño— ha encarcelado a la Mesa Nacional de HB y ha cerrado *Egin*, el primer periódico de ETA-HB. He aquí por qué, cara a las elecciones municipales de 1999, y también en reacción a un pacifismo ciudadano cada vez más extendido, el PNV se ve obligado a jugar (otra vez) la baza de la unidad de *todos* los nacionalistas vascos, y a pactar con EA (Eusko Alkartasuna) y *los radicales* un frente "popular" de *todos* los nacionalistas (el llamado Pacto de Lizarra). El fin declarado es hacer que tanto HB-EH (Herri Batasuna-Euskal Herritarrok) como ETA "bajen del monte" al sistema, pero en realidad se trata de subsanar una fuerte sangría del voto pro-nacionalista. Este frente nacionalista ha generado una grave situación en la que están por un lado los partidos estatales (el PSOE y el PP) y por otro los partidos nacionalistas —más un disminuido Izquierda Unida—. Por fin y sin ambages están enfrentados el macro- y el micro-nacionalismo. Y esto ha aumentado en el último año la crispación ciudadana y política en el País Vasco.

Dada esta situación, el quid de la cuestión sería, ¿por qué al final del siglo XX unos vascos pretenden negar —con el derecho de su parte— a otros vascos el pertenecer a su patria? Porque si los nacionalistas estatales y los españolizantes locales quieren negar la existencia de la patria o nación-estado de los nacionalistas vascos (los *abertzales*), estos últimos pretenden obligar a tragar por la fuerza a los no-nacionalistas su concepción minoritaria de lo "vasco" y su diseño de Euskadi. Por tanto, con toda lógica para los no-nacionalistas vascos (tanto los españolistas como los anacionalistas vascos) el entuerto está en que se les invita a formar parte de un País Vasco, y a "ser" vascos, pero según un modelo de vasquidad eligido por ultra-abertzales. Porque, al formarse el frente nacionalista vasco, éste asumió las tesis de la parte radical, es decir, del entorno inmediato de ETA.

Ahora bien, si anti- y no-nacionalistas vascos como los profesores Juaristi y Azurmendi niegan la existencia de la entidad Euskal Herria, hace poco en respuesta simétrica algunos seguidores de EH y ETA lograron que el Pleno del Ayuntamento de Rentería (Gipuzkoa) estudiase "la posibilidad de suprimir de la biblioteca municipal cuantos libros niegan la [existencia de la] nación vasca" (Mina 16). Aunque Javier Mina cuente esta anécdota sobre Rentería en clave humorística, es impagable como ilustración del grado de mutua denegación que existe hoy entre vascos abertzales y no- y anti-nacionalistas.

III

En los primeros años de la Transición, allá por los años ochenta, se barajaban distintas versiones de la teoría Represión/ Resistencia para explicar cómo una población tan heterogénea como la vasca pudo renacer como una unidad defensiva, y cuál fue la causa de la peculiar respuesta vasca —armada y violenta a partir de 1968— a la represión franquista. La más creíble es que la represión franquista en sí, en contra de sus propios intereses, logró fundir una población heterogénea, compuesta de autóctonos e inmigrados, en una unidad de resistencia, precisamente debido al carácter indiscriminado de una represión-opresión ciega. En cuanto a por qué sólo en el País Vasco se dio esta respuesta armada, hoy se tiende a reconocer que sobre todo los frecuentes estados de excepción, con la explícita suspensión de toda garantía de derecho constitucional, sirvieron en el País Vasco como forja de una nueva población rebelde.

Apoyándose en la idea propuesta por Juan Aranzadi en 1981, de la creación por ETA de una nueva "etnicidad", el investigador vascofrancés F. Juaréguiberry ha desarrollado un argumento que contribuye a aclarar la confusión que rodea la ideología del PNV y su relación con la izquierda radical (KAS-HB-EH). Lo que Jauréguiberry hace ver es cómo el nuevo nacionalismo (no distinto, sino superpuesto a la antigua variante peneuvista) se desarrolló como consecuencia de la fuerte represión. Si, razona Jauréguiberry, la popularidad de ETA alcanzó tales cotas en el momento preciso de los procesos de Burgos (1970), cuando la organización atravesaba una profunda crisis, esto significa que las dimensiones reales de ETA superaban con mucho su verdadera organización. ETA, entonces, sería "la punta de un iceberg" de resentimiento y oposición silenciosos provocados por cuarenta años de Franco (Jauréguiberry 229). Pero para que esa muda resistencia hallara esa voz y se convirtiera en un movimiento de masas hicieron falta años de discriminación *indiscriminada* contra los habitantes del país vasco.

A partir de 1939 la represión franquista repetía cotidianamente el mensaje de que los vascos eran distintos del resto de España, incluso que eran traidores a la patria. Eran diferentes del resto de España, pero eran todos uno en su porfía. De ese modo fueron fusionados en una masa homogénea, bien que ahora sólo eran homogéneos en su espíritu de resistencia, ya que, a partir de la década de 1950, la masiva inmigración al próspero País Vasco había destruído la base empírica de la ideología del viejo nacionalismo de la pureza de la "raza vasca". A la inversa, la represión indiscriminada contra toda la población de Euskadi, y no sólo contra los "vencidos" como en el resto de España (con la excepción de Catalunya), influyó en que los inmigrantes se fusionaran con los autóctonos que, a partir de 1970, se convirtieron en minoría. Al demostrar día tras día a *todos* los habitantes de Euskadi que sufrían la represión por el mero hecho de vivir allí, el franquismo forjó una nueva identidad vasca que Jauréguiberry llama "una identidad transgresora" (Jauréguiberry 230). Su hipótesis es que una resistencia pasiva compuesta por miles de transgresiones privadas e individuales desembocó en una resistencia activa que pasó a ser en la Transición una colectiva radical de votantes. Y abruptamente los antiguos símbolos culturales peneuvistas se convirtieron en los de *una nueva sociedad vasca clandestina* en busca de la libertad; y al ser la voz de esta sociedad clandestina, el propio nacionalismo vasco se tuvo que transformar. Con los procesos de Burgos de 1970 y el magnicidio de Carrero Blanco de 1973, los (nuevos) vascos fueron reconocidos universalmente como la vanguardia armada de la resistencia antifranquista y como habitantes ya de un nuevo "espacio de libertad".

¿Podemos decir que con Franco la represión fue dos veces más dura en el País Vasco que en el resto de España, alegando que allí la víctima fue la población entera, y no sólo (grosso modo) la mitad "republicana"? Si esto parece exagerado, Jauréguiberry ha concebido un método de cuantificación de esta represión en los años comprendidos entre 1968 y 1976 —la década antes de empezar la Transición. Y, basándose en las cifras extrapoladas, concluye que: a) esta generalización de las detenciones ("casi un habitante vasco por cada cien") no podía ser selectiva; no importaba quién eras, sino dónde estabas; b) la represión en el País Vasco fue incluso más dura porque las Fuerzas de Orden Público (FOP) nunca fueron naturales del lugar y los matices de la vida colectiva en una ciudad vasca para ellos eran un misterio; c) al convertirse en algo tan habitual, la detención perdió toda connotación de delincuencia y se convirtió en un distintivo de valor positivo (Jauréguiberry 233-34).

Pero incluso esta represión franquista "legal" apenas nos permite ver la realidad de la represión cotidiana contra vascos: los controles de carretera, los cacheos, las detenciones, los estados de excepción, etc. Para ilustrar el especial peso de esta represión y su naturaleza discriminatoria respecto del resto de España, sólo tenemos que analizar el último estado de excepción de Franco, que abarcó los meses de mayo, junio y julio de 1975. Para empezar, entre el 25 de abril y el 27 de mayo fueron detenidas unas 3.200 personas, 380 fueron juzgadas y encarceladas, 350 se exiliaron, seis perdieron la vida y dieciocho fueron heridas por arma de fuego, mientras que 45 fueron hospitalizadas tras sufrir graves torturas (Jauréguiberry 236-37). Amnistía Internacional calculaba que, durante este período de tres meses, fueron torturados al menos 250 detenidos. En Bilbao, las comisarías de policía estaban tan llenas que hubo de abrirse un campo de detención en Las Arenas. No es sorprendente, por tanto, hallar que, respecto de las demás regiones de España, este trato fuera, en cuanto al tipo y al grado, altamente discriminatorio.

Sobre este fondo es fácil percatarse de cómo —hasta 1975— una continua y cada vez más feroz represión pudo haber obrado la fusión de autóctonos e inmigrantes, proletariado y pequeña y media burguesía, hasta formar un movimiento de resistencia que, aunque asumiera muchos signos externos del viejo nacionalismo más conservador, era de tipo muy distinto. Jauréguiberry sostiene que lo que erosionó las antiguas señas de identidad de la versión esencialista del vasquismo fue la represión misma, que obligó a autóctonos e inmigrantes a reconocerse *como vascos* en lo que respecta a los símbolos ya existentes, aunque bastante cambiados respecto a su anterior contenido.

Podemos resumir esta aclaración de Jauréguiberry de la hipótesis explicativa Represión/ Resistencia diciendo que la fundamenta de verdad: su premisa de la decantación de nuevas energías en viejos símbolos está más que confirmada. No sólo eso, sino que también desvela la intención anti-vasca que transparenta gran parte del uso político actual de este modelo de Represión/ Resistencia cuando se trata de explicar hoy la violencia residual vasca. En parte, la intención política fue siempre desacreditar este hecho de la asimilación vasca de no-vascos, estrategia política utilizada por socialistas tanto contra el antiguo como contra el nuevo abertzalismo, para luego privilegiar otro valor: un *supuesto pluralismo* liberal-democrático.

Mientras que los anteriores estudiosos del nacionalismo vasco utilizaban explicaciones históricas, económicas o socio-económicas, Juaréguiberry, con los métodos de la psicología social y de la sociometría, toma más en consideración el factor subjetivo. Por ello ha podido explicar lo que sucesivos Gobiernos del postfranquismo han intentado reprimir: que, a pesar del hecho de que la inmigración inclinó la balanza demográfica de Vizcaya y Guipuzkoa a favor de los inmigrantes *no* vascos, el voto *abertzale* (nacionalista) siguió creciendo en la Comunidad Autónoma Vasca hasta aproximadamente 1987. Este hecho, tan desconcertante para "españolistas" como para vascos no-abertzales y anti-abertzales, se explica *en parte* por la tesis de Jauréguiberry: respondiendo al peso de la represión cotidiana, los propios inmigrantes eligieron ser vascos, eligieron la asimilación —y las nuevas señas de identidad vasca.[5]

Pero tanto autóctonos como inmigrados tuvieron que pagar un alto precio por esta fusión-asimilación. Y continuaron pagándolo empezada la Transición bajo gobiernos indudablemente más democráticos. La interpretación interesada del modelo causal

Represión/ Resistencia —que daría por finalizada la "legítima" resistencia de ETA una vez terminada la represión franquista en 1975—tampoco acepta que la represión franquista en el País Vasco no terminara con la llegada de la democracia. De hecho, las ocupaciones de Rentería por la Guardia Civil los días 11 al 16 de mayo de 1977, con UCD en el gobierno, o la violencia allí infligida a la población civil por la Policía Nacional, armada con barras y cadenas de hierro, en la apertura de las fiestas de La Magdalena el 20 de julio de 1983 (bajo un gobierno socialista) no fueron de naturaleza distinta a lo peor habido en Rentería durante el último estado de excepción impuesto en Euskadi.

Ahora bien, el resultado más grave del enquistamiento de este trauma y esta nueva "identidad transgresora" en el momento actual (11 julio de 1999) es su imborrable "*Antígona-ismo*", o sea, una incapacidad para vivir si no es en oposición a algún enemigo u Otro, autoritario o no. Como asevera tanto Juaristi como Azurmendi, esta incapacidad es la letra que entró con sangre durante el franquismo, y que veinticinco años de Transición no han podido borrar. Sin embargo, al ser este Antígona-ismo un problema generalizado entre la progresía española, por la cantidad y la ferocidad de los estados de excepción en Euskadi, el trauma resultante aquí echó los cimientos de la nueva conciencia identitaria vasca, *tanto abertzale como no-nacionalista y anti-abertzale*. Esta sí es una reacción post-traumática colectiva, el reflejo cultural de todo vasco contemporáneo, producido por casi cuarenta años de franquismo y no pocos de la Transición.

Y aquí no me refiero a la obviedad de que hoy unos 160.000 votantes de HB-EH creen a pies juntillas que Euskadi y el Estado español están en guerra. Con ser una aberración, esta creencia no es lo peor. Lo peor es que los vascos de hoy que sufren este estrés post-traumático no se conciban a sí mismos si no es como individuos enfrentados unos a otros, aunque sea a otros vascos. En este sentido comparto la sobria diagnosis de Azurmendi, aunque la haría extensible a los no-abertzales. Mikel Azurmendi dice que "la metáfora-raíz de la identidad abertzale consiste en verse en peligro a causa del *otro* [*español*]" (109). Por tanto agregaría a esta cita que también, y de la misma manera, la identidad *anti-nacionalista*, e incluso la *no-nacionalista*, consiste en verse en peligro a causa de un *otro* abertzale, y como atrapado en un juego de espejos sin fin.[6] He aquí por qué en Euskadi resulta plausible —como dice mi crítico de la nota 5— la demonización de todos: de la policía vasca y hasta de las mismas víctimas del terrorismo etarra. ¿No es el colmo que en Euskadi se ha llegado a decir de las víctimas mortales de ETA "que algo habrán hecho" —para merecer un tiro en la nuca?

IV

Ahora, resultaría vano pretender solucionar con un ensayo un problema que requiere una praxis política y "policial". Pero al final de la violencia, cuando sólo se crucen palabras, aún quedará esta mentalidad de los enfrentamientos, cuya solución sí es en parte teórica. Y para encontrar la salida de este laberinto vasco, quizás convendría fijarse en la convergencia —según Charles Taylor— entre los contenciosos nacidos de este frentismo político y social y los debates académico-filosóficos acerca del llamado multiculturalismo. Estos debates —exactamente como las polémicas entre no-nacionalistas y abertzales vascos— pueden caracterizarse como conflictos entre una visión "ilustrada" y una opuesta visión herderiana o particularista. De hecho, la postura "ilustrada" (o anti-nacionalista) se considera la más "moderna" y universalista y suele tachar la postura abertzale de retrógrada y romántica.

El hecho es que si acercamos un debate a otro, se iluminan mutuamente. Con más precisión, una solución ofrecida en el debate sobre multiculturalismo contiene también la posible solución para el enfrentamiento entre vascos abertzales, y vascos anti-nacionalistas y no-nacionalistas. Y la adaptabilidad de la solución multiculturalista al otro debate se debe a que en lugar de favorecer ni la parte abertzale ni la parte anti- y no-nacionalista, nos permite dirimir los contrarios y aprovechar ambas partes.

Aquí en primer lugar nos interesa la definición de multiculturalismo de Charles Taylor por lo que tiene de implícita justificación filosófica del particularismo o nacionalismo vasco. Según Taylor, el multiculturalismo tiene como premisa la noción de que "el reconocimiento por parte de los otros constituye una condición fundamental para la formación de la identidad personal del individual (sic)" (Viroli 17). El multiculturalismo, entonces, fomenta lo que Taylor llama "una política del reconocimiento". Ahora, desde el punto de vista liberal, siempre es perfectamente lícita la reivindicación por grupos sociales "de derechos particulares (sobre todo en lo que respecta a la tutela del idioma)"; y esto porque el liberal acepta como principio que la viabilidad de la lengua y de la cultura de un pueblo sean de rigor "para que el individuo pueda formar autónomamente su propia personalidad moral" (Viroli 17). Es decir, el multiculturalista —aunque parecería sumergido en un grupo— argumenta la autonomía e igualdad de los grupos con un fin en última instancia *individualista*. Por tanto, aunque parezca haber una aproximación entre la visión multiculturalista y la visión liberal de los derechos, Taylor insiste que la primera va más lejos que la segunda.

> Para Taylor... la política del reconocimiento y de la diferencia es en cambio radicalmente distinta del universalismo liberal: la primera exige que se reconozca y trate con particular respeto la identidad única (*unique identity*) de un grupo en concreto; la segunda exige, sin embargo, que todos los individuos puedan gozar del mismo conjunto de derechos. En una palabra: el universalismo liberal quiere ser ciego; el multiculturalismo exige que las diferencias estén a la vista...". (Viroli 17)

Como explica Maurizio Viroli en su reseña, esto quiere decir que el multiculturalismo no es lo mismo que el principio tradicional de la tolerancia, ni que el principio liberal de la no-discriminación. Según Viroli parafrasea a Taylor:

> El multiculturalismo reconoce tanto el principio de la tolerancia como el de la no-discriminación, pero exige algo más: el reconocimiento por parte de la comunidad del igual *status* de los distintos grupos culturales, así como un apoyo activo del estado para mantener con vida a los grupos culturales. (17)

Como sabemos, casi todos los liberales comulgan con el principio de la tolerancia, incluso con la meta de que se reconozca a todos los grupos distintos. En cambio, lo que el liberal no tolera es la pretensión de los multiculturalistas de que el estado promocione y mantenga esos grupos "diferentes." Desde el punto de vista liberal esto sería contraproducente para el estado en tanto sólo serviría para restar la lealtad del individuo al estado. Es obvio, siguiendo con la comparación, que en esto los *anti*-nacionalistas sobre todo serían homologables con los liberales. Exactamente como los liberales, siempre partidarios del *fair play*, los anti- y no-nacionalistas

58

abogarían por una igualdad de oportunidades para todos los grupos, aunque en la práctica esa igualdad resultase limitada a los mismos grupos liberales (cuando fueran mayoritarios).

Visto lo cual, una respuesta adecuada al multiculturalismo (o al abertzalismo conservador y radical) no es accesible ni por la vía "ilustrada", ni por la anti-nacionalista, ni por la liberal. Porque la polémica entre el multiculturalista (o el nacionalista) y el liberal está basada en que cada uno se aferra a una idea distinta de la vida moral y del individuo. Por una parte, apunta Maurizio Viroli,

> los liberales insisten en principios morales universales y en la idea de que el individual (sic) trasciende todo grupo cultural; por otra, los multiculturalistas [o nacionalistas] subrayan el carácter contextual, dialógico, de la vida moral del sujeto y, por ende, la importancia del vínculo con el grupo cultural. (18)

De hecho estamos acostumbrados a escuchar del anti-nacionalista que el abertzale tiene conciencia de "ameba", es decir que no sabe distinguirse de la conciencia del grupo dentro del que se mueve. Mientras que según el abertzale, el anti- y el no-nacionalista serían una especie de "conciencia desgraciada", intelectuales típicamente alienados de su núcleo social. La resolución que esgrime Michael Walzer —autor del libro que reseña Virolli— para esta polémica no sólo es anti-liberal sino que además aúna las dos partes enfrentadas. En otro libro, *Thick and Thin* (Claro y espeso), Walzer ha distinguido entre "una teoría moral 'clara' (universal, abstracta, referida a la humanidad y al individuo en general) y una teoría moral 'espesa' (local, específica, vinculada a la cultura particular y a la historia de un pueblo o un grupo)", pero con el propósito de subrayar, comenta Viroli,

> que ambas perspectivas son incompletas y que, para afrontar de manera justa y eficaz el problema de la convivencia pacífica entre diversos grupos culturales es necesario combinar ambas perspectivas, la universalista y la particularista. (18)

El razonamiento de Walzer se fundamenta en una concepción posmoderna del yo, al que considera cortado por varias divisiones. La primera división está relacionada con los distintos papeles que cada persona hace y los fines que persigue no sólo a lo largo de la vida sino cada día. Se es sindicalista o patrón, médico o paciente, y a cada caso corresponden responsabilidades y beneficios. Pero al mismo tiempo cada cual asume diferentes identidades eventuales; para Walzer uno/a se define respecto a su grupo particular nacional, la religión, o la adscripción política; se ve reflejado hoy sí, mañana no, en diferentes historias, grupos, y hasta lenguas, y cada uno depende de una identidad supraindividual, espesa y colectiva. En palabras de M. Viroli, "En el interior del yo posmoderno hablan distintas voces morales; somos capaces de autocrítica, tenemos dudas morales, angustias, incertidumbres". En base a esta concepción del yo polifacético, para Walzer los problemas de justicia local e internacional sólo pueden abordarse con "teorías complejas, densas y sutiles, [y] no con doctrinas únicamente sutiles o únicamente densas". La identidad de cada cual, en tanto vasco, o serbio, o esquimal,

> exige a pleno pulmón ser protegida y reconocida por un estado nacional; pero a esta voz se une la del ciudadano o la del individual (sic) que reclama derechos políticos y civiles; y aún una tercera, la de la pertenencia a la comunidad religiosa, que pide tolerancia. Puede ocurrir, sucede a menudo, que una parte de nosotros mismos se convierta en crítica de otra. (Viroli 18)

Dada la multiplicidad de cada yo, se requiere una nueva concepción pluralista de la justicia, lejos del sentido del viejo "pluralismo" liberal. Según concluye Walzer:

> Necesitamos ser tolerados y protegidos en tanto que ciudadanos del estado y miembros de grupos —*y también en tanto que ajenos a ambos*—. La autodeterminación ha de ser a la vez política y *personal* —ambas se interrelacionan, pero no son lo mismo—. La antigua forma de entender la diferencia, que vincula a los individuos con sus grupos autónomos o soberanos *encontrará resistencia entre* [los] *disidentes e individuos ambivalentes*. Pero cualquier nueva forma de comprensión que se centre *sólo en el disidente* encontrará resistencia entre hombres y mujeres que aún luchen por absorber, efectuar, elaborar, revisar y enjuiciar una tradición religiosa o cultural común. (Viroli 18)[7]

En opinión de Walzer, hay que olvidarse de viejas ideas imperiales y buscar "espacios justos" (M. Viroli) donde la gente, los grupos puedan vivir de acuerdo con su propio ethos y cultura. Y lógicamente esto requeriría soluciones diferentes para distintos grupos —estado independiente, comunidad autonómica, o incluso federación. En palabras de Viroli, para Walzer

> El punto de partida, si queremos reducir la intransigencia e intolerancia de los nacionalistas, debe ser la tolerancia y el reconocimiento. Si conseguimos que no se sientan amenazados, (...) los líderes nacionalistas no conseguirán hacer creer a nadie que amenazar a los otros sea el interés de la tribu. La historia alecciona: los fanáticos religiosos del siglo XVII se vuelven poco a poco inocuos desde el momento en que se les garantiza el derecho a practicar su religión (18).

En fin, la resolución combinatoria que ofrece Walzer consiste en contrapesar el empuje "centrífugo" del individuo con el abrazo de los "grupos culturales... de la sociedad civil", y al mismo tiempo aligerar el peso centrípeto de éstos con el empuje de los individuos "disidentes".

Y ahora, demos por terminado nuestro examen de la convergencia entre las dos polémicas con esta pregunta retórica de Michael Walzer: ¿Por qué una política parecida no iba a tener un efecto disuasorio para nuestros nacionalistas?

Sin embargo, ¿por qué tanta invectiva "ilustrada" hoy contra nacionalistas y abertzales, y tanto desprecio "liberal" contra multiculturalistas —ambas actitudes sin duda políticamente correctas? ¿Y cómo explicar la coincidencia de pro-multiculturalismo y anti-abertzalismo en las mismas mentes vascas ilustradas? No diría que cuarenta años de franquismo no causaran graves daños psicológicos en la población del resto de España, pero esa no es la cuestión aquí. Aquí se trata de deslindar por qué los anti- y no-nacionalistas del País Vasco no reconocen como normal y positiva la reiterada demanda (o requerimiento) de reconocimiento y de apoyo estatal de los nacionalistas. En mi opinión se trata de los efectos especialmente traumáticos de la "ocupación" franquista de Euskadi, y de los muchos "estados de excepción" durante y después del franquismo —sin descartar la represión civil violenta ejercida desde ETA.

Pero si después de veinticinco años de Transición democrática, "la herida patriótica" de Euskadi sigue abierta, también es un factor la actitud del "profesional" de la política vasca y nacional. Porque los mismos que en el primer momento de la Transición jaleaban cualquier gesto independentista de los abertzales conservadores o radicales, hoy se dedican a denigrar todo asomo de nacional-separatismo local. Ellos fueron, quizás sin pretenderlo, los primeros promotores del hoy existente "frentismo" a nivel local y nacional. Y ellos son los que hoy potencian ese yo monolítico de los votantes porque les va la vida y el voto en ello. He aquí por qué ahora los políticos tratan de extirpar todo polifacético yo postmoderno. No quieren para nada que se ventile el hecho de que existen vascos de lealtades diversas y hasta cruzadas: cívicas, religiosas y políticas; y que hay vascos capaces de votar al Partido Popular en las elecciones municipales de San Sebastián y a Eusko Alkartasuna en las elecciones generales, o viceversa. El profesional de la política vasca o española prefiere no reconocer que su votante puede ser un anti-nacionalista "muy vasco", un vasco-español, o un vasco-vasco muy socialista. Ellos, tanto los políticos abertzales como los políticos anti-nacionalistas, son los verdaderos enemigos de la comprensión mutua. Se oponen a los disidentes pero también trabajan por "el debilitamiento de las asociaciones de la sociedad civil y de los agrupamientos étnicos" (Viroli, 19). Porque ellos saben que cuando un grupo se siente débil y amenazado sus exigencias se vuelven más radicales. Pero el remedio, concluye Walzer, es potenciar ambos: *al grupo y al disidente*, porque

> Nuestros activistas religiosos o étnicos empiezan defendiendo los intereses de la propia comunidad, y terminan entrando a formar parte de coaliciones políticas, esforzándose por encontrar acomodo en formaciones equilibradas, y expresándose (cuando menos) en términos de bien común. La cohesividad (sic) del grupo vigoriza a sus miembros y la movilidad y ambición de los miembros más vigorosos liberaliza al grupo. (Viroli 19)

Quiere decirse que la promiscuidad civil y el proteísmo natural del ciudadano postmoderno conllevan un potente polimorfismo político, en contra del deseo de los mismos políticos. Y por ese camino se podría llegar a paliar los antagonismos innecesarios y a reducir los reflejos cívicos de este estrés post-traumático vasco.

Notas

1. El título "¡Malditos pueblos!" procede de un artículo de Opinión en *El País* (Madrid) del filósofo donostiarra Fernando Savater.
2. Como nota bibliográfica, véase sobre todo las ediciones inglesas de esta novela. Por errores de imprenta las americanas han perdido de vista las divisiones de la novela en capitulillos sin enumerar.
3. El subrayado es mío.
4. También Ortega y Gasset aludió al nacionalismo como enfermedad (contagiosa) en *España invertebrada* (1925).
5. La tesis de la represión de Jauréguiberry solo explicaría una fase *temprana* (pre-Transición) de esta sorprendente asimilación de inmigrantes en el País Vasco. Como ha observado un lector vasco del presente ensayo: "por una parte, hay un complejo asimilacionista de hacerse más vasco que nadie, lo que obliga a los inmigrantes a aparecer como los más abertzales; pero [por otra parte] ... silencias en tu trabajo el amedrentamiento de ETA. El voto abertzale entre emigrantes ha crecido sobre todo en los pequeños pueblos y comarcas cerradas, donde el miedo a aparecer como extraño, traidor y txakurra [miembro de las FOP] eran impresionantes. No parece que hayas tomado para nada en cuenta que aquí se ha estado matando a granel durante estos 20 años [de la Transición], y que ello motivaba interiorizar algo de culpa, en el sentido de pensar que algo de razón tendrán cuando se dejan matar y torturar por esa idea anti-Estado. Esta carencia es flagrante en tu escrito. No hay víctimas de verdad, solamente traumatizados. [...] Eso de que 'los propios inmigrantes eligieron ser vascos, etcetera', me suena a discurso hueco. ¿Eligieron sin coacción? ¿Qué hacía ETA mientras ellos elegían? Este silencio de la violencia etarra como factor psicológico para achantar al personal me ha dejado perplejo ante el altavoz potente que, en cambio, le has puesto a la violencia franquista".
6. Parece que en el País Vasco, a diferencia de la alienación postmoderna, persiste una férrea identidad grupal. En efecto, el EPT hace que hasta mentalidades "ilustradas" padezcan lo mismo y se enconen con la *otredad* nacionalista.
7. El subrayado es mío. Se podría formular a la tesis de Walzer una pregunta acerca de la viabilidad del concepto yo postmoderno, si se aplicara al entorno

vasco y/o español en general. Mi opinión personal —sin matizar— se esboza en la nota 6. Quizás habría que agregar la noción demográfica de que en España se daría un yo postmoderno debido a la masificación y alienación en las ciudades, pero mucho menos en los pequeños pueblos.

Obras Citadas

Azurmendi, Mikel. *La herida patriótica: la cultura del nacionalismo vasco.* Madrid: Taurus, 1998.

Caruth, Cathy. Ed. e introducción, *Trauma: Explorations in Memory.* Baltimore: The Johns Hopkins University Press, 1995.

Erikson, Kai. "Notes on Trauma and Community" en Caruth, ed. *Trauma: Explorations in Memory.* Baltimore: The Johns Hopkins University Press, 1995: 183-99.

Estornés Zubizarreta, Idoia. "Sobre torpeza y frentismo." *Historia* 1.4 (1999): 14.

Gutmann, Amy. Ed. *Multiculturalism: Examining the Politics of Recognition.* Princeton, N.Y.: Princeton University Press, 1994.

Jauréguiberry, Francis. *Question nationale et mouvements sociaux en Pays Basque Sud.* Thèse de doctorat de troisième cycle de sociologie sous la direction du Professeur A. Touraine. Paris: École de Hautes Études en Sciences Sociales, 1983.

Juaristi, Jon. *El bucle melancólico: Historias de Nacionalistas Vascos.* Madrid: Espasa Calpe, 1997.

Mina, Javier. "La biblioteca de Babel." *El País (del País Vasco).* 4 de abril, 1999: 2.

O'Brien, Connor Cruise. *Ancestral Voices: Religion and Nationalism in Ireland,* 2a ed. Chicago: The University of Chicago Press, 1995.

Savater, Fernando. "¡Malditos pueblos!" en *El País* (Madrid) 30 de abril, 1999: 17-18.

Taylor, Charles. "The Politics of Recognition" [1990] en Amy Gutmann (ed.), *Multiculturalism: Examining the Politics of Recognition.* Princeton, N.Y.: Princeton University Press, 1994: 25-73.

Viroli, Maurizio. "Multicultura e individualismo" en *Revista de libros* 26 (1999): 17-19.

Walzer, Michael. *Tratado sobre la tolerancia* (Barcelona: Paidós, 1998). Reseñado por Viroli, *Revista de libros* 26 (1999).

Woolf, Virginia. *Mrs. Dalloway* [1925]. London: Grafton Books, 1990.

4

History and Hauntology; or, What Does One Do with the Ghosts of the Past? Reflections on Spanish Film and Fiction of the Post-Franco Period

Jo Labanyi

In this essay I shall link a number of films and works of fiction produced in Spain during the last three decades. The question I shall be asking is what does a society—in particular, Spanish society of the transition and since—do with history; that is, what does it do with the ghosts of the past? Given current criticisms of contemporary Spanish culture, triggered by the 1992 quincentennial commemorations, for refusing to confront the traumas of the past, this is an important question. While agreeing that, in many respects, contemporary Spanish culture—obsessed with creating the image of a brash, young, cosmopolitan nation—is based on a rejection of the past, I want to stress the engagement with history by a considerable number of directors and writers, both older and young; and also to suggest, tentatively, that the current postmodern obsession with simulacra may be seen as a return of the past in spectral form.

Just as there are many kinds of ghosts (I shall be talking about werevolves, vampires, Frankenstein's monster as well as the politically displaced or "desaparecidos"), so there are various ways of dealing with them. One can refuse to see them or shut them out, as the official discourses of the State have always done with the various manifestations of the popular imaginary, where for good reasons ghost stories are endemic. One can cling to them obsessively through the pathological process of introjection that Freud called melancholia, allowing the past to take over the present and convert it into a "living death." Or one can offer them habitation in order to acknowledge their presence, through the healing introjection process that is mourning, which, for Freud, differs from melancholia in that it allows one to lay the ghosts of the past to rest by, precisely, acknowledging them as past. The first two options—denying the existence of ghosts, becoming possessed by them—in different ways result in a denial of history (through repression or through paralysis). The last option—accepting the past as past—is an acknowledgment of history, that allows one to live with its traces. As Derrida nicely puts it in *Specters of Marx*, ghosts must be exorcised not in order to chase them away but in order "this time to grant them the right [...] to [...] a hospitable memory [...] out of a concern for justice" (175). For ghosts, as the traces of those who have not been allowed to leave a trace (Derrida's formulation again)—are by definition the victims of history who return to demand reparation; that is, that their name, instead of being erased, be honoured. This concept helps explain why the ungrammatical term "los desaparecidos" (in English, "the disappeared"), which wrongly uses "desaparecer" as a transitive verb, so caught the imagination at the time of the military take-overs in Chile, Argentina and Uruguay: for it constructs the dead, by virtue of the fact that they have not just "disappeared" but have "been disappeared," as ghosts or revenants (to use the French term) who refuse to have their presence erased but insist on returning to demand that their name be honoured. Derrida has proposed the term "hauntology" as a new philosophical category of being—an alternative to ontology—appropriate to describe the status of history: that is, the past as that which is not and yet is there—or rather, here. That this "virtual space of spectrality" (Derrida 11) is somehow related to the simulacra of postmodernism is an idea that immediately suggests itself.

In their book *Memory and Modernity: Popular Culture in Latin America*, Rowe and Schelling recount a startling anecdote:

> There are conditions under which a massive erasure of memory can occur. A study, begun in 1985, of villas miserias (shanty towns) in Córdoba, Argentina, has revealed an absence of memory of the period of military government (1976-85), as compared with the years preceding it. This silence is not the result of fear: informants were not hesitant with information about their activities in the preceding period, details of which could equally be considered "subversive." Nor does it indicate a lack of knowledge, since the issue was what they remembered not about the country or the government but about their own lives. (119-20)

Rowe and Schelling suggest that the reason for this traumatic erasure of memory was the lack, during the period of military dictatorship, of any form of collective sphere other than that imposed by surveillance; that is, the lack of any space in which memories could be articulated. What is so striking here is that the casualty of this suppression of all forms of collective discourse should have been private memories. For popular memory—relying on oral rather than written transmission—requires some kind of collective space, even if it be reduced to that of the family (which is never a purely private sphere). When teaching adult Spanish students who grew up under Francoism, I have frequently been struck by the fact that the only historical knowledge they had about Spain's immediate past was transmitted to them by their families (and "family" here means a collective, extended family network).

Interesting work has been done in France by Pierre Nora (1984-93) on the notion of lieux de mémoire or "memory places": that is, the dependence of memories on attachment to some concrete site; for example, a monument or a landscape. This concept has also been developed by Raphael Samuel in his wonderful book *Theatres of Memory*. The sense of place in the films of Erice or the novels of Marsé and Llamazares is extraordinarily strong—but in all cases these are spaces where the possibility of collectivity and communication is denied or at best curtailed. One thinks of the oppressive silences in *El espíritu de la colmena* (1973) and *El sur* (1983); the image of snow blotting out the traces of landscape and with it memory in *Luna de lobos* (1985) and *Escenas de cine mudo* (1994), plus in both novels the image of the mine which forces memory underground into a disaster-prone space that threatens, and frequently causes, obliteration; while in Marsé's novels the barrio succeeds in keeping popular memory alive only in the form of dispersed, discontinuous, phantasmatic fragments. It is also worth noting that *El sur* and Marsé's novels focus on Andalusian migrants in the north, while Llamazares's novels deal with the Leonese maquis forced into hiding or (in *Escenas de cine mudo*) a series of travellers who pass through the Leonese mining village, while Llamazares is himself coming to terms with his own uprooting from his Leonese village now submerged beneath a pantano. In *Beatus Ille* (1986) and *El jinete polaco* (1991), Antonio Muñoz Molina similarly recreates his fictional Mágina—modelled on his own former hometown, Ubeda—through a return to roots by his protagonists from economic exile in Madrid and New York respectively. In all these cases, there is a traumatic crisis of memory related to a geographical displacement or "loss of place."

In *El sur*, Erice's disagreement with his producer halfway through making the film resulted in the scenes due to be shot in "the south" never being completed, with the felicitous result that, contrary to García Morales' story where Estrella goes to Seville and meets her father's former lover, in the film "the south" remains a ghostly presence, felt but invisible. In evoking "the south," Estrella is, of course, conjuring up the ghost of her dead Sevillan father, whose memory lives in her through the pendulum whose function is to divine the presence of that which is invisible: that is, ghosts. The film also changes the profession of her father's former lover to that of film star, reinforcing the notion of the past as ghost, for the human figure on screen is, literally, a shadow: a spectral presence that is and is not there. The cinema is also central to the topography of the barrio in Marsé's novels, where its spectral images form the basis of the construction of popular memory, allowing the past to endure as a ghostly presence that cannot be suppressed precisely because it lacks tangible form. The jumble of film images and snatches of historical memory in the adventure stories told by the boys in *Si te dicen que caí* (1973, authorized for publication in Spain 1976) makes the point that the status of history, particularly but not only under censorship, is that of ghost haunting the present: not there but there. The first of the family photographs on which Llamazares's *Escenas de cine mudo* is based consists in the young Julio standing in front of the stills outside the village cinema. It is the film stills, rather than the films themselves, that leave their trace in Marsé's work, as images of a spectral past that, unlike official versions of history, is discontinuous, lacking in causal logic, and for that very reason offers a space to let the ghosts of the past in, allowing popular memory to elaborate the ghost stories that are the stuff of oral history. Indeed, the boys' stories in *Si te dicen que caí* are attempts to conjure up the ghosts of the "desaparecidos" Marcos and Aurora/Carmen. The spectral quality of the film image is, I suggest, one of the reasons why it so "haunts" fiction of the post-Franco era, as the expression of a history that can be recovered only in spectral form. In this sense, one could argue that even those writers who, in true postmodernist fashion, replace history with a series of film images are, despite their apparent historical evasion, at least acknowledging the existence of ghosts. The phrase "post-Franco era," after all, defines it as a period haunted by a spectral Francoist past.

68

Photographs, like film stills, play an important role as images of a fragmentary, discontinuous, spectral past in *Si te dicen que caí*, as they do in Muñoz Molina's *Beatus Ille* and especially *El jinete polaco*, in which the past emerges from the gaps in between the photographs of Ramiro Retratista. Echoing Barthes's famous essay on photography (1984), Ramiro Retratista perceives his photographs as ghostly images of the dead: "cuando examinaba una foto recién hecha pensaba que a la larga sería, como todas, el retrato de un muerto, de modo que lo intranquilizaba siempre la molesta sospecha de no ser un fotógrafo, sino una especie de enterrador prematuro" (*El jinete* 93). But this is the case only because the photograph has the capacity to immortalize its subjects after death, in "una clandestina y universal resurrección de los muertos" bringing back to life "aquellas vidas que luego no quiso nadie recordar" (495). Indeed, as the narrator's girlfriend Nadia comments, the only person who cannot be brought back from the dead is the photographer himself, absent from his photographs (499). Ramiro Retratista's key photograph is, of course, that of the mummified body—a literal embodiment of a returning past—of the mysterious "emparedada," stories of whose discovery "haunted" the protagonist's childhood: a mummified corpse later replaced by a wax simulacrum, but nonetheless kept alive in the collective imaginary. Similarly, history enters *El espíritu de la colmena* as a ghostly presence via the prewar photograph of Ana's father with Unamuno. In *Escenas de cine mudo*, the "silent cinema" of the title consists in Llamazares's narrative animation of the "stills" comprised by the family snapshots kept by his mother.

Walter Benjamin has described the historian as collector or bricoleur, in the sense that he or she rummages around in the debris or litter left by the past, and reassembles the fragments in a new "constellation" that permits the articulation of that which has been left unvoiced (Benjamin 45-104; Frisby 187-265). Benjamin's historian—who looks for significance in fragments and details normally overlooked—is a historian of popular culture: that is, of trivia—for it is trivia that give us the "structure of feeling" that Raymond Williams saw as the key to understanding a particular period of history. Benjamin is to cultural history what Eisenstein is to film: that is, the theorist of montage. According to Benjamin's theory of cultural history as montage, the historian not only collects bits of rubble from amid the ruins of the past, but reduces the past to ruins and rubble—that is, broken bits and pieces—so it can be reassembled to create new meanings through the dialectical confrontation of fragments that normally are separate. One thinks here of the anarchist leader Durruti's magnificent reply to a foreign journalist during the Civil War: "We're not afraid of ruins" (qtd. in Cleminson 117). The historian's task is thus, not to put the uprooted fragments of the past back into their context, but to decontextualize even that which has not been reduced to ruins and rubble, allowing new relationships to be created. This, one may note, is exactly what the boys do with their aventis in Marsé's *Si te dicen que caí*, and what the protagonist and Nadia do as they rummage through the photographs and other objects in the trunk of the now dead Ramiro Retratista in Muñoz Molina's *El jinete polaco*. As excavator of ruins and "rubbish collector," Benjamin's cultural historian is a topographer, but one who defamiliarizes the maps made by official surveyors (whose function is to put everything in its "proper place") in order to create an alternative, fantasmagorical topography that can recover, not just things, but the dreams and desires attached to them which did not find realization as "fact": that is, popular history. Another image used by Benjamin is that of the photographer who produces a photographic negative of "normality," in which light and dark are reversed (this, one may note, reduces human figures to ghosts), and who can focus on a detail, or extract a detail and amplify it, destroying illusory official notions of history as continuity and allowing that which is normally overlooked to speak. Benjamin saw this as a materialist history, but it is also a history that, in acknowledging that which is normally rendered invisible (what Benjamin calls the "optical unconscious"), gives habitation to ghosts.

Ghosts, as Avery Gordon notes in her suggestive book *Ghostly Matters: Haunting and the Sociological Imagination*, give "embodiment" to those figures from the past who have been rendered invisible; that is, "desaparecidos." Likewise Benjamin's dialectical method of montage "animates" the fragmentary debris of history. Animation is precisely what Llamazares does to the snapshots that form the basis of *Escenas de cine mudo*, and also what Marsé does to the reproduction of Torrijos's execution on the carpet in *Si te dicen que caí*: in turning photographs and figure in the carpet into a form of silent cinema, they are giving the past a ghostly embodiment. Animation and montage are the cinematic techniques used by Basilio Martín Patino in his historical documentary films *Canciones para después de una guerra* (1971, authorized for release 1975) and *Caudillo* (1976), which construct an alternative history through the articulation of popular memory, combining voice-over personal memories with a varied range of cultural trivia (advertisements, comics, and above all popular film and song) intercut with newreel footage which concentrates on images of the debris of war and, above all, of the "desaparecidos" leaving for exile. The popular songs sing overwhelmingly of loss and absence, conjuring up the ghosts of history who have been rendered invisible. Patino's brilliant use of superimpositions and dissolves give the human figures in the documentary footage a ghostly quality appropriate to this evocation of the "disappeared," and reducing Franco and other official figures to the same ghostly status. But as ghosts, both the victims and the victors of history are a living presence that we are forced to acknowledge: the animation of newsreel footage or children's comics depicting Franco not only makes him ridiculous but reminds us that ghosts can be placated only if their presence is recognized. For these two films, Patino did a huge amount of archival work, "digging up" in Berlin previously unknown film footage in an excavation of popular memory that Benjamin would surely have admired. Worthy of Benjamin also is Patino's dialectical concept of montage which intercuts sequences moving in different directions (from right to left, from left to right), in a rapid succession of visual fragments lifted out of context and reorganized into a new constellation releasing alternative meanings. It is worth noting that *Caudillo* opens with an evocative sequence of ruins, including human ruins, left by the Civil War, leading directly into a pictorial representation of Franco, thereby constructed as a spectre inhabiting the ruins of the past.

For ruins are the favourite habitat of ghosts. The boys in *Si te dicen que caí* conjure up the ghosts of the past in the ruins of the crypt of the appropriately named church Las Ánimas, also frequented by Rosita in the later novella *Ronda del Guinardó* (1984). The fugitive or "desaparecido" in *El espíritu de la colmena* materializes as an apparition from an unknown past in a ruined, abandoned hut. As Paul Julian Smith has noted, Erice's film insists on the time-ravaged texture of walls and faces, giving both things and adult humans the quality of ruins: that is, relics haunted by the memory of the past.[1] Like Benjamin, Raphael Samuel describes the

71

historian of popular memory as a rubbish collector "scavenging among what others are busy engaged in throwing out or consigning to the incinerator" (20). The American historian of popular culture, Greil Marcus, in his collection of essays *The Dustbin of History*, bewails the contemporary tendency, in our obsession with the new, to scorn the past, as in phrases such as "It's history," which, as he notes, is a kind of contagious "language-germ" that means the opposite of what it says: "It means that there is no such thing as history, a past of burden and legacy" for "once something [...] is 'history,' it's over, and it is understood that it never existed at all"— "Gone—it's history" (Marcus 22-23). As he comments, "The result is a kind of euphoria, a weightless sense of freedom." Marcus notes that the phrase "dustbin of history" was coined by Trostsky in 1917 when he said of the Mensheviks: "you are bankrupts; your role is played out. Go where you belong from now on—into the dustbin of history." Since then, as Marcus wryly notes, we have been busy consigning history's losers to the "dustbin of history" in our mania for recording only success stories and our embarrassment at the existence of losers who contradict our Western obsession with progress. Marcus's essays in popular history are an attempt to write from inside the dustbin of history; that is, from inside the "historical hell" to which history's losers are assigned as ghostly "shades" or "shadows"—a dustbin or hell which is "a wasteland in which all are distant from each other, because this is a territory, unlike history, without any borders at all—without any means to a narrative, a language with which to tell a story" (Marcus 18). As Marcus puts it: "written history, which makes the common knowledge out of which our newspapers report the events of the day, creates its own refugees, displaced persons, men and women without a country, cast out of time, the living dead" (17). What makes these "refugees from history" (one thinks of the refugee in *El espíritu de la colmena*, who leaps from a train, a classic image of history as progress) the "living dead" is the fact that they are denied memory: not only because their story is not recorded by others, but because "the shame of stories they cannot tell and that no one would believe if they could" means that they "can barely credit even their own memories" (Marcus 20). It is crucial that the refugee in *El espíritu de la colmena* has no articulated or articulatable past. It is also important that, in *Beatus Ille*, we have no way of knowing how much of the historical reconstruction we are reading is the account of the

72

officially dead Solana—who "appears" to the protagonist Minaya in a cemetery—and how much of the narrative is written by Minaya. The novel's final postmodern twist, in which Solana reveals that he has trapped his biographer Minaya in his own narrative, but in which he also bequeathes his text (and his lover Inés) to Minaya, to be completed by him, foregrounds the impossibility of history's losers making public their own historical accounts, and the ethical imperative which demands that future generations take up their ghostly legacy, as an act of historical reparation.

As Marcus insists, the stories of such "refugees from history" do not make sense; they puncture the continuity of what we take for history as if they were "stories told by cranks" (37). Marcus notes that thriller writers have been able to capture the horror of the Holocaust in a way that historians rarely have, because they are not bent on explaining it; as Marcus comments, one does not explain an abyss, one locates it (59-62). It is the strong sense of place in Erice's films and Marsé's novels that captures the horror of a historical period traumatized by the prohibition on recalling the past through memory and narrative. Marsé's novels are "stories told by cranks," while Erice's films are focalized through the eyes of female children or adolescents who have not yet learnt to explain horror away. Marcus has Walter Benjamin in mind when he warns us to "Beware of the smooth surface of history, looking backwards, making everything make sense," because "It made no sense at the time, like a random series of jump cuts" (18): the first time Erice shows us the ruined hut where the "desaparecido" will materialize from nowhere, he does so through a series of jump cuts. In *El jinete polaco*, the protagonist compares his experience of history to that of watching a film lacking in continuity editing (247) or where the images succeed each other so fast that one loses the thread and cannot make out the connections (248); his reconstruction of the past, as he attempts to fill in the gaps between Ramiro Retratista's photographs, highlights these discontinuities rather than ironing them out. Marcus insists on the need to counter the deceptive seamlessness of what goes down as history (what he calls "history as disappearance"), which edits out the bits that do not fit the master narrative of success stories, by letting in through the cracks and disturbances (through the jump cuts) those parts of history that "survive only as haunts and fairy tales, accessible only as spectres and spooks" (Marcus 24). *El jinete polaco* "resurrects" a past kept alive through the ghost stories told to the narrator as a child, just as *Beatus Ille* literally "resurrects" its hero Solana, officially declared dead by the Civil Guard in the 1940s. Marcus's epigraphs include the Sex Pistols' line "We're the flowers in your dustbin" and Bakhtin's dictum "Nothing is absolutely dead; every meaning will have its homecoming festival."

Bakhtin, of course, is the chronicler of the popular cultural forms that, from the Renaissance onwards, were gradually forced underground by the growing division between "high" and "low" cultural forms. In writing from inside the "dustbin of history," Marcus is constructing an alternative history from discontinuous fragments of popular culture: pop music, pop art and popular literary forms such as the thriller. In much the same way, Patino's *Canciones para después de una guerra* creates a discontinuous alternative history out of snatches of popular song, rescued from the dustbin to which popular culture is so often consigned and recycled to form a "usable past"; indeed, the film shows how, in "los años del hambre," history's losers themselves recycled songs from earlier periods or songs written by the victors, investing them with alternative meanings as a strategy for coping with loss and bereavement. Snatches of popular song are also woven into the "aventis" or stories told by the boys in *Si te dicen que caí*, whose leader is Java, a "trapero" who recycles rubbish; indeed, many of the stories are told in his "trapería," which is also reputedly the hideout of the "desaparecido" Marcos, quite literally walled up in the "dustbin of history" (one thinks here also of the "emparedada," another of history's losers, in *El jinete polaco*). Images of rubbish and of hell run throughout *Si te dicen que caí* and *Ronda del Guinardó*; I would read these images not just as signs of moral and physical degradation, but as a metaphorical figure of the consignment of history's losers to the "dustbin of history" which at the same time is a "historical hell" inhabited by the living dead.

Which brings me to vampires, werewolves and other forms of the "undead." In chapter 21 of *Si te dicen que caí*, on the pretext of Luisito's death from tuberculosis, the boys tell the story of his visit to the Siamese Consulate, at the time of his father's second "disappearance," where his mother has been summoned to receive news of "un hermano desaparecido en la guerra" (303). The boys recount this episode in the form of a vampire story, which mobilizes the genre's diverse connotations.[2] Just before this vampire story starts, we are told of the tramp Mianet's stories of "niños que raptaban para chuparles la sangre": a "story told by a crank" which "explains" the prevalence of tuberculosis in "los años del hambre" as the vampirism of the poor by wealthy who, in drawing blood from kidnapped children to prolong their own life, turn them too into vampires who waste away for lack of lifeblood (303). The same popular explanation of tuberculosis is related in Muñoz Molina's *El jinete polaco* (77). Such popular "explanations" do not explain horror away; indeed, what could be more appropriate to capture the horror of the immediate postwar period than a horror story? True to form, in *Si te dicen que caí* the vampire in the boys' story appears to the tubercular Luisito immediately after he coughs up blood. It has been noted that stories of vampires (and of the kidnapping of children for organ transplants) have been rife in Peru and other parts of South America in recent years as a way of dealing with historical trauma.[3] The notion of the wealthy (particularly the moneylender) as vampires or bloodsuckers draining the poor is an old one, evidenced in Galdós's *La desheredada*, where Juan Bou calls the rich "sanguijuelas del pueblo."[4] El Tuerto, with his vampire-like dead eye, drains Luisito not just of his lifeblood but "también la memoria le vaciaron, el pobre nunca más llegó a acordarse de nada" (*Si te dicen* 309). For vampires are the "living dead" because they have no memory (and thus no shadow or reflection): the disease with which Luisito is infected is that of the amnesia of the regime, which the boys' stories, keeping the "desaparecidos" alive through narrative, are an attempt to stave off. It is loss of historical memory that allows the boys' fathers to degenerate from urban guerrillas into petty criminals. Vázquez Montalbán, in *Crónica sentimental de España* (1980), has also described the effects of Francoist repression and censorship as a "vampirización de la memoria." Sarnita, the chief teller of "aventis," in later life becomes a morgue attendant, who accompanies the dead in their historical underworld, keeping their memory alive through his own remembrance.

As all writers on the subject insist, vampires are close relatives of the werewolf: both predators on the living who are human and yet non-human. Vampire stories are complicated because the vampire turns his victims into vampires too; indeed, many vampire stories express pity for the vampire who is condemned to a living death (in *Si te dicen que caí*, El Tuerto has become a vampire because he previously was the victim of torture at the hands of Marcos and Aurora). Llamazares's *Luna de lobos* casts in the role of werewolf the rural guerrillas forced into clandestinity in the Cantabrian mountains after the civil war: predatory loners not of their own choosing; a "living dead" (repeatedly described as "muertos," "sombras" and "fantasmas") who bury themselves in caves or underground during the day, and emerge only at night. If the vampire has no memory, Llamazares's werewolves depend on memory: not their own but that of the collective in the form of the villagers and the Civil Guards who, out of love or terror, keep them alive as ghosts of the past through the stories they tell about them. In struggling to survive in the snow, the maquis are struggling against the threat of oblivion (whiteness/blankness). Greil Marcus laments the recent prevalence of apocalyptic narratives that assign the past to "history" in the sense of non-existence. It is important that Llamazares's novel is open-ended: the last of the maquis is expelled from the memory of his loved ones in the village and is left with no alternative but to "disappear" into exile, but at the end of the novel he is still alive and, most importantly, is telling his story.

The centrality to *El espíritu de la colmena* of Frankenstein's monster has been much commented on. While the monster has mostly been seen as an embodiment of the "otherness" which the Franco regime sought to repress by demonizing it—an association made explicit by Ana's equation of the monster with the refugee or "desaparecido"—it has also been connected with Ana's father, seen as an embodiment of patriarchal authority (Evans). Ana's father's connection with the monster is clear from the scene when he is filmed via his shadow in a retake of Murnau's classic vampire film *Nosferatu.* But there are problems with this interpretation, not so much because it casts the monster in the role of both victim and oppressor (we have seen how vampires are both), as because Ana's father—played by Fernando Fernán Gómez who, although never a political activist, had since the 1950s moved in opposition cultural circles—is a kindly figure, whose prewar association with Unamuno casts him as a Republican intellectual. I should like to suggest a different reading of the monster image in the film, whereby he represents not so much the demonization of the "other" as their assignment to the status of "living dead": Frankenstein created his monster out of body parts taken from a collection of corpses. In this sense, the monster stands as the embodiment, which returns to haunt the present, of a collective living death, which includes Ana's father as Republican intellectual denied self-expression except through his

76

private diary, just as Ana's mother can tell her story only through letters to a "desaparecido" or ghost. There is no suggestion in the film that the fugitive is Ana's mother's former lover, but they both share the condition of being ghosts of history. In offering the fugitive hospitality, Ana is carrying out Derrida's moral imperative of granting ghosts "the right [...] to [...] a hospitable memory [...] out of a concern for justice"—indeed, by giving him her father's watch, she is reinserting him into historical time. Ana is right to see the fugitive as the embodiment of the monster in James Whale's film for, as we have seen, films do not so much represent reality as embody it in the form of shadows or ghosts. Appropriately, the body of the "desaparecido" is laid out beneath the screen where the film *Frankenstein* had previously been shown. As in Patino's *Canciones, El espíritu de la colmena* insists on shots of the cinema audience watching the shadows on the screen, showing how ghosts are given embodiment in the collective memory which, after the show is over, can continue to tell their story.

The final words of the film, "Soy Ana," have encouraged readings which minimize its political significance by seeing it as a Freudian narrative of Ana's oedipal trajectory, as she learns to separate from parental figures and establish an autonomous identity. Avery Gordon, in her book *Ghostly Matters* (50-8), notes that Freud, while acknowledging the importance of haunting in his work on mourning and melancholia, nevertheless dehistoricizes it by theorizing it as a psychological projection. Indeed, she observes that Freud's early anthropological reading of spirits as a form of animism, whereby men introject the dead into themselves in the form of totemism, was leading him towards a historical theory of hauntology, but that he stepped back from this (just as he stepped back from acknowledging that his female patients were the victims of real seduction by the father), instead positing ghosts as a purely imaginary externalization of the inner contents of the unconscious. Derrida makes similar points about Marx's use of spectral imagery to figure the psychological projection that is bourgeois ideology (171-2). Gordon and Derrida insist that ghosts are not psychic projections, but the form in which the past lives on in the present. In this sense, Gordon insists that haunting is "neither pre-modern superstition nor individual psychosis" but "a constituent element of modern social life" (7). Faced with such a phenomenon, sociology—traditionally based on facts and statistics—does not know what to do and thus has joined the censors by insisting that ghosts do not exist. How, Avery asks, "do we reckon with what modern history has rendered ghostly? How do we develop a critical language to describe and analyze the affective, historical, and mnemonic structures of such hauntings?" (18). Her answer is found through readings of literature: Luisa Valenzuela's narratives of the "desaparecidos," Toni Morrison's stories of the returning ghosts of earlier generations of black slaves. I suggest that Erice's representation of Frankenstein's monster likewise makes the point that ghosts, while they require remembrance in human consciousness, have an objective existence as the embodiment of the past in the present. As Derrida reminds us, ghosts are not just the object of the gaze for they look at and summon us (7). This point is made by the culminating sequence of *El espíritu de la colmena* in which Frankenstein's monster appears to Ana, and in which something extremely important happens. The sequence starts with the subjective point-of-view shot so characteristic of the film, which constructs the monster as a psychic projection of Ana; but as it slips into a re-take of the scene from James Whale's *Frankenstein*—seen earlier in the film by us and Ana—in which the monster appears to the little girl by the lake, the camera suddenly changes position, filming both Ana and the monster from behind, from an objective vantage-point that belongs to no character. Thus the monster cannot be explained away as a projection of Ana's fantasy: it is "really there." Or rather, as befits a ghost of the past, it is and is not there, for it is a cinematic shadow: intangible but nonetheless embodied. The monster is thus a perfect illustration of the ontological (hauntological) status of history in the present.

In *Ghostly Matters*, Gordon condemns the hypervisiblity and superficiality of contemporary postmodern culture: "No shadows, no ghosts" (16). But in fact the recent burst of writing on hauntology is related to "the return of the real" which some critics (notaby Hal Foster in the book of that title) have proclaimed as the underside of the postmodern emphasis on simulacra. If the ghost is an embodiment of the real in the form of the simulacrum, then there is a sense in which postmodernity's conversion of reality into simulacra can be seen, not as the death of history, but as its return in spectral form. The term Hal Foster gives to this phenomenon is "traumatic realism" or, using a Lacanian pun, "troumatic realism" in the sense of a "trou" or gap in reality, for Lacan defines the traumatic as a missed encounter with the real (130, 132, 136). Ghosts are, precisely, the "might have beens" of history that return as an actualizable, embodied alternative reality. Fredric Jameson says something similar with his suggestive phrase: "Spectrality is [...] what makes the present waver" (qtd. in Gordon 168); that is, it opens up a hole in reality as we like to think we know it. As the monster appears to Ana, it troubles her image (his image) in the water, opening up a hole in comfortable notions of what is self and what is out there, what is present and what is an apparition of the past. Derrida insists that, just as there is a mode of production of the commodity, so there is "a mode of production of the phantom," through the process of mourning which, unlike melancholia which has no direct object, is always trigggered by a trauma (97). Hal Foster reminds us that the word "trauma" means "wound" (153): when the "desaparecido" disappears out of Ana's life, he leaves behind the tangible evidence of the blood from his wounds. The wounds of the dead body which we and Rosita confront at the end of *Ronda del Guinardó* do not help identify the victim but they provide tangible evidence of the suffering of history's losers, whose story could not be told.

Haunting, as Gordon puts it, is the result of "improperly buried bodies" (16): that of the unclaimed torture victim in *Ronda del Guinardó* whom the police want to see "dead and buried" in the sense of consigned to oblivion; that of the unknown fugitive in *El espíritu de la colmena*; that of the "emparedada" in *El jinete polaco*, or that of the officially dead Solana in *Beatus Ille*; that of the "desparecidos" evoked in the songs and images of *Canciones para después de una guerra*; that of the miners buried beneath the slagheaps in *Escenas de cine mudo*. But what should one do with improperly buried bodies: give them proper burial, or learn to live with their ghosts? Derrida advocates the second option: a "being-with-specters" that is a "politics of memory, of inheritance, and of generations" (xix). In *El jinete polaco*, the "emparedada" and the doctor don Mercurio (described in his old age as a living corpse) are revealed at the end to be the protagonist's great-great-grandparents, thus inserting the ghosts of the past into the family. The narrator's girlfried Nadia inherits Ramiro Retratista's photographs from her recently deceased father, again affirming inheritance. As Barthes notes, the photographs that most move us are family photographs (7). *El espíritu de la colmena*, *El sur* and *Si te dicen que caí* rely on family photographs to bring back to life a past—that of the Republic and the Civil War—that has been consigned to oblivion. The structuring of *Escenas de cine mudo* around the photographs in the family album assembled by the narrator's mother, inherited by him on her death, provides an image of history as discontinuous fragments held together by personal inheritance, just as the text of *Beatus Ille* is made possible by Minaya's acceptance of the officially dead Solana's legacy, in the form of his story or voice.

In *El jinete polaco*, it is the protagonist's postmodern profession as international interpreter—secondhand transmitter of a global Babel of voices—that enables him to respond to the summons of the ghosts of the past, which, via Ramiro Retratista's photographs, beckon him back to the historical roots he had attempted to put behind him. The novel's first part is titled "El reino de las voces": to hear voices is analogous to seeing ghosts. But ghosts cannot make their own voice heard; they rely on an interpreter to speak for them. The postmodern stress on the impossibility of direct access to the past may be a response to the ubiquitousness of the media, advertising and heritage industries, which convert history into a consumer commodity; but it can also be seen as a recognition of the spectral quality of the traces left by the past on the present, and of the moral imperative that requires us to bear witness to "the traces of those who were not allowed to leave a trace"; namely, ghosts. In a country that has emerged from forty years of cultural repression, the task of making reparation to the ghosts of the past—that is, to those relegated to the status of living dead, denied voice and memory—is considerable. Derrida's notion that history occupies in the present a "virtual space of spectrality" contradicts the notion that postmodernism signifies an "end of history," suggesting rather that it should be seen as a "return of history" in the form of the revenant. The fact that Spain returned to democracy at the height of the postmodern vogue for "virtual reality" should not necessarily be bemoaned as having prevented an engagement with the past. Perhaps instead we should consider the ways in which postmodernism, by breaking with empiricist concepts of mimesis, allows us to recognize the existence and importance of ghosts.

Notes

1. Unpublished talk to Film Seminar, Department of Spanish, Queen Mary and Westfield College, University of London, 1997.
2. For an excellent exploration of the symbolic potential of the vampire genre, see Gelder 1994.
3. See the unpublished paper "Cronos and the political economy of vampirism: notes on a historical constellation" by my colleague at Birkbeck College, John Kraniauskas.
4. Tannahill (1996: 167-88) shows that the vampire myth, often but not only in this sense, predates its nineteenth-century literary manifestations by several centuries in the popular imagination, notably in the "vampire epidemic" that swept Hungary, Moravia, Silesia and Poland in the late seventeenth and first half of the eighteenth centures.

Works Cited

Barthes, Roland. *Camera Lucida*. London: Fontana, 1984.

Benjamin, Walter. *One-Way Street*. London: Verso, 1997.

Cleminson, Richard. "Beyond Tradition and 'Modernity': The Cultural and Sexual Politics of Spanish Anarchism." In *Spanish Cultural Studies: An Introduction. The Struggle for Modernity*. Ed. Helen Graham and Jo Labanyi. Oxford: Oxford University Press, 1995: 116-23.

Derrida, Jacques. *Specters of Marx: The State of the Debt, the Work of Mourning, and the New International*. New York and London: Routledge, 1994.

Erice, Víctor. *El espíritu de la colmena* (film), 1973.

—— (1983). *El sur* (film)

Evans, Peter W. "El espíritu de la colmena: the monster, the place of the father, and growing up in the dictatorship." *Vida Hispánica* 31.3 (1982): 13-17

Foster, Hal. *The Return of the Real: The Avant-Garde at the End of the Century*. Cambridge, Mass. and London: MIT Press, 1996.

Frisby, David. *Fragments of Modernity*. Cambridge: Polity Press, 1988.

Gelder, Ken. *Reading the Vampire*. London and New York: Routledge, 1994.

Gordon, Avery F. *Ghostly Matters: Haunting and the Sociological Imagination*. Minneapolis and London: University of Minnesota Press, 1997.

Llamazares, Julio. *Luna de lobos*. Barcelona: Seix Barral, 1985.

——. *Escenas de cine mudo*. Barcelona: Seix Barral, 1994.

Marcus, Greil. *The Dustbin of History*. London: Picador, 1994.

Juan Marsé. *Si te dicen que caí*. Mexico: Editorial Novaro, 1973.

——. *Ronda del Guinardó*. Barcelona: Seix Barral, 1984.

Martín Patino, Basilio. *Canciones para después de una guerra* (film), 1971.

——. *Caudillo* (film), 1976.

Muñoz Molina, Antonio. *Beatus Ille*. Barcelona: Seix Barral, 1986.

——. *El jinete polaco*. Barcelona: Planeta, 1991.

Rowe, William and Vivian Schelling. *Memory and Modernity: Popular Culture in Latin America*. London and New York: Verso, 1991.

Samuel, Ralph. *Theatres of Memory*. London and New York: Verso, 1994.

Tannahill, Reay. *Flesh and Blood: A History of the Cannibal Complex*, revised edition. London: Abacus, 1996.

Vázquez Montalbán, Manuel. *Crónica sentimental de España: una mirada irreverente a tres décadas de mitos y de ensueños*. Barcelona: Bruguera, 1980.

5

Short of Memory: the Reclamation of the Past Since the Spanish Transition to Democracy

Joan Ramon Resina

> ¿Han notado que el horizonte de los recuerdos está algo más alto que la línea de visión y que, lo mismo que el cine, obliga a levantar la cabeza?
>
> Gonzalo Contreras, *La ciudad anterior*.

Social Versus Historical Memory

Proposing historical memory as a topic for reflection—but whose memory, why precisely historical and not social, political, cultural, or popular?—presupposes that this kind of memory is intrinsically problematic. To raise this issue is to suggest that historical recollection is precarious or threatened. It is to assume, furthermore, that historical remembrance is a normal function of societies, just as memory, without adjectives, is a constitutive faculty of individuals—meaning, of course, not the banality that this faculty is common to all but that memory constitutes the subject. The second of these two assumptions, namely that societies are endowed with the basic apparatus of historical remembrance, is plainly mistaken. Certainly, all known societies "remember" to the extent that they reproduce themselves in the more or less consciously upheld image of their past—through ritual, epic works, myth, kinship laws, song, or a pantheon of gods, saints, or heroes; in short, through a cosmology. But historical memory is a more specialized kind of "recollection." It is also a recent one—barely two hundred years old, perhaps a little over that, depending on whether Vico is counted as an exponent of the modern historical consciousness.

I am not forgetting Herodotus, Thucydides, Livius, Beda, or the great medieval chroniclers: Muntaner, Desclot, the Castilian

Primera Crónica General, nor Renaissance spirits like Machiavelli. I am merely pointing out that when one speaks about historical memory, its control, erasure, or "assassination," it is a specific discourse that is in question, precisely the discourse that emerged as a specialized branch of the human sciences or *Geisteswissenschaften* in the nineteenth century—a discourse based on protocols of research and documentation of "facts," which are treated as witnesses of events and must be scrupulously reconstructed before their meaning and validity can be formally established. Granted that this discourse covers only a part of the debate about the memory crisis in contemporary Spain, I would offer that it stands at the center of the more general polemic associated with the representation of the past.

This centrality remains even if one concedes that the agent of public remembrance is not the scholarly community of historians but a vague entity which, following Maurice Halbwachs, I will call the "collective memory." This term's ambiguity frees us from having to resort to the even vaguer and ideologically boobytrapped term "nation," while allowing for systemic amplitude. I mean the following: although contemporary debates about the loss or suppression of memory engage a variety of discourses, which include politics, the press, literature, cinema, and the media, the memory these discourses refer to is assumed to rely on a rigorously documented organization of "facts" corresponding to "historical truth."

Although intertwined, Halbwachs's categories "historical memory" and "collective memory" ought to be kept distinct, not as one separates the wheat from the chaff, but in terms of their discreet mechanics, protocols, and scope. The distinction is important because, while there is no doubt that Spain's transition to a monarchical regime was associated with a memory crisis, it is not certain that the crisis was of the historical memory. Despite insinuations to the contrary, the evidence indicates that erosion of the past affected not so much the field of historiography as the areas related to sensory experience and the virtual space of the collective memory. This possibility will be discussed below in the subdivisions devoted to each of these areas: the senses, the collective memory as explored in the novel and film, and the surplus of history in a competitive market of discourses about the past.

84

The Making of Memory

Those who denounce the problematic transmission of the past in the decades after Franco's death rarely acknowledge that distorting and forgetting may be essential to remembering. Nearly everyone involved in the debate has ignored that even under the best of political circumstances, the past is not available in its totality and that whatever we remember of it at a given time and place depends on the nature of the institutions that organize social life. As Michael Schudson puts it: "memories are prepared, planned, and rehearsed socially as well as individually. Experiences attended to by powerful social institutions are likely to be better preserved than experiences less favored by rich institutional rememberers" (359). This point must be born in mind when considering the clash between different memory-agencies in contemporary Spain.

The recent war for multimedia space between the two great consortia, Telefónica and Grupo Prisa, each associated with the interests of one of Spain's largest political parties, PP and PSOE respectively, bodes ill for social memories that find themselves outside of or, worse, in the way of those interests. This problem is also illustrated by memory discrepancies and downright tensions between institutions which are circumscribed in their scope, such as those representing the minority (or minoritized) nationalities,[1] and memories programed by state institutions or facilitated by powerful concerns which share the state's view on the usefulness of a given past and on whether and how it should be incorporated into present knowledge and practice.

An example of convergence between state and private interest is furnished by Spain's largest newspapers. Since its appearance in 1976, *El País* has become a hegemonic instrument for encoding and enforcing knowledges about Spain. No other daily, and especially no regional newspaper representing the viewpoint of the peripheral nationalities, has either the readership or the public status needed to challenge the mnemonic politics of this powerful opinion-shaper. In this, as in other instances of de facto monopoly, ostensible competition masks the market's inherent captivity. *ABC*, despite its partially different agenda and large share of the newspaper market, raises no challenge to hegemonic thought, being in fact the second wheel on the state's axis of printed opinion. The same is true of regionally hegemonic dailies, like Barcelona's *La Vanguardia* or Valencia's *Las Provincias*.

The point is not that monopolies distort and repress—both actions are intrinsic to memory construction—but that they do so without acknowledging the purposes served by those practices. Like other "fixing" practices, monopolies on social memory preempt the continuum and refuse access to alternative knowledges. The problem lies not just with the fact that newspapers have an archival function and accrue documentary value over time. It also has to do with the circumstance that newspapers, like other social institutions, mediate information to which individuals resort without themselves processing it mnemonically or checking its validity against the experienced or tested structures of the past. In other words, along with data that constitute so-called information, newspapers transmit structures of relevance and semantic guidelines which shape the reader's orientation to the past. As Schudson notes: "The individual's capacity to make use of the past piggybacks on the social and cultural practices of memory" (347).

Current debates on historical amnesia are not so much about the loss of the past as about the politics of memory. The dispute is really over which fragments of the past are being refloated and which are allowed to sink. As Marek-Marsel Mesulam observes, "All acts of recall are also acts of imagination, retrospective reinterpretations, mini-confabulations. The tendency for distortion is not a consequence of a deficiency in brain function but a reflection of adaptive evolution. Rewards are not given for veridical reproduction but for the adaptive value of what is recalled" (382). For his part, Salvador Cardús, discussing Ferran Canyameres's autobiographical writings, usefully distinguishes between memory and remembrance. Who was Ferran Canyameres? The question is not likely to elicit a confident answer. And that is precisely the point. Canyameres was a prominent figure in business and political circles during the second Spanish Republic and an important presence in the postwar exile community; he was also a prolific writer—of novels and, especially, of diaries and memoirs. Now he is a forgotten person. Forgotten in spite of his lifelong obsession with preserving every fact, every detail about his life; forgotten not because of the insufficiency but because of the excess of the autobiographical record. Forgotten, in effect, because, as Cardús points out, Canyameres did not respect the rules of memory construction ("Memòria i relat" 11). Those rules include selection, elimination, resort to anachronisms, cohesion of point of view; in a word, interpretation. And interpretation is lacking in Canyameres's autobiographical writings; they contain too many remembrances and too little memory.

Remembrance refers to past experiences which are accessible to an individual. Memory is constructed with the data of those experiences, but it is eminently social. Canyameres's case is instructive. His autobiography reflects the accumulative scheme of the chronicle without reaching the status of historical memory. Halbwachs had pointed out that our memory depends on our temporal milieu as much as on personal impressions and remembrances. As a sociologist, he was aware of contextual determinants and emphasized the distinctiveness of historical meaning, carefully distinguishing it from the mere cataloguing of facts: "By the term 'history' we must understand, then, not a chronological sequence of events and dates, but whatever distinguishes one period from all others" (*The Collective Memory* 57). Canyameres filled many pages with the chronicle of his life but failed to conjure a distinct personality through an act of narrative enchantment—the only thing that could have made his autobiography memorable.

The act that Canyameres failed to perform is normally present in memory work. According to Schudson, memory comprises four processes of distortion: distanciation, instrumentalization, narrativization, and conventionalization (348). Without these processes, "true" memory would never reach the mark of historical memory. While an absolutely accurate memory would amount to a purely mechanical production, recollection entails a complex network of functions serving the purpose of biological and social adaptation. Unreliability may in fact be a condition of successful remembrance. As Mesulam explains: "It could even be argued that a superior talent for veridical recall could constitute a sign of brain disease. In some types of autism, for example, otherwise mentally retarded individuals, also known as 'idiot savants,' are capable of remarkable feats of accurate recall. These individuals cannot reorganize facts creatively, and their phenomenal memory ability is of little benefit (and is often an impediment) in the pursuit of life achievements" (382-83). The locus classicus of such a disease is

Borges's "Funes el memorioso," a story about a man who cannot forget anything he has ever thought.

For most human beings, remembering is inseparable from distorting and forgetting. To retrieve the past is also to encode it. Sensations and images of lived experience become memories as they are integrated into modes of thought and behavior which flow from society to the reminiscing subject (Halbwachs "On Collective Memory" 51). Such encodings proceed strategically in view of present or anticipated needs, which are themselves layered in memory, affecting the sense and depth of retrieval. However, one may ask: if selectivity and distortion are structural to recollection, and if, as Renan observed, ignorance and error with respect to the past are necessary to create political states (qtd. in Rubert de Ventós 112), what is then so surprising about historical memory undergoing modifications during the Spanish Transition? Why all the stir about history? Before tackling this question, let us be clear that the concept of political transition is meaningful only to the extent that it conveys a genuine recreation of the state, which perforce will also transform the oppositional strategies that brought about the change. If, as Paul Connerton claims, society is itself a form of memory, then a profound reorganization of the state must also reform social memory along with the institutions that promote it.

Induced Amnesia

The beginning of an answer to the questions raised above may lie in Peter Burke's observation that history is not just written by the victors but is also forgotten by them (106). Losers cannot afford to forget. They need to brood over the past, on what went wrong and why, in the vain hope of standing once more at the decisive crossroads. Their memory is compulsive. If one claims that the Spanish Transition was characterized by programmed amnesia, one posits implicitly the existence of a critical memory and therewith of losers. Certainly, the Spanish Transition was not a win-win game, nor were losers all on the side of the Francoist forces or all winners in the ranks of the opposition. Notwithstanding the "disenchantment" of prominent intellectuals,[2] the Transition satisfied a majority sufficiently for it to cling passionately, more than twenty years later, to an unamended Constitution which was

88

crafted under the shadow of the bayonets. Identifying the losers of that political sea-change is easy enough. One need only consider which political forces became the pariahs of the new regime, which have been more vilified, denied access to the most influential media, pushed to the margins of the political space. Which ones, in short, have needed to exert themselves the most in order to preserve their share of the social memory, and with it the memory of what the Transition was really about.

At the beginning of *Galíndez* (1990), Manuel Vázquez Montalbán's gripping novel about the suppression of the historical memory, a female American student and a young Spanish politician of the then governing Socialist Party (PSOE) stand before a monument to a Basque politician who disappeared in exile. The student is writing a dissertation about Jesús Galíndez and wishes to retrace the steps leading to his still unexplained abduction in New York in 1956. She looks intently at the monument and the landscape, while the young Socialist, who is getting cold and impatient, talks about men's fashion and makes sexual remarks. Soon she gives up her scrutiny and is ready to go. "¿Qué tal el monumento?" he asks. "Ridículo." "Ya te dije que aquí nadie sabía quién era ese Galíndez. A mí como si me hablaras de Tutankamón." "Para ti," she answers, "la prehistoria terminó hace diez años." "Más o menos. Y estoy tranquilo sin memoria o con muy poca memoria histórica. La verdad es que no entiendo por qué tú vas por la vida fisgando en las memorias históricas ajenas. Ni siquiera vives bien de eso" (12). The person who talks like this is in charge of the Ministry of Culture's budget, at a time—the nineteen-eighties—when this Ministry lavishly and indiscriminately financed Madrid's highly publicized postmodern look.

In the next scene the couple visits the politician's relatives on a Basque farm. Here the reader finds the counterpart to the winner's amnesia. The two men on the farm have themselves a political past. The father is an old Communist militant, and the son has been involved in the Basque armed struggle. Both have served time in the same prison. Now they lead quiet lives away from the world and from politics, except for the occasional reprisals they suffer on account of their past militancy. Ten years ago, the older man explains, civil guards in plain clothes set the house on fire. That happened after Franco's death, in the new-fangled democratic state. "Ahora, tranquilo. Ya todo está en calma," his young PSOE nephew reassures him. He alludes, of course, to the idea that the real Transition was ushered in by the Socialists. "Y una mierda," replies the old man. "Tranquilo no. Amnésico. Yo si no estoy amnésico no estoy tranquilo. Pero no me muevo para que éste no se mueva, que un día me lo iban a traer acribillado y eso no lo soportaría la Amparitxu, ni yo" (21). The old man alludes to the darkest chapter in the history of Spanish Socialism: the dirty war against partisans of the Basque independence struggle. Vázquez Montalbán traces a line between the young Socialist's irresponsible attitude towards the past and the know-nothing, ask-nothing approach to his office, which indulges in a vain optimism fraught with unknown corpses. On the losers' side, however, amnesia is a survival strategy, the surest and safest way of adapting to the new historical dispensation.

A critical writer like Vázquez Montalbán and a radical politician of a different persuasion, Pilar Rahola, coincide in their grim view of Spain's political Transition as a deliberate turning-off of the collective memory. Rahola too believes that an oblivious culture is depriving individuals of the capacity to respond to newer and more sophisticated control strategies: "Però tinc la impressió que el pacte —inconscientment o conscient— de la transició política no va ser un pacte de no-agressió sinó d'automutilació, com una mena de lobotomia col·lectiva que ens va extirpar la memòria entesa com a mecanisme d'alerta. I ara ja no som capaços de reconèixer-los, de reconèixer els signes, d'activar els mecanismes de defensa. Es aquí, en la brutal i sobtada normalització dels agressors a tota cultura de llibertat, on ens hem tornat vulnerables i febles" (*Avui* 3 May, 1998).

On the other side of the political spectrum, the desire for oblivion is conspicuous, and forgetting is identified with progress and democratic freedom. On February 23, 1998, while presenting a history book in the Spanish Cortes, Vicepresident of the Government Francisco Alvarez-Cascos said he was gratified that after seventeen years citizens had already forgotten the failed coup d'état of February 23, 1981. In his view, this development evinced the consolidation of political freedom ("El cop d'Estat", *Avui* 24 February, 1998). The joy of forgetting (or of others' forgetfulness) may well be related to the normalization of the previously abnormal, as Rahola suggests. In effect, Vicepresident Alvarez-Cascos celebrated the fact that his party was gradually shedding its shadow in the collective consciousness. Casting his party as a political Schlemil, he hoped that no one would notice that it was precisely the Partido Popular's coming to power that finally put temptations of unconstitutional adventures to rest. Moving in counterpoint, José Borrell, the one-time Socialist candidate to the Government's presidency, outdid his electoral rivals in defining memory's desirable time span. Decrying the public attention brought to his party by the judicial process against state terrorism, Borrell declared that "sería triste que lo que ocurrió hace más de quince años distraiga la atención de nuestra sociedad de los grandes retos que hemos de afrontar" (*Avui* 28 July, 1998).[3]

Unquestionably, the post-Francoist volatilization of certain aspects of the past was a form of censorship—politicians and journalists repressing something they did not want to face for personal reasons or to protect the interests of political and economic clans. But disrememberance was also motivated by the need to achieve political consensus and to facilitate the eventual alternation of power. A comparable oblivion of recent history is said to have helped naturalize an unfamiliar democratic mentality in post-Nazi Germany (Mommsen 89). Although here too, as in post-Franco Spain, political apathy and an ostensible lack of feeling for the dead and the displaced may have been "only the most obvious external symtom of a deeply rooted, obstinate and occasionally brutal refusal to confront and come to terms with that which actually happened" (Arendt 25). A self-protective refusal to look hard at the facts may be common after severe crises. Kirk Savage claims that the primary function of American Civil War memorials was to ensure "systematic cultural repression, carried out in the guise of reconciliation and harmony" (qtd. in Olick and Robbins 127).

Conceivably, in Spain the exit from fascism was shorter and safer through an implacable unreferentiality. In the end the need for reconciliation and a broad consensus determined the ideological mutation of the Spanish left towards positions bordering on and finally indiscernible from those of their conservative antagonists.[4] It is important, nonetheless, to understand that, just as memory reaches back over relatively long stretches of time, its dissipation does not occur overnight. The politics of oblivion that conditioned the Francoist regime's metamorphosis had been prepared over a long period of time. Commenting on the readjustment of history in school textbooks in the mid-sixties, Carolyn Boyd notes that "[t]he regime that in 1964 celebrated '25 years of peace' instead of its victory over the 'anti-Spain' now found it preferable to cover 'the rancors and animosities of other times, perhaps bathed in blood [...] with a discreet veil of transcendence and forgetfulness and better, with the tunic of solidarity and Christian fraternity" (292).

As this process of transcendence entered the dangerous balance of the Transition, much of the oppositional memory evaporated to the point where, to use David Lowenthal's phrase, the past began to look like a foreign country. Officialdom strained to rid Spain of its traditional aspect by promoting a postmodern look which found its conscious parody in Almodóvar's films of the eighties and its unintended one in the claim that Madrid is Spain's most New Yorkian city (uttered unselfconsciously by a person interviewed for the documentary film, *Spain, Ten Years After* [1985]).

While Spain was forging its postmodernity (understood there as an ultramodernity), the past became a country where old people had once lived: an irrelevance. Or else a concept associated with movements of national vindication, such as the Basque and the Catalan, which needed historical legitimation for their claims. This "residualism" was possible because a state exists not so much territorially as temporally. Its coherence depends more on the integration of time and subjectivity than on the preservation of its borders. In promoting Spain's postmodern look, the Socialist government acted on the insight that, since historical memory depends on a prior balance of power, it tends to preserve that balance. Rather than radically restructuring the state, the Socialists stimulated change where they could. In the eighties that meant altering the perception of Spain's temporality. Hence the eagerness and sometimes recklessness with which they sped up the country's modernization.

Compared with the transitions undergone by other Western dictatorships in this last quarter of a century, from Chile to Poland, Spain's journey into modernity seems unexceptional. Over and above the ideological agendas of the various opposition movements, the true locomotive of historical change—to use Marx's metaphor—was not the revolution but the market.[5] It was the market's implacable logic that pushed Spain, from the sixties on, out of the autarchy and into reformist policies leading up to the Moncloa pact and the Constitution of 1978. And the market it was that produced a rupture in the collective memory which consensus-oriented politicians cautiously avoided in the public domain. As is wellknown, the market depends on designed obsolescence; each new commodity advertises the demise of a previous one, throws it into history's dustbin. This goes, of course, for history itself understood as a commodity, as a repertoire of intellectual contents that can suddenly appear old-fashioned, outdated, and consequently irrelevant. As the prime engine of modernization, the market tends to appear as a permanent transition from a past that is constantly being neutralized.

Spain's insertion into the market economy goes a long way towards explaining the Transition's temporal imprecision and the confusion of those who insist on anchoring it in politically significant events. Failure to understand the market's mnemonic logic accounts for the widely divergent assessments concerning the Transition's span. It also explains the general sense that the Transition remains incomplete,[6] that it petered out at some point, or else never truly happened (cf. González Casanova's book on the subject, *El cambio inacabable*).

The Transition, I submit, is neither here nor there. Trying to localize it in reference to power shifts like the 1982 Socialist electoral victory, or to megarites of self-celebration such as the 1992 Olympic games or the Quincentennial of Columbus's first transatlantic journey, makes no sense. The Socialist government, incidentally, did not organize this commemoration in the spirit of restitution of the historical memory but with the design of retrospectively founding Spain's claim to modernity.[7] Rather than an actual event, the Transition was the special effect (in the cinematographic sense, too) of a collective installation in a present that wished itself absolute: the present of the market. This present is paradoxical and yet quite real. The old-fashioned present used to be the site of memory, since memory, as Richard Terdiman puts it, is the modality of our relation to the past (7). Or, expressed in reverse, "Memory stabilizes subjects and constitutes the present. It is the name we give to the faculty that sustains continuity in collective and in individual experience" (Terdiman 8). The market inaugurates another kind of present by amputating the past. This present produces itself by constantly severing its moorings. As a result, it not only destabilizes subjects and entire communities but itself becomes a modality of time out of time, an eternal transition blind to its origins or destination. Change is this present's highest value and identity its most suspect concept.

The Senses in Transition

The past disappears at different levels. On one of these levels the Transition cannibalized the liberal conception of the state's political complexity. A simplified democracy administrated by political agencies was superposed onto a developing market economy. The result was a shrinking multiparty system tending towards bipartisanship thanks to electoral laws that discourage fragmentation of the vote and transfer power from civil society to the parties. This liberal implosion created the conditions for a *Historikerstreit*, which will be discussed in the last part of this essay.

Notwithstanding these public repercussions, the market's effect on memory is strongest at the level of bodily experience, the level, that is, of material culture. Discussing the European economic integration, of which the Spanish Transition was an episode, Nadia Seremetakis notes the vanishing of tastes, aromas, and textures from the contemporary European margins. In her view, the market's drive towards integration entails a massive intervention in the everyday cultures of the European periphery, determining what regional varieties of basic products, including food staples, can be grown, marketed, and exported (3). An emphasis on the ethical superiority of the "universal" over the local further rationalizes the market, while consumers are acculturated through the importation of the universal commodity, which they welcome as something exotic to their traditional milieus. As Seremetakis so crisply puts it: "Here a regional diversity is substituted by a surplus over-production" (3). This process is far-reaching. By eliminating the sensory elements that distinguished regional cultures from each other, this intervention puts pressure on a whole array of factors essential to the reproduction of social identities and meanings.

As an example of the volatilization of sensory memory, consider Josep Pla's vast compendium of the sensory experiences formerly available to a Southern European culture which has undergone intense modernization. Pla records the wealth of sensory knowledges, memories, and histories associated with a corner of the Mediterranean. In order to do this he activates a precise, concrete vocabulary suited to this region's material culture—a language that is itself part and parcel of that culture's sensory experience. Pla wrote against the grain of contemporary trends, anticipating the

94

future vindication of his work when, nostalgic for the wisdom of the senses, readers will look for its literary traces. However, whether the vocabulary itself can survive the dissipation of the experience is an open question. Will words survive sensory amnesia? Language itself is being streamlined in the age of the global market. This trend is especially visible in regional languages caught between international communications and the official languages which define the public spheres of communication and experience. In order not to disappear entirely from public life, these languages are forced to shed their syntactical and semantic peculiarities (the memory sites of their cultures) and to pattern themselves after the dominant languages. Thus they are turning into ever more synthetic idioms, temporarily buoyed by the discharge of expressions and perceptions which had conformed specific cultural identities.

Over and above the political will to bury the past, material memory recedes as the senses are being eroded. The irony of this development is that it has taken place in the midst of semi-official hedonism.[8] But then, as Seremetakis points out, "The structure of modern sensory experience is inherently ironic. The sensory sphere is experienced in such a manner that profound transformations occurring in it or imposed on it are rendered imperceptible to the individual eye" (19). This infrascopic reconditioning of experience makes everyday life the site for far-reaching historical transformations. Under these circumstances history can be altered most effectively, because this is where it is least visible. Not by chance is the everyday often opposed to the historical—Unamuno, for example, considered it a repository of permanence, a realm of anonymous reproduction of collective life. More recently, with the *longue durée*, Braudel incorporated the structures of collective inertia and glacier-pace change into historiography proper. The *longue durée* refers to the framework of social practices which are determined by large-scale processes that elude individual attention and intentionality. For Braudel these processes and slow-motion change are the motor of profound historical transformations. It is possible to assert that political history privileges the narrative of change and transition, while the everyday is experienced as a denarrativized continuum, closer to biological than to historical time. A powerful social technology detaches political events from the everyday and endows them with a dynamism that appears to inhere in them, producing the illusion that they and they alone are the contents of contemporary narrativity.

Memory Tensions in the Novel and Film of the Nineteen-Eighties: Antonio Muñoz Molina and Basilio Martín Patino

The clash between public narratives of change and the transformation of the sensory environment was an object for cultural reflection in the eighties and early nineties. During that exhilarating decade of Spain's modernization, there appeared a number of literary works steeped in nostalgia and, occasionally, in the utopian resolution of the gap between memory and experience. Examples of a nostalgic subjectivity can be found in some detective novels of Manuel Vázquez Montalbán, or in films like José Luis Garci's *Volver a empezar*. The suturing of memory and its object is illustrated by Carmen Martín Gaite's *La reina de las nieves* (1994). Some of these works focused deliberately on the question of narrative authority. Antonio Muñoz Molina's first novel, *Beatus Ille* (1986), to mention one example in this category, has to do with the struggle for the narrative upper hand between a reductive past transformed by an infatuated memory and a banal present which inscribes the history of the places it has evacuated. In this novel a naive literary historian moves into a zone of amnesia wielding a few formulaic historical tools, among them the pseudocategory of generation and the nearly epic conception of the pre-Civil War poet. Awkwardly, he interrogates the patina on fetishized mirrors, furniture, and photographs, forgetting that, as Arthur C. Danto warned, "Objects do not wear their histories on their surfaces" (44), and that, as Seremetakis points out, the senses do not yield the material world up for consumption but defer it, changing it into memory (29). The young man who walks into his uncle's house as if he walked straight into the past and moves among objects and people (including the woman he makes love with) as if they were ghosts from the historical beyond forgets that the objects he comes into contact with are only clues to an *other* time, that they are a semiosis. Ignoring the imaginary dimension of remembrance and oblivious to the fact that he is—according to Eliot's words in the novel's epigraph—"mixing memory and desire," he falls prey to literature, trapped, literally, by the book that he had hoped to retrieve. The title of Muñoz Molina's novel thus refers not only to the bucolic tradition, counterpointed here by the theme of paradise as the scene of betrayal, cruelty, and cowardice but also to the protagonist's naive blessedness.

The programmed obsolescence of regional experience and its related sensory memories is the theme of another novel by the same author. *El jinete polaco* (1991) is in many ways paradigmatic for the Transition. Dramatizing the disappearance of an obsolete social model, the novel supports and even reinforces ideological axioms central to that model. The Transition resulted from the dictatorship's biological exhaustion, but it assured a democratic afterlife for ideas and persons threatened by ideological depletion. *El jinete polaco* registers this situation by presenting the Bildungsroman-like cycle of a Spaniard's first unhappy but finally reintegrated national consciousness. More important, however, from the point of view of social memory, are the many passages in which a local sensory specificity mediates a mesh of close-knit memories, which appear in ghostly unreality or in a state of swift, irreversible corruption. An allegory of the ghostly character of memory is foregrounded in the figure of a mummy, which is, literally, the source and obsessive point of return for mnemonic reflections. This brittle remain of an organic, sensual reality functions both as a memory of spent sexual joy and a memento mori linking present joy to historical corruption.

In *El jinete polaco* the narrative point of view stands at the site where memory fades as such and its contents merge unrecognized with personal and social existence. The very concept of Transition supposes that the social subject is positioned at a historical watershed, from which it can survey the receding past without as yet discerning the new dominant view. The contrast between the loss of the habitual and the onslaught of the unfamiliar gives rise to a sense of passing time. Returning to his provincial town after spending years abroad, the narrator remarks: "es la incesante comparación entre lo que recuerdo y lo que miro la causa de que sólo en esta ciudad pueda cobrar una conciencia tan clara y obsesiva del tiempo" (550). The past fades away from the collective imaginary, living on in time enclosures from which the present brutally extricates itelf. Running away from an asylum where old men and women outlive themselves, the narrator declares: "Yo oigo sus voces, pero no quiero que me atrapen, ahora advierto el peligro de aventurarse demasiado en la memoria o en las mentiras de otros, incluso en las de uno mismo" (572). Evasion is here a euphemism for repression. It reflects a sense of memory's mythic dimension, from which personal remembrance is not entirely segregated, although it denounces the lure of the collective past. In this way the narrator traces a false dichotomy between his memory and the memories of others, when in fact the decisive dichotomy is that between public and private memories. The private is colonized through a process of anonymization in which the public consciousness partakes of the same ghostly quality as the shipwrecked memories of yore.

> Tú a lo mejor no lo sabes, porque vives fuera y no te fijas, pero la gente que conocíamos está cambiando mucho. Es como en una película de marcianos que vi hace poco en la televisión. Los extraterrestres llegan a un pueblo y en lugar de conquistarlo con pistolas de rayos se apoderan del alma de la gente. Tú estás con tu mujer, o con algún amigo, y al principio no le notas nada, pero luego ves que tiene los ojos como vacíos y que anda un poco rígido y es que ya se ha convertido en marciano. Alguien que es todavía normal da una cabezada y cuando vuelve a abrir los ojos ya es otro, aunque sigue hablando igual y tiene la misma cara. (428)

Colonization, spectralization, deprivation of the sense of self throw into relief the anachronistic side not only of experiences that suddenly make no sense anymore but also of the elements that infiltrate the local mesh of collective memories and, altering their sensory structure, make a clean slate available for new social reinscriptions. In restrospect the narrator recognizes that the fetishized American singers he used to listen to in a jukebox were voices from the past. By the time they reached his provincial town they had ceased to exist, even if they continued to exert a modernity effect, like dead stars shining thousands of light years away from the place where they flickered out.

Pondering that the voices from the jukebox announced a long-vanished freedom, the narrator observes: "Ibamos a llegar tarde al mundo, pero no lo sabíamos, nos preparábamos avariciosamente para asistir a una fiesta que ya había terminado" (345-46). An anachronistic party defines well enough the politically constructed and officially encouraged ludism which characterized the Transition. The highly praised *movida* or *revolución de los esqueletos*—a phrase that betrays the political unconscious of that decade, which was dominated by fear of closeted skeletons—was a potlatch-like consumption of the surpluses of the Western youth movement of the sixties and seventies, which had largely bypassed Spain. It was also an inauguration party celebrating Spain's overdue normalization in a Western world consisting of NATO and EEC membership.

The skeletons' revolution manifested the spectralization of a public memory filled with the skeletons of a distant war and a recent dictatorship. Muñoz Molina's novel alludes to this unintended effect of the new youth culture. However, the most explicit (and poetic) rendition of the conflict between public and private memory, between the political Transition and the everyday, is Basilio Martín Patino's film, *Los paraísos perdidos* (1985). As the film begins, someone, an old woman, is dying in a modern hospital. A generational change, a biological fact, preconditions everything else. The middle-aged daughter of an exiled university professor (Charo López) returns to her family's town in Central Spain to fulfill her dying mother's wish. "Madre quería reconstruir la casa," she explains. The house, in an advanced state of disrepair, is an apt image for the public memory of Spain's recent past. Assuming the existence of a political will to retrieve the intellectual patrimony from the previous regime's zone of amnesia, Charo looks around for help. After some debate, the town hall grants a marble plaque. The vicerector of Salamanca's university, presumably the school where her father used to teach, recommends selling his archive to an American university or seeking a commercial sponsor, a bank, or perhaps Coca Cola. The Socialist government's Minister of Culture pays lip service to the foundation's interest, but he is visibly incommoded by its political significance: "Lo que podríamos llamar una cierta significación de lo republicano no tiene por qué ser conflictivo. Eso es historia y ahí está." But he cuts the discussion short through a masterful performance in which he criticizes radicalism ("el maximalismo") and praises the PSOE's realpolitik: "pero las únicas mejoras posibles hoy por hoy están aquí, y aquí no hay más cera que la que arde." Amnesia, in other words, has become realism's imperative. Between these scenes, the protagonist visits a friend in a home for the elderly. Here, in the underside of Spain's boastful renovation, an old man reminisces about the war, while Charo's young cousin grows impatient. Another old man (Francisco Rabal) pronounces the Transition's catchword, like someone commiting moral suicide: "lo importante es enterrar la memoria, olvidar el pasado." As if beckoned by these words, the next shot shows an ambulance taking away the body of an inmate, presumably dead.

The film subtly counterpoises a woman's reconnection with the past (a past mediated by cultural displacement—the protagonist has grown up in Germany) with memory's poetic dimension. As she wanders about town and the camera reveals the ruins of a church, the house's iron gate, and the abandoned inner yard, her voice in off reads from Hölderlin's *Hyperion*: "¿A qué otro sitio podría huir de mí si no tuviera los días queridos de mi juventud? Como un espíritu que no encuentra ningún descanso, vuelvo a las regiones abandonadas de mi vida." These regions are undergoing a metamorphosis, which the camera captures much more faithfully than the peppy discourse of the young, newly established politicians. After registering the stills from a recent *destape* film, *Una noche en coche cama*, shown in the anachronistically named Cine Imperio, the camera cuts across to a medium shot of three old women, spooky apparitions from a society that is quickly fading.

After finding her father's books gathering dust on the floor, her voice in off continues: "cansado de la vida preguntas al fin: ¿dónde estáis ahora, ideales de mi juventud?" Although voiced over and with a defamiliarizing effect on the images, the *Hyperion* lines are diegetically justified. The protagonist is translating the poem into Spanish and vaguely convinces an old friend of hers, Miguel, to undertake its publication. Yet, this project will not be fulfilled either, because as she completes the translation in the early hours after a night of camaraderie and love, she is only minutes away from her last disappointment. Her visit to Miguel's house reveals a contrast between the uninhabitable sites of memory and the comfortable places of oblivion. The sight of his villa prompts her to ask: "¿Todavía quedan estas casas?" Miguel (Juan Diego) replies: "Tuve mucha suerte, se la compré a un canónigo. Está todavía por arreglar. Son mis pequeñas compensaciones." The shamed self-effacement of the *nouveau riche* is as conspicuous as the ideological displacement. Traditionally, the Catholic church enjoyed a near monopoly on Spain's mythic markers; now a falsely modest, because ideologically vested, entrepreneurial class has taken over society's reins and privileged spaces. It is fitting that this class is represented by a publisher, since it controls the narrations that circulate and are disseminated. It is not necessary to speculate with the hollowness of its cultural mission, for the rhetoric gives away the political reality. In this instance the tale-telling words are "luck" and "small compensations." The former dissembles a political process of swapping and accommodation, while the latter raises the question of what is being compensated. With this subterfuge, Miguel hopes to disguise the political continuity linking him to the house's previous owner, a continuity that politics denies but the everyday confirms in the stubborn memory of the material world.

If Miguel's villa represents continuity, the "republican" house stands in the center of the renovated town as a "cultural zone of non-contemporaneity" (Seremetakis's term). This would-be monument (literally, a remembrance) to the republican past stands in the town's square across from the church. On the edge of but not quite in public space, the house is a repository of private memories and a potential public archive. The irony of this virtuality runs deep, because the protagonist, a woman with a life elsewhere, is thinking about exchanging that life for the phantom of the life she might have lived in this square. She browses through the ruins of that potential past, trying to find the material reasons for a subjective discontinuity that matches the country's break with its immediate past. Interviewed as a local celebrity, she is asked: "¿Qué se siente al volver?" To which she replies with the following reflection:

> En cuanto a lo de volver, yo diría que más que volver se trata de empezar una nueva etapa en mi vida. Quizá esta vez la definitiva. Ya es hora, ¿no? En cualquier caso, esta vuelta me serviría de disculpa para cambiar yo también. Creo que en la vida hay que saber dar un corte, un esquinazo a tiempo.

She is talking about the need for a transition predicated on rupture. Yet, by calling on the semantics of return, she discloses the relation between her desire for rupture and her consciousness of the past. And that prompts the next question: "¿La condiciona a usted mucho, me da la impresión, en uno u otro sentido, el pasado, la memoria?" To which she gives a perfectly ambiguous reply: "No sé, lo que ocurre es que la memoria puede ser un depósito de felicidad si los recuerdos son hermosos o enriquecedores. Pero también la memoria puede ser una especie de pesadilla si no nos liberamos de ella." Memory can turn into an unbearable debt, as she later admits to Miguel. Like her mother, she is becoming a hostage to the past.

Trying to rebuild the house as it had been half a century before (trying, therefore, to erase fifty years of history) is an unbearable obligation. "A mamá se le metió en la cabeza restaurar la casa como era hace cincuenta años. Empieza a haber problemas y a mí se me viene todo encima. Me agobia, me agobia mucho, Miguel." A symbol of the past that interrupts the present's linearity, the house is at once an intended site of historical memory and a zone of socially created amnesia. As Bachelard puts it, "Not only our memories, but the things we have forgotten are 'housed'" (xxxiii). Standing in the middle of an aesthetically rejuvenated town, the exile's house frames the sacrificial space of undesired but stubborn memory.

A memory that will not let up, that insists on being there in its paradoxical nonpresence, is the territory of the ghost. The house of forgotten memories is a haunted place. It spooks those who live in the reduced present of that which is on display. For them the ghost is a jarring experience. Lurking in the shadows of rejected reality, it bears witness to the existence of discontinuities in the happy narrative of modernity at last. It runs against the grain of socioeconomic currents that treat material experiences and the lives invested in them as so much dust. *Dust*, as Seremetakis explains, is created by any perceptual stance that treats the object world as a nullity that casts no meaning into our bodies, or recovers no stories from our past (12). Dust is all the protagonist's young cousin can see in the old house. Nonetheless, the house speaks through its objects, not least through the books which are slowly turning into dust. While Charo can tap objects from memories that have long been out of sight ("He encontrado en un desván la vieja casa de muñecas con que jugó mi madre, con que he jugado yo"), her cousin feels uncomfortable in the shadow of his world made of visibilities (at various moments in the film he toys with a video recorder). It is not surprising to hear him declaring: "A mí no me gusta esta casa, está llena de fantasmas." The ghost is a form of visual latency, a symptom of a socially mandated invisibility. As such, it announces a complex system of permissions and prohibitions (Kipnis, qtd. in Gordon 15), whose alteration or denial expresses itself in the dread aroused by haunting experiences.

The film itself is built upon the ghostly principle. Tension develops between the visible and the unrepresentable every time that a voice, detached from the images, intrudes into the present of the film. I refer of course to the lines from *Hyperion*, voiced over

102

the visual sequences at different intervals. Coming from a different age and culture, the poet's words point out, within the world's incessant shipwreck, the persistence of an island of memory which the poet imagines indestructible but the film shows to be in an advanced state of devastation. Towards the end of the film the three friends, Charo, Miguel, and Benito (Alfredo Landa), who represent the generation of the Transition, are finishing supper in the old house, while below, in the packed public square, the young post-Franco generation is dancing in joyful oblivion of the country's past and present divisions. This youth knows nothing about ghosts and lives up to Spain's "ludic culture." (Benito remarks on the fact that girls now do not wear bras, a sign of the new sexual liberation.) But for those who remember, the contrast between private memory and public knowledge prompts a melancholy reflection on life's losses, indulgently hedged by the Transition's material benefits:

> Benito: ¿O es que ahora no vivimos mejor?
> Miguel: Sí, eso sí. Bueno, menos mal que perdemos memoria.
> Benito: ¿Tú has perdido memoria? Pues yo la debo tener de elefante.
> Miguel: Los elefantes no sé, pero los no elefantes parece ser que perdemos cien mil neuronas al día, irrecuperables según dicen, a partir de los treinta y cinco años, así que vete echando las cuentas.

At this point Charo, as if musing to herself, outbids the festive spirit by proposing a potlatch: "¿Te imaginas qué fácil sería organizar una pira descomunal con todo esto? ¡Qué liberación!" She is referring to the objects and books in the house, the traces of her personal past, but also to collective ghosts weighing on her generation like a debt. She dreams of a new beginning, which is of course as mythical as the paradise she is beginning to give up for lost, and as oblivious as the bliss of those who are dancing in the square below. A new beginning would release her from the patrimonial debt (symbolized in her pledge to rebuild the house), inducting her into an absolute present free from memory and inherited obligations. But the fresh innocence would be payed for by a loss of purpose, for it is from the tension that anachronism installs in the present that a sense of direction emerges. As Derrida claims, only the debt of justice to the past engenders responsibility for the future. The future rushes in through the subject's striving for a balance that eludes particularly those who seek it in a continuous present: "Sans cette *non-*

contemporanéité à soi du present vivant, sans ce qui secrètement le désajuste, sans cette responsabilité et ce respect pour la justice à l'égard de ceux qui *ne sont pas là*, de ceux qui ne sont plus ou ne sont pas encore *présents et vivants*, quel sens y aurait-il à poser la question 'où?', 'où demain?' (*'whither?'*)" (16).

Impertinent Memory

At the beginning of this reflection I suggested that the battleground for remembrance is not so much the field of historiography as the everyday experiences through which the collective memory is shaped, reformed, or erased. I have also implied that this quiet revolution in customs and perceptions may be inextricably related to forgetting, so that Derrida's phrase—"Puis, une fois la tâche révolutionnaire accomplie, alors survient nécessairement l'amnésie" (182)—may be true also of an explicitly antirevolutionary program for change, such as the Spanish Transition was. Cynically one might say that, once Spain was integrated into the world market, the memories of the Civil War and the dictatorship became superfluous, even counterproductive, and amnesia set in.

Setting off this statement is a remarkable development in the Spanish publishing industry during the Transition. When censorship was lifted, a surge of memoirs and autobiographical writings concerning the Civil War and the Franco years flooded the bookstalls. Part of this literature responded to adaptive needs. A case in point is Pedro Laín Entralgo's *Descargo de conciencia* (1976), which triggered a parodic critique in Juan Marsé's *La muchacha de las bragas de oro* (1978). In the social atmosphere of the Transition, permeated by discretion and the need for consensus, a great deal of this literature appeared as an anachronistic irrelevance. Furthermore, like the revisionist memoirs of ex-Francoists, those by Republican figures seemed to have little more than gestural value. If they looked back, it was in order not to be petrified within the abandoned city of the delegitimated past.

This memoristic literature anticipates an issue that will surface two decades later in the debate over historical memory. I refer to the question of narrativity and its relation to historiographic legitimacy. According to Seremetakis: "As the zones of amnesia and the unsaid expand in tandem with the increasingly formulaic and selective reproduction of public memory, the issue of narrativity becomes a zone of increasing political and cultural tension" (19). That the issue of narrativity is inseparable from the conflict of interpretations of the past can be illustrated by reference to a recent polemic involving the nature and purpose of the Spanish Civil War. An indelible datum in the Catalan collective memory is the anti-Catalan thrust of the Spanish *Movimiento Nacional*, which entailed a different degree of postwar repression in Catalonia. Spanish historiography does not register this datum, around which one of the Transition's great zones of amnesia continues to expand. As a result, recollections of this episode elicit irate denial from a political and intellectual establishment heavily invested in the status quo. As Adorno once said, "in the house of the hangman one should not speak of the noose, otherwise one might seem to harbor resentment" (89).

Such was Eduardo Mendoza's reaction to the petition formulated by Esquerra Republicana de Catalunya's Secretary General, Josep Lluís Carod-Rovira, to the effect that the Spanish government should apologize for human rights violations perpetrated during the Franco regime. Mendoza's argument against this proposal hinges on the idea that a democratically constituted government, even one that is ruled by a party founded and integrated by former Francoist ministers and supporters, has no moral obligation in connection with the War and the dictatorship. If anything, says Mendoza, this government is itself a victim of the war. In his view, the specificity of the repression in Catalonia is dissolved by the general character of the Civil War, which renders the war's nationalistic aspect irrelevant or, in Mendoza's word, ridiculous. According to him, the fact that people were killed throughout Spain debunks claims that the fascist coup and the ensuing repression were selectively accented ("El senyor Carod-Rovira demana comptes," *Avui* 21 December 1998). In spite of unambiguous evidence in support of the view that Catalonia's autonomy was uppermost in the conspirators' decision to rise against the Republic,[9] or the documented intensity and idiosyncrasy of Catalonia's postwar repression,[10] Mendoza's position is not only widely held but is actually hegemonic. When the nation-state is the only legitimate analytical frame, the issue of collective responsibility dissolves in the reflection that the state cannot reasonably apologize to itself, because it cannot fulfill simultaneously the roles of culprit and victim.

There are certainly arguments to question the appropriateness of using remembrance reductively, and it is true that vindication through memory can be a form of vengeance adjoining suprahistorical and infracritical territory. Dagmar Barnouw raises precisely this objection to Jewish attempts to keep the Holocaust above history and protected from discussion (6). But it is equally certain that postwar, democratic German governments have not claimed unaccountability on the technically unimpeachable but morally unacceptable pretense that they *too* were victims of Nazism. If answerability, in this case, retains the burden of guilt and financial *Wiedergutmachung* as the price for national continuity, how can avoidance be justified when the demand for political responsibility involves no more than an apology? In point of fact, Spain's governing party is not only far from accepting formal historical responsibilities but is still incapable of distancing itself morally from its fascist antecedents. On September 14, 1999, sixty years after the end of the Civil War, this party rejected a motion of the Spanish Congress to formally condemn the military putsch against the Second Spanish Republic. Such inability for moral self-conquest or even strategic detachment undermines all arguments for the disengagement and lifting of historical responsibility on account of the political changes articulated during the Transition.

Reactions like Mendoza's overlook the reason why proposals such as Carod-Rovira's are important.[11] It is not a question of belatedly assigning liabilities which the Transition pledged to disregard but of defining the future political commonality and securing the ethical premises on which that commonality can reasonably stand. Defensiveness on this issue is suspect. Reluctance to honor the victims is not indicative of a desire to break free of the past but of the past living on in the present. That which is negated as a cause of the Civil War and at the core of the repression, namely the unbending loathing against the smaller nationalities, makes a *comeback* in a new historical avatar. The survival of the nuclear pathos of Francoism within democracy is far more troubling than the marginal existence of self-confessed fascist nostalgia outside democracy. It is this survival under ideological erasure, this spectralized but robust permanence, that imposes blindness to the present and oblivion of the recent past.

Historical memory plays a crucial role in shaping the points of view from which social and political actors understand themselves and each other. As Jürgen Habermas observes in relation to the historical liabilities of the German Federal Republic, national traditions and mentalities that have long been assimilated reach back to a time well before the beginning of the present democratic regime (49). His reflection could contribute to centering the recently reopened debate about the national significance of the Spanish Civil War. The relevant question is not whether responsibilities can be adjudicated retroactively but whether the hegemonic culture contained normative grounds for justifying the aggression against the heteronationalities (Habermas 50). This is, of course, a question for political as well as academic historians of the various state-defined disciplines (historiography, the philological disciplines, art and literary history, philosophy, and so on). If such normative grounds are present in the conception of the Spanish state, then it is reasonable to suspect that silencing them during the Transition contributed to a politico-cultural matrix that imperils the coexistence of the various nations within Spain. In fact, coexistence is already compromised by the unspoken persistence of premises that permeated an undemocratic demeanor in the past.

I suspect that Carod-Rovira intended his proposition as a cathartic way of dispelling the mentalities that contributed to the fascist aggression against Spain's heteronational entities. Unacknowledged, those attitudes have gathered strength in the post-Francoist state. Only by surmounting the present state of denial and fixing the democratic limits of normative representations can consciousness break loose from mental habits and lay a solid basis for inter-national respect and equality within the state. On that basis alone can a contractual form of political coexistence function.

Against Mendoza's denial of differentiations within the fabric of fascist violence, one can argue that recognizing the specificities of the aggression is justified by the War's political nature and purpose. That a hierarchy of hostilities existed was felt even by those Catalans who supported the Spanish "National Movement" against their own national group. A hierarchy clearly stated in the motto, "antes roja que rota." However, my purpose is not to adjudicate in the dispute but to point out its theoretical core. Mendoza accused Carod-Rovira of playing with history ("ho fa jugant amb la història" ["El senyor Carod-Rovira"]). He added that history may justify diverse interpretations, but all of them must be ruled by some fundamental traits, which, one suspects, must be underpinned by a

107

broad consensus. Implicitly, Mendoza refuted poststructuralist claims that language construes the historical referent and assumed the obligation of providing a warranty for one's discourse about the past. As stated, his position respects history's empirical bottom line, the days and works of the dead. That is a surprising position for a novelist who plays with history. Mendoza has built up his literary career on the practice of dislocating history by subjecting historiographic (that is, ethically committed) discourse to the vagaries of genre and, often, to a banalizing lightness which redeems itself through humor but is hardly consonant with history's "fundamental traits." This is true not only of his first novel, *La verdad sobre el caso Savolta* (1975), which Jacques Maurice relates to the Transition's horizon of expectations, but also of *La ciudad de los prodigios* (1986) and of his recent novel about the postwar, *Una comedia ligera* (1996).

For a writer whose works establish their own criteria of truth satisfaction, it is strange to dismiss as ridiculous a discourse (Carod-Rovira's) that Mendoza himself calls iterative. Are not repetition and compulsiveness the signs of a trauma seeking release in the way suggested by Carod-Rovira, namely through admission? As Derrida says about discourse that is persistent, "When a discourse *holds* in some way, it is [...] because it has been opened up on the basis of some traumatizing event, by an upsetting question that does not let one rest [...] and because it nevertheless resists the destruction begun by this traumatism" (qtd. in Wyschogrod 178). What this means is that such a discourse is laden with affect (but is it not true of all discourses about the past?), and affect is not only an undeniable aspect of the novel but also, perhaps primarily, an aspect of the historian's responsibility for the past. As Edith Wyschogrod puts it, the claim of the heterological historian (the one who recognizes the otherness of the past) "is not merely 'I remember the affect of the other,' but 'I am responsible for re-membering the affect of the other'" (178).

The rubbing point in Mendoza's dispute with Carod-Rovira is not so much disagreement about the "fundamental traits" of the past as about the otherness of those traits. It is not a question of the past becoming scarce and of conflicts breaking out for its control. On the contrary, today, as Michael Schudson suggests, "the past may be increasingly a superabundant resource, and conflict may emerge not from its scarcity but from its superfluity" (361). For his part,

Charles Maier finds in contemporary society a "surfeit of memory," which, in his view, runs counter to the Enlightenment dream of "progress toward civic enfranchisement and growing equality" and leads instead towards a "narrow ethnicity" that "aspires preeminently to the recognition by other groups of its own suffering and victimhood" (150). Maier's essay is so full of qualifications that it is hard to know whether he is for or against keeping alive the memory of transgressions of what we might call "the human civic code." It is just as hard to decide whether it is the distracting potential of memory when it becomes a survival strategy—or, as he neatly puts it, "a strategy to come to terms with survival" (140)—or the proliferation of survivors with memories that shake his confidence in the politics of recognition as promoter of civic value. It is clear, however, that he is vexed by the spectacularization and instrumentalization of traumatic memory, and in that respect it is equally difficult to disagree with him.

Both Maier and Schudson diagnose problems that arise from overloaded memories. Despite the rhetoric about the disappearance of historical memory, we are far more conscious about the past than at any other time. But then, the surplus of memories circulating in larger or smaller channels begs the question: who does the remembering? For whom? With what means and for what purpose? In obligation or reponsibility towards whom? With what warranties? In short, this surplus of memories and remembering agents raises the question about the legitimacy of the memory deployed.

At its limit, the conflict of interpretations may restrict historical discourse to socially legitimated individuals, like those who handle regulated substances. Impatient with the political tampering with history, Javier Tusell recommended precisely this measure in order to prevent what he calls "the alternative use of History." Tusell reasons that those who are not sanctioned to practice historical interpretation often abuse the pastness of the past, its temporal difference, for the benefit of a thesis about the present ("El uso alternativo"). Probably the presentist bias should be discouraged, although this "use" of the past is hardly limited to marginal or ad hoc manipulation. On the contrary, it is found squarely in the midst of historiography itself, as Hobsbawm and Ranger's influential *The Invention of Tradition* amply demonstrates. Yet Tusell himself offers a striking example of this spurious use of temporal difference for the benefit of an interpretation of a present event. "Goebbels en Arrasate" is the title of another article he published in *El País*. Remembering Kristallnacht and Auschwitz, Tusell identifies ETA terrorism and the Holocaust. Furthermore, he claims that the 21% of Basque voters who supported Herri Batasuna (the Basque independence party linked to the armed struggle) played the same role as those Germans whose endorsement of Hitler made possible the gassing of Jews (14). Independently from one's assessment of the role of violence in the Basque country, one thing is clear: Tusell indulges in what he himself has called "the alternative use of History."

Considering the fate of victims in different genocides, Wyschogrod asks if it is legitimate to create a single historical persona in the absence of linguistic, cultural, and economic ties (13). The same question can be asked about the executioners. Is it not disingenuous to speak about the industrialization of ETA horror or about Ortega Lara's resemblance to a Jew from Auschwitz when he was liberated by the Spanish police? Even if one feels the outrage that Tusell tries to convey with this extrapolation of meaning from a heteronomous constellation, Wyschogrod's caution should still prevail: "For the historian it is not a question of how likenesses are to be posited predicatively." The very attempt to compare incommensurables presupposes a logic of difference and thus begs the question (14). Furthermore, if the Basque conflict with the Spanish state must be explained by the Holocaust, are not these historical phenomena themselves wrenched from historical understanding and rendered unintelligible?

Knowing how to deal with incommensurables is the touchstone of history. It requires commitment and is linked to the ethics of naming. The name that we attribute to the other calls up a false presence and erases its otherness. As Wyschogrod observes, names do not designate properties. Neither are they propositions to which truth or falsity can be attributed. Only the referent can be the object of attributions whose truth or falsity can be asserted or established. Names, on the other hand, especially common names, "can be conferred to demean or even to consign to death" (Wyschogrod 13). Above all, they encode those who are named or renamed in a system of references with particular meanings and affects. Naming has been a deliberate strategy in the conflict of historical interpretations. We have seen that strategy in Tusell's predication of identity between the Nazi organization of mass killings and the guerrilla tactics employed by the armed faction of Basque independentism. Tusell, like many Spanish intellectuals, deploys the term "nationalist" in order to predicate an identity between incommensurable social and historical realities. Using this nomer attributively and pseudoreferentially subjects realities to a temporal and geographic warp at the same time that it occludes the operative political relations. This process has gone so far that today the Spanish press distinguishes as a matter of course between democratic parties (those that support the centralized nation state) and nationalist parties (those that advocate a multinational state and extensive devolution).

For those who hide their own nationalism behind the structures of the nation state, peripheral nationalism, "the nationalisms," as the term goes in reference to Basque and Catalan demands for devolution or self-determination, is a political aberration with the same characteristics, objectives, and consequences everywhere, at any time, under any conditions. In 1996, during the war in Bosnia, and then again in 1999, as the Kosovo crisis was raging, Spanish newspapers brimmed with condemnations of nationalism. Most of these condemnations had the value of expletives; they were characterized by thinness of analysis and the incapacity to concentrate on the ostensible referent. The conflicts in the Balkans have been used repeatedly as an excuse to castigate Basque and Catalan national reivindications. For some years, dire warnings about Spain's alleged balkanization have been commonplace in centralist discourse.

In an article entitled "Nacionalismo" (*El País* 6 April, 1999), novelist Rosa Montero candidly expresses the purpose of strategic naming. "Quiero creer," says Montero, "que [...] la palabra nacionalista estará tan justamente desprestigiada que la consideraremos un insulto." Certainly, it is as an insult that the (nationalist) Spanish press uses the term in reference to Basque and Catalan-specific parties, while reserving the term "democratic" for the centralist parties. Derogation is one of the functions of naming when applied to the other. So are exclusion and amnesia-creation. In this form of naming, as in magic, names are the true referents. Subjects, on the other hand, are not called up as witnesses with regard to the truth or falsity of that which is attributed to them. Categorical derogation depends on the capacity of hegemonic discourse to create subsystems of marked elements while organizing itself around nonmarked positions: bourgeois universalism, male neutrality, statal patriotism.

I cannot enter here into an analysis of the distinct historical phenomena alluded to by the reductive term "los nacionalismos," or simply "el nacionalismo." This extreme reduction, incidentally, subtends Jon Juaristi's twice awarded book, *El bucle melancólico* (1997), which represents national liberation movements as a pathological phenomenon from which only a heroic resolution can keep the author, a self-styled modern Odysseus, on the side of reason—*raison d'état* (268).[12] It is enough to point out that these strategies of memory confinement marshall predicates which are attached to an affect-laden system of historical references. By deploying such predicates, the historian displaces the referential object and bypasses the obligation to contemporize with the dead. Although archival material is readily available, "antinationalist" intellectuals generally fail to appear at the cognitive rendezvous with the otherness they lump together by means of common predication. Hence they overlook the violence involved in suppressing alterity. In *El nacionalismo catalán como factor de modernización*, Vicente Cacho Viu spells out the democratizing and modernizing influence the Catalan national movement had for the entirety of the Spanish state. In its way of dealing with a heterological nationality, this book is a rare Spanish instance of an outsider's ethical discharge of the historian's obligation towards the other.

Strategies of naming bring me to the last narratological problem I wish to discuss in relation to the conflict of historical interpretation. Histories proliferate according to the need to countenance a society's ghosts. The historian gives a face to the faceless dead, the unknown, silent, or silenced ones. During the Transition new histories seemed to emerge from the great zones of amnesia; histories that were not grounded in the accepted historical discourse. Such histories were not just other but were often unreconcilable with those bequeathed by state-oriented historiography. Their emergence amounted to a deregulation of memory, lifting the state monopoly on the past. This situation can be described with the analogy that Toni Morrison uses to describe the nature of her work: "You know, they straightened out the Mississippi River in places, to make room for houses and livable acreage. Occasionally the river

112

floods these places. 'Floods' is the word they use, but in fact it is not flooding; it is remembering. Remembering where it used to be" (305).

The Conflict of Historical Memories

Two decades of deregulated remembrace have brought on alarm and re-regulation proposals. The most conflictive of these proposals was the 1997 Humanities decree devised by Esperanza Aguirre, Minister of Education in the conservative government of José María Aznar. At the core of her decree was history, the teaching of which the Minister was eager to coordinate throughout Spain. This eagerness set the new government off from Francoism's relative unconcern with this discipline.[13] In fact, though, the beleaguered Humanities project stemmed less from the government's preoccupation with the precision of the historical memory imparted to the young than from the alarm triggered by the existence of competing memories.[14] In the government's view, a centrally devised program in state history should override the statutory educational jurisdiction of the autonomous nationalities.

The polemic around the government's proposal to regulate the teaching of history throughout the state prompted several intellectuals to intervene. *El País* published a series of articles with a similarly centralist outlook. Among these interventions, Muñoz Molina's was the most explicit in endorsing the government's goal. Speaking of "los simulacros de historia que alientan los nacionalismos de ahora," he denounced the Catalan and Basque memories of the Spanish Civil War. To be sure, Muñoz Molina did not wish to be ranged as a conservative. He explicitly abominated Francoist historiography. It was wrong, he said, because it falsified Spanish history, eliminating or distorting the chapters associated with the liberal tradition. Yet, Spanish history, as he conceives it, reflects a system of relevances deemed homogeneously valid throughout the state and organized in a strict hierarchy. Catalan and Basque histories, for example, are not disciplines in their own right; they are "partial histories" which—purified of the national dross—"enrich" the common history of all Spaniards. Only when channeled through this "common" history can those incomplete narratives be incorporated into the history of mankind ("La historia y el olvido").

113

Inadvertently, Muñoz Molina reasserts the nineteenth-century historiographic model based on the creation of nation states. This model reflected the mandated assimilation of regional memories into one dominant version of the national past. The dominant version, nevertheless, succeeded only insofar as it was mediated by local categories, as A. Confino has shown for the German nation (Olick and Robbins 118). Such a model of a "common" history censures the chapters of internal aggression or the forgeries perpetrated along the consolidation of the linear narrative of commonality. When he denounces the historical "simulacra" allegedly fostered by the peripheral nationalities of the Spanish state, Muñoz Molina does not for a second consider that Spanish history, as handed down, is a massive simulacrum, all the more intractable for its tight fusion of "knowledge" with power. Instead, he treats the recent past as an exceptional phase of the national development and proposes other, not so new anchoring points for the master narrative of Spanish nationalism. Switching to a supposedly more objective story about the construction of the state, he believes that a more congenial picture emerges which preserves, nonetheless, the dominant traits of Castile-centrism.

Muñoz Molina's viewpoint, typical for a whole array of post-Franco intellectuals, justifies Edward Shils's observation that "traditional patterns of belief and conduct [...] are very insistent; they will not wholly release their grip on those who would suspend or abolish them" (200). This observation was confirmed once more after the conservative landslide in the Spanish general elections of March 2000. It would be inappropriate to speak of a new political culture and a new tone in the media, for nationalistic retrenchment began well under PSOE supremacy, but it is fair to say that the recent upsurge of traditional values and rhetoric has reached a degree that was unprecedented in the Transition. Buoyed up by their absolute majority in the Cortes, the conservatives quickly announced their intention to refloat the Humanities decree as an unnegotiable and unadjournable part of their political program. The necessary academic legitimation for this diaphanous political move came soon thereafter, and as if made to order, when the Real Academia de la Historia presented a report on the teaching of history in secondary schools throughout Spain on June 27, 2000. Claiming to be the meditated result of a long and laborious collection of detailed information, this document raises the alarm at the "very troubling" ways in which History is being taught in secondary schools. Some of these ways are methodological, having to do with the preeminence of "interdisciplinarity" and of an analytical rather than a strictly memoristic approach to history. The Real Academia criticizes that students are taught notions of metahistory and are made aware of the significance of the historian's conceptual tools at the expense, so the report claims, of "the historical process," by which the Real Academia clearly understands the chronological articulation of events (of certain privileged events, as we will see). Its methodological critique is so schematic that it seems merely pro-forma. In any case, when it complains that some textbooks do not display, unbroken, the chronological succession of events from Antiquity to the present, the report does not betray the slightest consciousness that this traditional articulation is far from an objective characteristic of the events themselves. Nor that, if time is the elementary dimension of history, not only the quality of time but also other human-related variables are responsible for the relevance of "events" and their configuration in a historical frame of reference which, like the constellations in the sky, will change according to time, place, and the instruments available to the beholder.

The report's emphasis lies plainly in its attack on the (statutorily guaranteed) educational competences of the historical nationalities, which come under fire for, allegedly, diffusing "the Spanish historical process" or even overwhelming it through the "particular vision of the past of this or that Autonomous Community." These objections are as familiar as they are riddled with contradictions. The first one has to do with the idea that the report is a non-political, scientifically rigorous evaluation of the pedagogical approach to "the historical process," an object over which the Academia, as a state institution on the same footing as the Army or the Judiciary, has a vested curatorial power. This power supposedly gives it the authority to protect "history" from becoming a political instrument at the hands of "the nationalities and regions of the Spanish State," "according to the expression that was fashionable during the transition years," the report adds, forgetting that this is the actual wording of the Spanish Constitution. The comment is neither gratuitous nor incidental. By attributing one of the foundational categories of the democratic state (namely, the distinction between nationalities and regions) to an obsolete rhetorical fad, the Academia undermines the legal foundations of the post-Francoist Spanish state, casting them in the false light of temporary concessions to the spirit of a bygone era. Another grievous contradiction is that between "the Spanish historical process" and the "particular vision of the past of this or that Autonomous Community." Assuming the existence of "a historical process" that happens to be essentially Spanish, it can only refer to the history of the Spanish state or else to "history" as configured through the prism of that state's system of relevances. In that case, it cannot be overlooked that the view of the past, as configured through the systems of relevances of the various nationalities and regions, may differ from the view canonized by the Real (and therefore monarchical) Academia de la Historia, without ceasing for a moment to be part and parcel of that self-same state's "process."

By attacking "sociologism," "economicism," and "pedagogism," the Academia's report undermines the disciplinary supports for the general validity it claims for the "historical process," while its onslaught against the "particularlism" of substatal viewpoints calls into question the specificity of historical research and the inductive nature of historical knowledge. Coming from a traditional branch of the state, it may not be altogether coincidental that the Academia's understanding of the "historical process" is tautological. It privileges "contents" that can be considered constitutive of the state; in other words, events and people whose selection and relative importance are dictated by the state's present configuration. Hence, "Los grandes personajes y los acontecimientos políticos deberán servir para formar el armazón de la disciplina, en la que habrán de presentarse, en sus interdependencias, lo económico, lo social y lo cultural." The great characters of the past, with monarchs and statesmen at the forefront, are, like the events privileged by this official historiography, the markers of a particular political configuration: that of the unified and centralized national state. With their help the state becomes as self-referential as the framework through which we are summoned to examine the authentic and impartial relation of the past.

Leaving aside the grave methodological shortcomings of the Academia's report,[15] its worse aspect is the presumption to watch over the shoulder of the educational departments of the so-called autonomous governments and over the shoulder of each school board and each school teacher. Advocating for a centrally conceived

116

curriculum, which in fact already dictates 55% to 65% of the contents of the history courses taught in the secondary schools of the autonomous communities with educational competence, the Real Academia de la Historia exacerbates the interference of "political circumstances," which it bemoans in the teaching of history, looking back nostalgically to some former time when that which it calls "general [Spanish] history" or "common [Spanish] history" was unchallenged for good, forcible reasons.

The plea for a unified history of the nation state can be opposed by the democratic demand that history be available to competing identities. Insistence on a government regulated teaching of history can be taken as one more step towards supressing the memory of the groups that were sacrificed in the creation of "the common history." The conflict of historical memories, of which the Real Academia's report is merely the latest manifestation, disguises the issue of the state's responsibility towards those others (women, peasants, national minorities and marginal religious groups) whose ghosts have never been officially called up. But the Real Academia's plea for an objective history is as likely to sanction the jarring viewpoints of the victims as the Conference of Spanish Bishops is to admit the Church's complicity with the coup-d'état and the dictatorship. As Pierre Vidal-Naquet observes, "De toutes les historiographies, la pire est évidemment l'historiographie d'État, et les États admettent rarement le fait d'avoir été criminels" (161).

Preventing a version of history from accruing undue power and becoming hegemonic is desirable even from the point of view of the dominant identity, for a society is a metaphor for the articulation of a great many differentiated and often conflictive actions, expectations, and imaginings, each with an irreducible temporality of its own. To straitjacket these temporal processes into a synchronous model based on a single deposit of memories would stymie the society's dynamism. Above all, the difficulty of alternative histories in asserting themselves should not be mistaken for their illegitimacy. Action does not happen unimpeded in a free, ideologically pliant medium, and reaction must be reckoned with. To understand the recent flare-up in the conflict of memories, one should ponder anthropologist Josep R. Llobera's assertion that "The Catalan nation has lived in a politically and culturally repressive state, and has consequently a pronounced deficit of historical memories of its own (ethno)nation, though it has been fed with a

117

diet of state history which ignores or perverts the (ethno)national history" (332). Llobera agrees with Muñoz Molina that there is a proliferation of memories but sees this situation in a very different light. He simply accepts that "multinational states that engage in historical reconstruction with the view of homogenising a given population within a dominant national culture and language, may have to compete with alternative ethnonational visions—even if the latter tend to be projected in a weaker light" (332). Llobera understands the limitations of institutionally disadvantaged memories, but he is careful to point out that the accusations of suppression or perversion of "historical truth" are reversible, in part because they are the consequence of different evaluations of what is relevant, what weighs more on the historian's consciousness of his or her debt to the past. The issue of relevance involves, in effect, an ethical question passed off as an epistemological one.

Llobera's viewpoint, steeped in respect for the historical memories of so-called peripheral nationalisms, is, predictably, more receptive to otherness than the discourse of self-styled "antinationalist" intellectuals. Such rhetoric, however, is deliberately confusing. In Spain today, "antinationalism" is indistinguishable from good old fashioned nationalism, and "antinationalists," who often repeat, unawares, the utterances of notorious fascist leaders, have become ideological mainstays of the homogenizing, centrally controlled nation-state. In contrast, Llobera's "peripheral" viewpoint welcomes the surplus of the past and accepts the rivalry between those who represent different patterns of recollection and different areas of amnesia. The struggle for the past is unavoidable, but it should not proceed by closing the distance between the ghost and the death-erasing historian's discourse. Instead it should accept the relation between the rememberer's social identity and the stretch of the past offered up to recollection. In Peter Burke's crisp formulation: "Given the multiplicity of social identities, and the coexistence of rival memories, alternative memories (family memories, local memories, class memories, national memories, and so on), it is surely more fruitful to think in pluralistic terms about the uses of memories to different social groups, who may well have different views about what is significant or 'worthy of memory'" (107).

Must we conclude, in a poststructuralist vein, that historical memory is merely an effect of poetic structures? Or that the zones

118

of amnesia and recollection can be designated at will? The answer to both questions is no. The (re)construction of alternative memories proceeds out of a sense of urgency prompted by an obligation to the dead. On these terms, (re)construction is a doomed attempt to retrieve those who have been sucked into oblivion's black hole. In the face of massive investments in silence, the enterprise can be heroic, but it only attains moral authority if it establishes a balanced relation to the available data. Recovering tracts of historical amnesia for the collective memory is comparable to filling the ocean with polders. Every step taken in the direction of the abyss must be secured against the onrush of scepticism and denial. Such work must be constantly and patiently renewed with a view to discharging the debt with the past, and it must be done, contrary to the protocols of ordinary justice, by patiently carrying the burden of proof and painstakingly revisiting the historical fault lines where evidence can be gathered. The historian who rejects the metaphysics of traditional history—the history of the state—must invert the point of view, even at the risk, as Foucault put it, "of adopting the famous perspective of frogs" (155). As he explained, effective history is concrete; it trades with those things nearest to it; it has no fear of looking down and measuring things in their intensity. "Effective history," in short, "studies what is closest, but in abrupt dispossession, so as to seize it from a distance" (156). That is the way to consort with ghosts: in insurmountable proximity. Such a refusal of the single, hierarchized perspective that looks on distances and plausible abstractions is necessary if the historian wishes to reinsert the witnessing absence of the departed into the historical continuum. Ghostly voices must be listened to, but that which the voices convey must be painstakingly documented, so that a bedrock of proof meets the attempts to monopolize memory. The need for impregnable evidence, always a requirement of serious historiography, is all the more decisive for the alternative historian, who—to paraphrase Vidal-Naquet's recommendation in a different context—must not offer his flank to the habituated reflections, not of state intellectuals whose opinion matters little, but quite simply of honest people (184).

Notes

1. Cf. Salvador Cardús's critique of the term "minority" and his proposal for an alternative in "Sobre algunes dificultats." See also Cardús and Estruch (351).

2. A spurious term in this context, since it presupposes the previous "enchantment" of intellectuals whose distinguishing trait was precisely that they remained critical throughout this process. For a discussion of the term "disenchantment," see Resina 57-59.

3. The syndrome of excessive historical memory seems to affect all political leaders, who feel that amnesiac voters and militants would be more conveniently stewarded by the parties. Thus, in the aftermath of the elections of March 12, 2000, in which his party came out of the polls with a steadily low rate of endorsement, Josep-Lluís Carod-Rovira declared: "A ERC [Esquerra Republicana de Catalunya] pesa massa la memòria històrica, s'és massa esclau dels objectius finals, s'està massa pendent de l'ortodòxia ideològica, factors tots ells que, amb d'altres, en dificulten l'ascens" ("Després de la batalla," March 22, 2000). Memory and purpose, the two Janus faces of history, and the attendant set of knowledges and ideas that subtend classic political philosophy now give way to the autonomously political. Poll approval becomes the measure of what can be legitimately known, pursued, or even integrated into the pragmatic consciousness of political action.

4. Instances of ideological coincidence are legion. They are perhaps most striking in the Socialist realignment with the Francoist ideal of a nationalized Spain strongly defined by the state apparatus. Attacking the plurinational state proposed by the Basque and Catalan administrations, the Socialist candidate to the Government's presidency, José Borrell, said recently that he refuses to accept that "España esté enterrada, junto a Franco, en el Valle de los Caídos" ("Spain remains buried, next to Franco, in the Valley of the Fallen") (*Avui* 11 Feb., 1999).

5. Revolution was never in the cards. As Rafael Borràs pointed out, the much-lauded consensus was a transaction between reformist Francoists who understood that the political system could not be preserved unchanged and a very weak left. In Borràs's words, "Santiago Carrillo era perfectamente consciente de que no

solamente no podía asaltar el Palacio de Invierno, sino que no podía asaltar ni siquiera la casita de verano" (Barranco 61).

6. As I was formatting the camera-ready manuscript of this book, Rosa Montero announced in *El País* that the Transition had been finally completed, one full quarter of a century after Franco's death. Speaking about the staggering victory of the Partido Popular in the elections of March 12, 2000, she wrote: "Tengo la sensación de que éste es el verdadero final de la Transición, la prueba definitiva de nuestra madurez democrática," endorsing what the same party had vaunted during the 1996 electoral campaign that handed limited power over to it four years earlier ("Progresismo"). There is no trace of irony in her statement. In retrospect, this "verdadero final" is a fitting conclusion for the "Transition" story, exposing what the entire operation was about.

7. See in this connection the Minister of Culture's public statement on the occasion, and note the programmatic title of his talk (Solé-Tura 16).

8. In the eighties, Madrid's popular Socialist major, Enrique Tierno Galván, found the best of demagogic formulas, condescendingly urging fellow citizens to enjoy themselves. Tierno was probably the first politician to exploit the "ethics" of self-gratification during the Transition.

9. See, for example, the following articles by José Antonio Primo de Rivera: "Traidores" (*Arriba* 12, 6 June 1935); "Cataluña y el 6 de octubre" (*Arriba* 34, 5 March, 1936); "El separatismo sin máscara" (*Falange Española* 14, 12 July 1934); "España es irrevocable" (*Falange Española* 15, 19 July 1934), reprinted in Primo de Rivera, *Obras completas*. See also José Antonio's letter of 24 September 1934 to General Franco (delivered by Ramón Serrano Súñer), in which the leader of Falange Española instigates the General to forestall the danger posed to Spain's "unity" by Catalonia's autonomy (Primo de Rivera I, 434-6). Those who cling to the idea that the Civil War was fundamentally a class war within a society of co-nationals might consider Paul Preston's observation that in the Francoist Academia General Militar "[t]here were virtually no cadets from the regions with historic aspirations to independence, Galicia, the Basque Country and Catalonia, and therefore no one to counter the idea that in the regions resided the enemy within" (39).

10. Skeptics would do well to consult Josep Benet's *Catalunya sota el règim franquista*. A Spanish translation is available: *Cataluña bajo el régimen franquista*, Barcelona: Editorial Blume, 1979.

11. The motion was presented again one year and a half later by Esquerra Republicana de Catalunya's Parliamentary deputy Joan Ridao, inviting the Spanish State, in the person of the President of the Government, and the

hierarchy of the Spanish Catholic Church through the Bishops' Conference, to manifest official regret for the injustices committed during Francoism and for their complicity with the dictatorship and its crimes. Recalling that some proceedings of military trials remain under military jurisdiction and are illegally kept from public scrutiny, Ridao alerted that the present democracy should not be "an alibi for silence and oblivion" (Carbó).

12. The Odyssean metaphor is unfortunate. If the nation is hallucinated by souls gone astray on a return voyage to nowhere, what is this homeward bound figure doing here? Is Ithaca, then, a figment of the seafarer's delirium? Does not Odysseus drive away the usurpers from his ancestral home, his own *herria*? To what melancholy mast, on what battered vessel, did Juaristi tie himself up in order to resist the call of a particular nature turned song and a particular history turned legend, or viceversa?

13. The irrelevance of history and the corresponding onset of historical amnesia preceded the Transition but were in fact motivated by the forces that produced it. Thus Carolyn Boyd notes: "Having embraced economic and social modernization and thus no longer dependent on its peculiar reading of the national past to justify Spain's 'difference' from Europe, the regime now seemed determined to deny history any functional educational role whatsoever" (292).

14. The defeated proposal was to resurface in the Popular Party's campaign for the general elections of March 12, 2000. Having won by a wide margin, the Popular Party was quick to announce its plans to implement the Humanities reform. Although no longer Minister of Education, Esperanza Aguirre, now president of the Senate, wasted no time reminding the President of the Government about his pledge to decree the project's implementation ("Aguirre").

15. As it turned out, none of the Academia's members in Catalonia were consulted during the elaboration of the study. Apparently, they were incognizant about the contents of the report until its publication. To make the matter even more confusing, after the *coup-d'éffet* had been achieved, an official spokesman of the Real Academia declared that the academicians had not examined any of the textbooks used in Catalonia and that, in fact, they had not found anything of concern in this autonomous community.

Works Cited

Adorno, Theodor W. "The Meaning of Working Through the Past." Trans. Henry W. Pickford. *Critical Models: Interventions and Catchwords.* New York: Columbia UP, 1998: 89-103.

"Aguirre confia a veure 'per fi' la implantació del decret d'humanitats." *Avui Digital* 31 March, 2000.

Arendt, Hannah. *Besuch in Deutschland.* Trans. Eike Geisel. Berlin: Rotbuch, 1993.

Bachelard, Gaston. *Poetics of Space.* Trans. Maria Jolas. Boston: Beacon Press, 1999.

Barnouw, Dagmar. "Time, Memory, and the Uses of Remembrance." *Alexander von Humboldt-Magazin* 73 (1999): 3-10.

Barranco, Justo. "Entrevista a Rafael Borràs, editor barcelonés homenajeado en la Feria del Libro de Madrid." *La Vanguardia* 31 May, 1998: 61, 63.

Benet, Josep. *Catalunya sota el règim franquista.* Paris: Edicions Catalanes de París, 1973.

Boyd, Carolyn P. *Historia Patria: Politics, History, and National Identity in Spain, 1875-1975.* Princeton, N.J.: Princeton University Press, 1997.

Burke, Peter. "History as Social Memory." *Memory: History, Culture and the Mind.* Ed. Thomas Butler. Oxford: Basil Blackwell, 1989: 97-113.

Cacho Viu, Vicente. *El nacionalismo catalán como factor de modernización.* Barcelona: Quaderns Crema and Amigos de la Residencia de Estudiantes, 1998.

Carbó, Ismael. "ERC proposa que Aznar i l'Església demanin perdó pel franquisme," *Avui Digital* 21 June 2000.

Cardús, Salvador. "Memòria i relat biogràfic. A propòsit de Ferran Canyameres." *Ciutat* 7 (1998): 8-13.

———. "On Some Difficulties in the Theoretical Analysis of Nationalism." International Symposium on Nationalisms As an Object of Study in the Social Sciences. Fundació Jaume Bofill, November 7-9, 1996. Published in Catalan translation: "Sobre algunes dificultats en l'anàlisi teòrica del nacionalisme." *Nacionalisme i Ciències Socials.* Barcelona: Editorial Mediterrània, 1997: 9-13.

Cardús, Salvador and Joan Estruch. "Politically Correct Anti-Nationalism." *International Social Science Journal* 47 (1995): 347-52.

Carod-Rovira, Josep-Lluís. "Després de la batalla." *Avui Digital* 22 March, 2000.

Connerton, Paul. *How Societies Remember.* Cambridge: Cambridge UP, 1989.

Contreras, Gonzalo. *La ciudad anterior.* Santiago: Editorial Planeta Chilena, 1991.

"El cop d'Estat, una data més per a la història." *Avui Digital* 24 February, 1998.

Danto, Arthur C. *The Transfiguration of the Commonplace.* Cambridge, Massachusetts: Harvard UP, 1981.

Derrida, Jacques. *Spectres de Marx.* Paris: Galilée, 1993.

Foucault, Michel. *Language, Counter-Memory, Practice.* Ed. Donald F. Bouchard. Trans. Donald F. Bouchard and Sherry Simon. Ithaca, New York: Cornell UP, 1977.

González Casanova, J. A. *El cambio inacabable (1975-1985).* Barcelona: Anthropos, 1986.

Gordon, Avery F. *Ghostly Matters: Haunting and the Sociological Imagination.* Minneapolis: University of Minnesota Press, 1997.

Habermas, Jürgen. "Über den öffentlichen Gebrauch der Historie." *Die postnationale Konstellation.* Frankfurt am Main: Suhrkamp, 1998: 47-61.

Halbwachs, Maurice. *The Collective Memory.* Trans. Francis J. Ditter, Jr. and Vida Yazdi Ditter. New York: Harper and Row, 1980.

———. *On Collective Memory.* Ed. and trans. Lewis A. Coser. Chicago: The University of Chicago Press, 1992.

Hobsbawm, E., and T. Ranger, eds. *The Invention of Tradition.* Cambridge: Cambridge University Press, 1983.

Juaristi, Jon. *El bucle melancólico: Historias de nacionalistas vascos.* Madrid: Espasa-Calpe, 1997.

Llobera, Josep R. "The Role of Historical Memory in Catalan National Identity." *Social Anthropology* 6 (1998): 331-42.

Maier, Charles S. "A Surfeit of Memory? Reflections on History, Melancholy and Denial." *History and Memory* 5. 2 (1993): 136-52.

Martín Patino, Basilio. *Los paraísos perdidos* (film), 1985.

Maurice, Jacques. "De la manipulation de l'Histoire dans *La verdad sobre el caso Savolta..*" *La Renovation du Roman Espagnol Depuis 1975.* Ed. Yvan Lissorgues. Toulousse: Presses Universitaires du Mirail, 1991: 75-85.

Mendoza, Eduardo. "El senyor Carod-Rovira demana comptes." *Avui Digital* 21 December, 1998.

Mesulam, Marek-Marsel. "Notes on the Cerebral Topography of Memory and Memory Distortion: A Neurologist's Perspective." *Memory Distortion. How Minds, Brains, and Societies Reconstruct the Past.* Ed. Daniel L. Schacter. Cambridge, Massachusetts: Harvard UP, 1997: 379-85.

Mommsen, Wolfgang J. "Die Vergangenheit, die nicht vergehen will." *Gegen den Versuch, Vergangenheit zu verbiegen.* Ed. Hilmar Hoffmann. Frankfurt am Main: Athenäum, 1987: 83-93.

Montero, Rosa. "Nacionalismo." *El País Digital* 6 April, 1999.

——. "Progresismo." *El País Digital* 21 March, 2000.

Morrison, Toni. "The Site of Memory." *Out There: Marginalization and Contemporary Cultures.* Ed. Russell Ferguson, Martha Gever, Trinh T. Minh-ha, and Cornell West. New York: The New Museum of Contemporary Art, Cambridge, Massachusetts: The MIT Press, 1990: 299-305.

Muñoz Molina, Antonio. *Beatus Ille.* Barcelona: Seix Barral, 1986.

——. "La historia y el olvido." *El País Digital* 28 November, 1997.

——. *El jinete polaco.* Barcelona: Planeta, 1991.

Olick, Jeffrey K. and Joyce Robbins. "Social Memory Studies: From 'Collective Memory' to the Historical Sociology of Mnemonic Practices." *Annual Review of Sociology* 24 (1998): 105-40.

Preston, Paul. *The Politics of Revenge: Fascism and the Military in Twentieth-Century Spain.* London: Unwin Hyman, 1990.

Primo de Rivera, José Antonio. *Obras Completas. Discursos y escritos (1922-1936).* 2 vols. Madrid: Instituto de Estudios Políticos, 1976.

Rahola, Pilar. "El cant, si t'arriba, Puig Antich, pren-lo com un crit." *Avui Digital* 3 May, 1998.

Real Academia de la Historia. "Informe sobre los textos y cursos de historia en los centros de enseñanza media." *El País Digital* 28 June, 2000.

Resina, Joan Ramon. *El cadáver en la cocina: La novela criminal en la cultura del desencanto.* Barcelona: Anthropos, 1997.

Rubert de Ventós, Xavier. *De la identidad a la independencia: la nueva transición.* Trans. Francesc Roca. Barcelona: Anagrama, 1999.

Schudson, Michael. "Dynamics of Distortion in Collective Memory." *Memory Distortion. How Minds, Brains, and Societies Reconstruct the Past.* Ed. Daniel L. Schacter. Cambridge, Masssachusetts: Harvard UP, 1997: 347-64.

Seremetakis, C. Nadia. "The Memory of the Senses." *The Senses Still: Perception and Memory as Material Culture in Modernity*. Ed. C. Nadia Seremetakis. Chicago: The University of Chicago Press, 1994: 1-43.

Shils, Edward. *Tradition*. Chicago: The University of Chicago Press, 1981.

Solé Tura, Jordi. *1492: La dimensión real del mundo moderno*. Conferencia del Ministro de Cultura, Jordi Solé Tura, pronunciada en el Club Siglo XXI de Madrid, el 24 de febrero de 1992. Madrid: Subdirección de Estudios, Documentación y Publicaciones, 1992.

Terdiman, Richard. *Present Past: Modernity and the Memory Crisis*. Ithaca: Cornell University Press, 1993.

Tusell, Javier. "Goebbels en Arrasate." *El País* 5 July, 1997: 14.

——. "El uso alternativo de la Historia." *El País Digital* 23 July, 1998.

Vázquez Montalbán, Manuel. *Galíndez*. Barcelona: Seix Barral, 1990.

Vidal-Naquet, Pierre. *Les Assassins de la mémoire*. Paris: La Découverte, 1987.

Wyschogrod, Edith. *An Ethics of Remembering: History, Heterology, and the Nameless Others*. Chicago: The University of Chicago Press, 1998.

6

Oblivion and Remembrance: the Double Desire of Muñoz Molina's *El jinete polaco*

David K. Herzberger

El jinete polaco (1991) begins with a moment of critical awareness for the main character, Manuel. He awakens (physically) in the middle of the night and begins (mentally) a chronotopic exploration that embraces much of the time and space of his past. This exploration represents for him a radical transformation, one that generates personal and historical perturbations in the way that he perceives the perplexities of living, and one that defines as well the content of the form of *El jinete polaco*. For nearly two decades Manuel has viewed memory as a pernicious attachment to other times and places, and has sought to isolate himself within the present by dissociating himself from all that has come before. In this instant of awakening, however, he calls forth the time and space of his hometown, Mágina, thus compelling him to imagine himself outside of the protective insularity of the present: "Se incorporó para buscar un cigarrillo en la mesa de noche y sólo entonces se dio cuenta de lo tarde que era al ver la hora en el despertador, y calculó instintivamente la hora que sería en Mágina. Ya habría amanecido, su padre estaría en el mercado ordenando la hortaliza húmeda y brillante sobre el mostrador de mármol..." (12). Manuel's sudden desire to fuse temporal and spatial frames for which he previously allowed no connection triggers in his life what Michel de Certeau has called "an efficacious meandering" (xviii)—a peripatetic journey in which the long suppressed past emerges to question Manuel and thereby call his existence into question. In other words, the memory which Manuel had forcefully kept in abeyance now corrupts the pure present tense he had so insistently forged by means of his willed forgetting. As a result, he is compelled to examine those moments of the past when the future had not yet been decided and when the meaning of his existence was still open to the uncertain horizon of expectation.

The pattern of Manuel's efficacious meandering between past and present is not an uncommon one among fictional characters of the twentieth century. Nor, for that matter, is his long-held desire to erase from memory all that he had known and been. From Nietzsche's nineteenth-century admonition to forget the past and engage the horizons of the future with creative freedom, to Proust's and Faulkner's urgent commingling of past and present to demonstrate how our understanding of one turns upon the impingement of the other, the shifting function of time and space in fiction has emerged as an ontologically slippery but critical component for the nurturing and defining of character identities. In *El jinete polaco*, Manuel's literal and symbolic awakening stems from his conscious decision to reinvest his identity in the past when for nearly two decades he had attempted precisely the opposite. Indeed, he had lived suspended in a temporal amorphousness which served to annul all affect derived from the expected accumulation of experience and perception. As a result, he persistently located himself amid immense patches of oblivion, secure only in a carefully constructed presentness which expelled other times and spaces from the here and now of his existence.

Manuel sees the decision to abandon his hometown eighteen years earlier as an unavoidable entailment. In a general way, the historical context of his youth in Mágina provided the impetus for his felt need to rid himself of the past. The burden of Francoism (both as tradition and story) and the emptiness of the transition to democracy define for him the parameters of a double-edged dissent: he renounces the spent meaning of history shaped by the old regime and also scorns the meaningless present whose value to the young adults of Mágina is measured only by its potential to negate the flatness of their lives. Mágina seems perpetually to distend this flatness rather than diminish it, hence the youths regularly desire to be someone else and to be located in some other place. To be perceived as an outsider, to be identified as a foreigner, became the singular goal of Manuel and his friends during the early years of their lives: "Me iría... y cuando volviera, si volvía, yo también sería un forastero, un renegado, un nómada" (204).

The urgency to forswear his previous life, however, is spurred not merely by a desire to repudiate the culture of Mágina in an abstract, psychological sense by adopting the latest popular customs from abroad (although as adolescents Manuel and his friends mimicked the counterculture of drugs and embraced the rock music of Jim Morrison). Nor is it compelled by a projected return to the town once foreignness has been affirmed and the stain of Mágina has been erased in some indefinite future time. Instead, Manuel pursues the harsh extirpation of experiences and objects whose filiation with Mágina is unbearable:

> Me da rabia poseer cosas, libros de fotografías, discos, carpetas de recortes... armarios llenos de ropa sin usar, cartas inútiles que no serán contestadas pero que nunca llegan a tirarse, libros que ya no serán leídos... es como una selva en la que hubiera que estar manejando sin descanso [sic] el machete para que no vuelva a cerrarse la espesura, como una casa comida por las termitas de la que hay que irse cuanto antes..., abandonando el peso muerto, las costumbres, las cosas, la ropa usada, los libros inútiles, incluso los recuerdos.... (395)

Manuel's perception of Mágina is saturated with traditions and values that both weigh him down and incite revulsion. The provisory intrusions and intolerant circumscription of the town eventually afford him a succinct template for forgetting: "quería no estar atado a nada ni a nadie y no tener raíces" (259). Manuel's desire thus impels him not toward a fusion of horizons (past and future) but toward an unremitting dislocation of one from the other. In other words, his desire for difference and separation produces a self-coerced form of amnesia in which he lives with a keen sense of his detachment from past time as well as an awareness of the fragility of such detachment. Certainly he has not emerged into selfhood from a fortuitous confluence of forces which he at once shapes and is shaped by. Indeed, his life is defined largely by absence. He suspects that the removal of his being from being-in time cannot sustain him for long, hence he travels from one space to another with vacuous persistence, as if his constant movement will prevent the past from catching up with him.

There is clearly a practical reason, however, for Manuel to declare the impertinence of his past. Mágina represents for him all that has checked his growth and progress, all that has compelled conformity from those whose lives are connected firmly to a time and space which seem able only to intensify stagnation. This is the case above all for Manuel's family, who are enmeshed in an on-goingness (of space, values, history, etc.) and are unable to

129

disengage themselves from the cycle of bland repetition. As Manuel sees it, memory for his family relates less to having done great things in the past and wishing to do them again than to a stifling enshrinement of the dead. Their inability to blot out the past, to project themselves toward a future horizon unfettered by historical memory, represents for Manuel the tragic failure of their lives: "Pensé con desdén, con rencor, casi con odio, que estaban como muertos, que se pasaban así la mayor parte de sus vidas, impotentes, atados a la tierra, invocando fantasmas" (234).

Manuel's compulsion to forget therefore stems from his perception of the past (of history) as a collection of inert deposits that virtually preclude the possibility of change and growth. Forgetting comes to function for him as a kind of exorcism in which he can escape from positing origins which press hard against his desire to emerge from the past. His resistance to historical and personal memory, and to the space associated with both, leads him to shun Mágina in favor of the transient life of an interpreter whose purpose is designed less to pursue the future than to deny the past. He aspires neither to community nor to the temporal foundations of community (tradition, history, continuity), and thus hopes to evade the complex of socio-historical relations which resonate throughout Spain during the waning years of Francoism and the early years of democracy. It is in fact precisely for this reason that the painting of *El jinete polaco* serves as the recurrent metaphor of Manuel's nomadic existence. He finds in the painting the ambiguous configuration of his disconnectedness:

> [...] la figura del jinete que cabalga por un paisaje donde muy pronto amanecerá o acaba de hacerse de noche, un viajero solitario y tranquilo, alerta, orgulloso, casi sonriente, que da la espalda a una colina donde se distingue la sombra de un castillo y parece cabalgar sin propósito hacia algún lugar que no puede verse en el cuadro y cuyo nombre nadie sabe, igual que tampoco sabe nadie el nombre del jinete ni la longitud y latitud del país por donde está cabalgando. (18)

Manuel's understanding of the painting is critical for several reasons, all of which point to the overriding tensions in the novel between remembering and forgetting. First of all, as Manuel sees it, the painting posits its own temporal ambiguity—the viewer cannot distinguish if the horseman rides into a new day or into the night. It is a moment at once frozen in time and removed from time, thus dissolving the markers which humans generally use to measure temporal flow. Manuel of course identifies with such ambiguity, since for the past eighteen years temporal indices which distinguish present and past for him have been superseded by an on-going presentness. Futhermore, the horseman's journey "sin propósito" confirms not only the absence of a horizon of expectation for Manuel in the future, but also draws out the thinness of his present. His is a life with scant meaning, underscored by his ambling about without a discernible purpose. Perhaps most importantly, the temporal ambiguity of the painting is complemented by its spatial ambiguity, both of which suggest a kind of liquifying amorphousness that points to the pleasure and deception of the rider's existence. For Manuel, of course, there is a desire for such uncertainty yet a wistfulness for something more concrete. In this sense, the painting hints at an inevitable ending. After all, the rider is "cabalgando," and the fact that he has turned his back and rides from the castle on the hill hints at the impossibility of remaining forever removed from the accretions of time and space as existential determinants. In other words, despite the signs of historical oblivion which permeate the painting, the horseman nonetheless remains located in some place and some time—even if these can be determined somewhat intangibly through their absence.

The persistence and inevitability of time and space vaguely intimated by the painting are not easily dismissed by Manuel even as he defines his life attempting to exclude them. For indeed, they seep into his consciousness and serve to intensify his desire to escape everything associated with them. In a family and a town overrun with the meanings and uses of memory, where the aggregate of shifting images, ancestors, friends, and stories is endlessly recomposed, Manuel's willed forgetting is both powerful and insistent. His need not just to sever the past from the present but to expunge it from his language, intensifies the willed anomie of his existence. Manuel's work as an interpreter thus emerges as a decisive avatar of his rootlessness. As he moves from one city to another and from one time zone to another to work at international conferences, he uses language (the most temporal of epistemological tools) to avoid all time and space which lie outside the immediacy of the present: "Huyo en secreto, cumplo con una ficticia aplicación mis tareas, converso en dos o tres idiomas igual que si viajara por países o vidas a los que no pertenezco, sin un minuto de retraso entro en la cabina de traducción que me ha sido asignada, compruebo el micrófono, los auriculares, eludo la tentación de encender un cigarrillo, oigo una voz que habla y procuro repetir en español sus palabras sin que me importe lo que dicen..." (80). Manuel's work isolates him in space (he translates from a booth, removed from all community) and in time—his language is intended to repeat simultaneously the language of others. This daily affirmation of solitude nurtures his consciousness of self as living cut off from everything except the present. More importantly, however, it leads eventually to his awareness of the deficiency of the present and to the realization of his incapacity *to be*.

El jinete polaco can thus be seen as a work that posits the destruction of historical memory only to reveal the impossibility of such a proposition. The impossibility is not affirmed *per se*, but rather the will to obliterate time is revealed throughout the novel as a fatal error. Manuel seeks to unmoor himself from the temporal and spatial atavism of Mágina with the hope of authenticating discontinuity. It is of course a discontinuity grounded in loss and absence and is therefore presented as both empty and destructive. While Manuel discerns the infinite flow of time as he views the painting of the horseman, he also grasps his own finite understanding of time. The Civil War, his youth in postwar Spain and later the transition to democracy have no standing as discrete moments which bear diverse meanings, for there is no differentiation amid the formlessness into which Manuel relegates all time outside of the present. Hence both the personal and historical sense of identity for Manuel have little to do with key events most often used as historical markers. To the contrary, normal temporal signs become divorced from temporal distinctiveness and thereby deliquesce into forced oblivion. Unlike his parents and grandparents, therefore, and unlike Spanish society as a whole during the nearly two decades of his youth spent in Mágina, Manuel finds only deceit in the past.

As I have suggested, however, Manuel comes to understand that his is a double deceit. For in the end (which serves as the beginning of the novel), rather than celebrate the presence of the present, he despairs of its corrosive deficiencies. His awareness of these deficiencies leads to a more damning recognition of the abyss between what he perceives as the usefulness of forgetting and the inevitable truths of remembering:

> [U]no, si quiere, se puede volver tan maleable como un trozo de arcilla, contar su vida al mismo tiempo que la inventa, modificar, tachar, atribuirse una memoria y una forma de hablar que no le pertenecen, borrar meses, años enteros, ciudades, historias de mujeres. Era tan fácil que no me daba cuenta de que también era peligroso, porque la mentira, una vez inventada, actúa por sí misma y es un ácido que carcome irreparablemente la verdad, sobre todo cuando uno carece de puntos firmes de referencia y sólo tiene puntos de fuga.... (396)

The cult of the past by Manuel's family served to check the acceleration of the future toward possibilities capable of spinning out of control.[1] Indeed, cultivating the past became for them not simply a way to assuage troublesome disjunctions which threatened comfortable continuities, but a way to authenticate history as the necessary antecedent for all that they perceive as permanent in their lives. In contrast, Manuel's response to his family's constant evocation of the past turns upon an overdetermination of the present: he posits the absence of an origin in an attempt to define himself unfettered by spatial and temporal restrictions and untied to meanings generated by others. But as Muñoz Molina shows throughout *El jinete polaco* (as if the novel were written for this purpose), neither an overcommitment to the past nor its abandonment is able to bring about the vital commingling of the "has been" of the individual with the "yet to be." If we pose the question, why does Manuel desire to remember after eighteen years of calculated amnesia, why does he evoke the past when he had claimed its utter sterility, the answer comes easily: it is because he is able finally to envisage time projected beyond the present—time perceived and used as "becoming." But the future cannot stand alone—it will be defined only by evoking the fullness of temporal horizons both present and past. Indeed, Manuel comes to affirm that it is participation in the past, not its suspension, which makes the idea of a future possible. In this way, the chronotopic core of Manuel's re-cognition of life moves to the fore:

> Pero no es verdad, descubro al mirar el reloj que brilla sobre la mesa de noche, ésta no es la hora de Mágina, y no sólo porque yo esté en otro

133

continente y al otro lado de un océano, sino porque estos relojes no sirven para medir un tiempo que únicamente ha existido en esa ciudad, no sé cuando, en todos los pasados y porvenires que fueron necesarios para que ahora yo sea quien soy, para que los rostros y las edades de los vivos y de los muertos se congregaran ante mí como en el baúl insondable de Ramiro Retratista, para que Nadia sucediera en mi vida. (31)

It is important to bear in mind here that it is not the past *per se* which immediately impinges upon Manuel and forces its way into his consciousness. Instead, it is the sudden and deep awareness of his future with Nadia that triggers his desire to recover the past and to link himself with the time and space of Mágina: "vinculados [Manuel y Nadia]... por las voces y los testimonios de un mundo que irrumpía en ellos viniendo del pasado..." (10).

Nadia's appearance in Manuel's life in the present, however, provides not only the impetus for his exploration of the past but also the vehicle. The trunk full of photos inherited from her father, who in turn had received them many years earlier from the photographer (Ramón Retratista), allows her and Manuel to suture together the stranded objects and stories of their past and to give significance and presence to what previously had been insignificant and absent. Over the course of ten days in Nadia's apartment (and over the course as well of nearly the entire novel) Manuel and Nadia examine the photos and remember. Remembering becomes significant in their lives for any number of reasons, but two stand as highly pertinent both to their immediate context and to the ascription of meaning to history: 1) the linking of temporal horizons reverses Manuel's static and stagnant sense of presentness—that is to say, it reverses the oblivion of history; 2) their evocation of the past underscores the ineradicability of storytelling—of narration— as the basis for positing a diversity of meanings rather than for creating a single truth.

The past thus sets for Manuel not only a parameter within which he can frame stories, but also becomes an operative component of the stories themselves. The thickness of memory molded by the photos enables Manuel to undertake (as Henry James once wrote about Conrad's *Chance*) "a prolonged and hovering flight of the subjective" (254) over the outstretched terrain of Mágina during the twentieth century. Both the time and space of Mágina are critical to this process because Manuel constructs himself in his memory of the town. Each one of the streets, houses, and restaurants which Manuel knew as a youth thus becomes a semaphore of the self he had previously wished to annul but which now permeates his consciousness. Manuel also recognizes himself in the sensations produced by his newly-discovered memory, and he undertakes a Proustian journey nourished now by desire and need.[2] But his memory of a place (Mágina) allows him more than merely to gain sensations—it allows him, more importantly, to discover his own being as a temporal and spatial projection. For indeed, when Manuel arrives in Mágina he finds that he is already there. This transition from present to past and from absence to presence, reconnects memory and history to being when once it had been severed, and reveals to Manuel how a glance cast into the depths of time is also a glance cast into the depths of space: "a su alrededor, en su conciencia, en su mirada, hasta en la superficie de su piel, todas las cosas irradiaban vínculos en el espacio y en el tiempo" (16).

Manuel is keenly aware that the past is both detached from the horizon of the present and fused with it, and that the space of Mágina adheres to both temporal planes at once. At the same time, he comes to recognize that his being is not one plane *or* the other, but is to be found in the rapport which binds the two. Yet while "finding" plays a key role, the re-cognizing of the self turns more upon creation than discovery, more upon desire than awareness. This means, in a practical sense, that while detachment from desire and the effort to forget once drove Manuel to engage only the pure present, where telling was replaced by acting, the regeneration of desire now exposes the full spectrum of time and compels narration: "[M]e doy cuenta de que por primera vez en mi vida soy yo quien cuenta y no quien escucha..." (180). Manuel explores past time fully conscious of the perpetual and even radical discontinuity of the elements composing it. The photographs before him are like memory itself—collections of moments which are able to occupy variable positions with respect to all others, given order (if not stability) by the narrator. Manuel clearly sees himself as part of a story shaped by chronology and causality. He understands that historical forces shape his life but he perceives as well that these often lie beyond his range of control. More significantly, however, he recognizes that the past as he evokes it is not a natural sequence of events inevitably told in a specific way, but rather both a sequential and simultaneous accretion of events constructed by narrative tradition and by decisions consciously and unconsciously made. Thus it is not simply what he narrates that creates his sense of self but the way in which he perceives how narration counters oblivion and coerces meaning. It is a coercion not bereft of truth—"no quiero modificar en su origen el curso del tiempo, sólo concederme unas pocas imágenes que pueden no ser del todo falsas" (194)—but thickly vexed by both collective and individual need:

> Hasta ahora supuse que en la conservación de un recuerdo intervenían a medias el azar y una especie de conciencia biográfica. Poco a poco... empiezo a entender que en casi todos los recuerdos comunes hay escondida una estrategia de mentira, que no eran más que arbitrarios despojos lo que yo tomé por trofeos o reliquias: que casi nada ha sido como yo creía que fue, como alguien, dentro de mí, un archivero deshonesto, un narrador paciente y oculto, embustero, asiduo, me contaba que era. (193)

As I have suggested, Manuel willfully calls forth fragments of time tightly connected to fragments of space. But as occurs with time, while the actual content of that space slowly bleeds into his consciousness (e.g., the fields where he toiled, the bars where he drank, the school where he studied) and infuses fullness where once there was emptiness, his perception of "how" supersedes the adequacy of "what" (content). Further, as occurs with his conception of time, Manuel first takes space for a continuum whose wholeness is self-evident and easily understood. He quickly perceives, however, that it is not simply a matter of exploring a particular space, but of positioning oneself in relation to that space. Like time, space grows from an ensemble of aspects and points of view whose totality reveals not truth but meaning as it is connected to desire. Manuel makes the critical point when his spatial perspective filters through Nadia, the object of his love: "Siento que vuelvo a Mágina por primera vez porque he llegado desde un lugar donde no estuve nunca. No vuelvo de la huida ni del rencor, sino de ti, no veo la ciudad únicamente a través de mi memoria, sino también de la tuya..." (526). Memory spatializes time (and vice versa) for Manuel, and both are integrated into the larger enterprise of overcoming the willed amnesia and forgetting of the past two decades.

136

In the end, therefore, Manuel embraces recollection over oblivion and does so by replacing a period of dearth with a period of plenitude. His success in discovering what he had once renounced reveals his critical awareness that there can be no permanent loss of historical memory, only temporary amnesia that is self-afflicted. Manuel's amnesia is perhaps best viewed as a form of failed temporal suicide—failed not only because of the pressure which time inevitably exerts on him both chronologically and psychologically, but also because of Manuel's own recognition of his desire for temporal fullness. After eighteen years of negation the horizon of expectation once again asserts its presence to dislodge the emptiness of Manuel's present, but it can only do so by drawing into consciousness spatial memories long abandoned. Manuel's desire is doubly powerful in this instance for it compels the recollection of scattered events from the past as well as the organization of those events within narrative form. This (re)constructive process is decidedly muddled—the evocation of the past as well as its retelling cannot remain detached from the contingencies of memory and discourse. Of course, there is a cost to the telling of the story. Manuel may ultimately recall more the way he tells it than the way it happened, thus posing a threat to the authenticity of memory by laying bare the protean nature of its assertions. Yet clearly in the novel, remembering and telling are shown to be risks worth taking. Both the individual and historical perspectives conveyed in *El jinete polaco* reach into the depths of time and space in order to represent a present no longer congealed and stilled, but vital and hopeful. Manuel had sought to maintain his life as a blank page but now realizes that it is an unavoidable palimpsest. Hence the suppression of time (past and future) is revealed in the novel as a cheerless end game. Time evoked, through memory and within narration, is affirmed as the only way to defeat the game—if only for a while.

Notes

1. The contentious issue of memory and creating the past has consequences for both meaning and behavior beyond the individual in Francoist Spain. For a discussion of these matters as they relate to historiography see my essay in *PMLA*.

2. It is important to distinguish here between desire and need. In general terms, desire is vital and procreative. It impels the self towards enrichment and suggests that process is more central to being than end or result. In contrast, when desire seeks only to reach an end (i.e., when the individual desires the end of desiring), then need supplants desire. As a result, the kinetic personage of desire, who is always a being-in-process, now yields to the static individual of need, whose self is actualized and thus, ironically, destroyed. For a succinct overview of this idea see Thomas Docherty.

Works Cited

Certeau, Michel de. *The Practice of Everyday Life*. Trans. S. Randall. Berkeley: University of California Press, 1984.

Docherty, Thomas. *Reading (Absent) Character*. Oxford: Clarendon Press, 1983.

Herzberger, David K. "Narrating the Past: History and the Novel of Memory in the Postwar Spanish Novel." *PMLA* 106 (1991): 34-45.

James, Henry. "The New Novel." *Theory of Fiction*. Ed. J.A. Miller. Lincoln: University of Nebraska Press, 1972: 252-56.

Muñoz Molina, Antonio. *El jinete polaco*. Barcelona: Planeta, 1991.

El tabú del franquismo vivido en la narrativa de Mendoza, Marías y Muñoz Molina

Maarten Steenmeijer

Introducción

Varios años después de la muerte de Franco (el 20 de noviembre de 1975), muchas calles españolas todavía llevaban el nombre del dictador y seguía intacto el ostentoso símbolo de la Falange en los muros de muchísimos pueblos. ¿Por qué no habían desaparecido, junto con el viejo sistema político, estos residuos de la dictadura? Quizás para no ofender a los millones de adeptos de Franco que seguían recordando con afecto al dictador y añoraban "los cuarenta años de paz". O quizás fuera por temor a la extrema derecha, de cuyo poder y combatividad España se percató bruscamente en la noche del 23 de febrero de 1981. Pero lo más probable es que fuera por indiferencia: Franco no era un tema como para enfadarse, sino que se había convertido en un fenómeno insignificante, anodino.

Se trata de una actitud que está estrechamente vinculada al proceso de modernización que, según parecía, había llevado al país a un estado de euforia sin precedentes: por fin los españoles eran libres, por fin eran europeos, por fin eran *modernos*. Estaban demasiado ocupados con el futuro como para preocuparse del pasado. También el ritmo acuciante en que se producían los cambios contribuyó a que el pasado fuera desapareciendo de la vista con una asombrosa velocidad. Hasta el punto de que en la prensa democrática aparecieron noticias alarmantes diciendo que, para muchos jóvenes crecidos en la democracia, Franco había llegado a tener el mismo status que, por ejemplo, Carlos I, es decir, era un personaje que no tenía nada que ver con el tiempo en que vivían, sino que pertenecía a un pasado remoto.

Esta indiferencia o negligencia no era sólo el producto de la transición sino que, en realidad, se había implantado ya en el periodo en que España, a pesar de todos los esfuerzos de Franco para mantener cerrado el país, iba entablando contactos con la cultura de la libertad que reinaba al norte de los Pirineos, un proceso inevitable e irreversible debido a, entre otros factores, la televisión (que, gracias a la creciente prosperidad, hacía su aparición en muchos hogares), a los turistas (cuyo número iba aumentando de forma espectacular) y a los cientos de miles de emigrantes españoles que durante las vacaciones traían sus experiencias, observaciones, impresiones e historias "europeas" a su tierra.

Por todo ello las generaciones que habían nacido y crecido en la dictadura tuvieron en perspectiva otra realidad que aquella en la que vivían. Así pudieron desarrollar una forma singular de libertad-en-la-opresión cuyas características principales eran un altivo desprecio por la propia cultura y, al mismo tiempo, un extraordinario interés y aprecio por todo lo que venía de fuera. Se trata de una mentalidad que iba a arraigar profundamente y que sigue vigente hasta el día de hoy. Es significativo en este contexto, por ejemplo, que no fuera un español sino un inglés quien escribió la primera biografía exhaustiva de Franco (Preston, 1993).

Nadie duda de que la Guerra Civil y el franquismo fueron un desastre para la literatura. Las razones son muchas: la censura, la falta de una infraestructura, la muerte de algunos de los valores más importantes durante la Guerra Civil (García Lorca, Machado, Unamuno, Valle-Inclán) y el exilio de la mayoría de los autores que habían sobrevivido la guerra. Así se cortó el importante y prometedor proceso de modernización que vivió la literatura española en las primeras décadas del siglo veinte, y se quedaron huérfanos los autores principiantes.

No es de extrañar, pues, que muchos autores de la posguerra incurrieran en un realismo tradicional cuando no trasnochado, sobre todo si se tiene en cuenta que muchos de ellos se sentían llamados a mostrar en sus novelas lo que la España oficial trataba de escamotear con una retórica rimbombante: el terror del estado, el colaboracionismo de la Iglesia, el oportunismo de la burguesía, el atraso de grandes partes de la población, la pobreza, el hambre, la falsificación de la historia…

En los años sesenta muchos valores consagrados (Camilo José Cela, Miguel Delibes, Juan Goytisolo y muchos otros) se sacudieron el yugo del realismo social y retomaron el hilo de las innovaciones de la preguerra cortado por la dictadura. Es cierto que esto significó un gran paso hacia adelante para la narrativa, pero igual lo es que en un importante aspecto la narrativa seguía estancada, puesto que no cambió de temática: la narrativa seguía centrándose en —obsesionándose con— la España de la Guerra Civil y de la dictadura. Por mucho que la narrativa quisiera combatir la política y cultura oficiales —en un principio con su compromiso político, luego con su experimentalismo—, no pudo evitar ser, en cierto sentido, tan estrecha de miras como el régimen contra el que se rebelaba. Y si había una cosa que querían evitar las siguientes generaciones de autores, fue ser estrechas de miras. Hay que tener en cuenta que no habían vivido de forma consciente los primeros —y peores— años del franquismo, sino que habían crecido en una época en que iban abriéndose las puertas al extranjero, por más que el régimen intentara evitarlo. Se trata, pues, de autores que no estaban tan traumatizados por la guerra y sus consecuencias como las generaciones anteriores y que en su adolescencia habían tenido más posibilidades de ampliar sus horizontes.

Eran éstas unas circunstancias muy favorables para que naciera una tenaz alergia a los tiempos y la situación en que esta generación de autores había crecido. Se podría decir, incluso, que para ellos el periodo del franquismo como tema literario se iba convirtiendo en poco menos que un tabú. Un ejemplo representativo sería Eduardo Mendoza, cuyas primeras cuatro novelas se agrupan alrededor de este episodio traumático y desdeñado de la historia reciente de España: *La verdad sobre el caso Savolta* (1975) y *La ciudad de los prodigios* (1986) tienen su acción en un periodo anterior a la Guerra Civil, *El misterio de la cripta embrujada* (1979) y *El laberinto de las aceitunas* (1982) durante la transición.

Unos pocos años después de haber terminado *La ciudad de los prodigios*, Mendoza dijo que vislumbraba un cambio a este respecto y que este vacío significativo estaba en vías de llenarse:

> Yo creo […] que hay ahora una generación, a la que yo pertenezco, que está llegando a la madurez, de la edad y de la profesionalidad, y que están empezando a contar su experiencia personal. Esta generación tiene la peculiaridad de ser la única generación del mundo que vivió el fascismo completamente, en todos sus ciclos. Nació dentro del fascismo, fue educada en el fascismo y lo vio envejecer y volverse caduco y ñoño y morir de muerte natural y dejar una herencia y transformarse de una militancia de banderas y tambores en una cosa mucho más sutil que seguía

informando toda la vida pero que ya no necesitaba expresarse por medio de símbolos y estandartes. No tenía ni siquiera que exponer su filosofía porque ya estaba en la vida cotidiana, en la educación, en la información, en el lenguaje. Los que vivimos esta experiencia, [...] única en el mundo [...], tenemos este bagaje que nos ha marcado y que creo que es interesante empezar a contar. (Steenmeijer, "Barcelona" 11)

La pregunta que me propongo contestar aquí es hasta qué punto estos pronósticos de Mendoza se han materializado. Dicho de otra manera: ¿el periodo del franquismo ha dejado de ser un tabú para los autores de su generación? Intentaré esbozar una respuesta a base de un comentario de la obra de Eduardo Mendoza (1943) a partir de *La ciudad de los prodigios*, de Javier Marías (1951) y de Antonio Muñoz Molina (1956), que se encuentran entre los autores más productivos, polifacéticos y traducidos de la época postfranquista[1]

El caso Mendoza: la falta de urgencia

Como cabía esperar en vistas de las afirmaciones arriba citadas, en la obra de Mendoza se ha producido un cambio notable: dos de las cuatro novelas que publicó después de *La ciudad de los prodigios* —*El año del diluvio* (1992) y *Una comedia ligera* (1996)— tienen como fondo la dictadura franquista. La primera novela evoca un mundo antiguo que está a punto de tener que renunciar a sus costumbres y tradiciones en favor de los nuevos tiempos que avanzan: el interior de Cataluña a principios de los años cincuenta, cuando, según la novela, el antiguo poder rural estaba en vías de extinción, los maquis aparecían como bandoleros románticos reinando en las montañas y el gobierno regional aún no se había hecho cargo de la sanidad. El tema de la modernidad que va invadiendo la vida tradicional está entretejido con la vida de sor Consuelo. Como madre superiora acaba de recibir el mando del necesitado hospital de un pequeño pueblo, que con la llegada de un hospital financiado por el Estado amenaza convertirse en un caso desahuciado. En busca de ayuda económica, llama a la puerta de Augusto Aixelà de Collbató, un cacique atractivo e indolente, el último descendiente sin hijos de una vieja familia de terratenientes, que simpatiza con el franquismo.

142

En el curso de las arduas negociaciones con este aristócrata la monja ejemplar se da cuenta, con gran estupor, de que está enamorándose del cacique. La toma de conciencia de sus sentimientos y la consiguiente confusión mental se expresan de manera discreta y serena. Pero después de que la monja ha hecho el amor con el terrateniente, el ritmo de la novela se acelera bruscamente y los acontecimientos (unos aún más improbables que otros) y los géneros y subgéneros (novela sentimental, novela de guerra, novela política, novela de aventuras, novela psicológica, elegía rural, melodrama, culebrón) se entremezclan dando tumbos los unos sobre los otros. Por ser tan abrupto, brusco y extremado, este cambio no convence como representación icónica de la transición de tradición a modernidad, sino que convierte *El año del diluvio* en una caricatura indefinida e insatisfactoria.

Si la segunda mitad de *El año del diluvio* es abrumadora, *Una comedia ligera* se caracteriza precisamente por un ritmo lento. La novela tiene la extensión de *La ciudad de los prodigios*, y en cierto sentido puede ser considerada como una continuación de esta obra anterior. La historia transcurre a finales de los años cuarenta, cuando Barcelona había dejado de ser una ciudad de prodigios por algún tiempo ya. Sin darse ninguna prisa, Mendoza nos presenta al autor de comedias Carlos Prullàs merodeando durante un par de días por la capital catalana cortada del mundo. A poco más de la mitad de la novela se produce el asesinato que alterará la vida de Prullàs y se descorre un poco el velo detrás del cual se esconde la Barcelona prohibida: la gente marginada, el hampa, las prostitutas, los estafadores, los autores disidentes, los conspiradores políticos. A partir de aquí Barcelona deja de ser una ciudad de una sola dimensión. También en la profesión de Prullàs las cosas dejan de ser lo que eran: sus comedias están pasando de moda, ya que ahora el público "pide ideas profundas y emociones fuertes: una nueva percepción de la realidad" (50), con lo que el autor parece aludir al existencialismo y el realismo social que iban a cambiar el clima cultural y literario del país. El autor de comedias es lo bastante oportunista como para extender el brazo hasta donde le llega la manga: deja su profesión y se convierte en un hombre de negocios.

Prullàs es una personalidad gris en una realidad gris y, por consiguiente, un símbolo evidente de su tiempo. Sin embargo, el protagonista y la historia de la que forma parte son demasiado singulares como para considerar *Una comedia ligera* como la novela de un trauma colectivo. Diría incluso que su significado programático o metaliterario es mayor que su significado referencial. Sería exagerado, quizás, considerar a Prullàs como un alter ego de Mendoza, pero no lo es relacionar la falta de *urgencia* que transmite *Una comedia ligera* con las ideas programáticas afirmadas recientemente por el autor, según el cual la novela, por los cambios drásticos vividos por el género en el curso del siglo veinte (vanguardia, modernismo, postmodernismo), ha perdido mucho de su importancia. "Hoy la novela se ha convertido en una forma honesta, civilizada e instructiva de entretenimiento […] y los lectores de novela, en simples consumidores de novela" ("La novela" 23). Sea como fuere, considerando el año de nacimiento de Mendoza —1943—, es muy poco probable que el autor catalán haya querido ficcionalizar sus propias vivencias del franquismo en estas dos novelas ubicadas en la dictadura. En el fondo, pues, el enfoque y el planteamiento de *El año del diluvio* y *Una comedia ligera* no se distinguen de los de sus novelas anteriores.

Un español a regañadientes: Javier Marías

España brilla por su ausencia en la primera novela de Javier Marías, *Los dominios del lobo*, escrita en su mayor parte en el verano de 1969, cuando "el joven Marías" (*dixit* Juan Benet) —que aún no había cumplido dieciocho años— estuvo en París. El libro —una crónica de familia tan curiosa como cautivadora, escrita en un estilo muy transparente y llena de subintrigas— transcurre completamente en los Estados Unidos. El planteamiento de Marías fue insólito: para escribir *Los dominios del lobo* se había basado en no menos de ochenta y cinco películas —la gran mayoría de ellas norteamericanas de los años treinta, cuarenta y cincuenta— que había visto en París durante las seis semanas que estuvo allí. El caso es que Marías estaba seguro de una cosa cuando se escapó a París, como escribe en el prólogo que añadió a una edición posterior:

> […] yo no deseaba escribir *necesariamente* sobre España ni *necesariamente* como un novelista español. Las razones para este rechazo (tan global como injusto) eran de orden literario y de orden político, pero no es este el lugar para exponerlas ni para refutarlas. Sólo quiero llamar la atención sobre el hecho de que este desdén inicial por *lo español* (en tanto

que identificado simplistamente con *lo franquista*) lo compartía con la mayoría de los miembros de mi generación —la primera nacida después de 1939—, según pronto averigüé. (11)

Los dominios del lobo no es representativa de las novelas con las que luego iba a consagrarse Marías, pero con respecto a este rechazo de *lo español* (y no sólo "identificado simplistamente con *lo franquista*") el autor madrileño ha seguido siendo fiel, en esencia, a la poética de su primera novela. Es cierto que los protagonistas/narradores hiperconscientes de novelas como *Todas las almas*, *Corazón tan blanco* y *Mañana después de la batalla piensa en mí* tienen la nacionalidad española, pero se trata de un hecho de poca importancia en el contexto de sus "relatos", que no tratan de España sino que transmiten un singular sentimiento de vida, una manera muy particular de pensar, un lenguaje y estilo muy propios y, al mismo tiempo, universales. Los narradores de Marías son solipsistas empedernidos que prefieren mantenerse a cierta distancia de la vida, incluida la propia. Estos voyeurs de la existencia no paran de dialogar consigo mismo, construyendo así una imponente fortaleza de historias, observaciones, razonamientos y explicaciones alrededor de ellos mismos tras la cual se atrincheran. Pero por grandes que sean sus capacidades verbales, su retórica, su perspicacia y sus mecanismos de defensa, no pueden, empero, evitar que su conciencia sea invadida por la sensación inquietante y ominosa de que la existencia humana en general y la suya en particular abarca mucho más de lo que ellos pueden dominar y quieren saber. Por más que prefieran que no fuera así, resulta que, al fin y al cabo, ellos no son capaces de seguir manteniéndose a una distancia superior de ese fenómeno caprichoso e imposible de controlar que es la vida.

Pero en la impresionante serie de novelas y libros de cuentos en que da cuerpo a esta fascinante temática, el propio Marías sí ha sabido guardar distancia del tema de "España como problema". Hay que destacar que se trata de una cuestión estética y no moral. No es que Marías crea que España es por definición un tema inferior o sin interés, sino que se presta más al ensayo que a la novela. (Ver Steenmeijer, "Bedriegen".)

Marías —que también como ensayista y columnista tiene una gran reputación— habla con conocimiento de causa puesto que muchos de sus ensayos y columnas se centran en "España como problema", y en ellos Marías sí se revela como un autor comprometido. Con su despiadada crítica de las manías y malas costumbres de sus compatriotas, Marías forma parte de una tradición literaria muy española, aunque sea a pesar suyo: la de Quevedo, Larra, Clarín, Valle-Inclán y otros españoles a regañadientes.

Quien lee las columnas reunidas en *Mano de sombra* (1997) y *Seré amado cuando falte* (1999) no tiene más remedio que concluir que hay pocas cosas en España que funcionan. Asignándose a sí mismo el papel del *gentleman*, Marías denuncia los abusos menores y mayores de sus compatriotas en, entre otras cosas, la política, la justicia, la organización penitenciaria, Telefónica, Correos, la vida pública, los modales, el lenguaje contemporáneo, la manera de vestir (¡la proliferación de varones que, en verano, lucen sin vergüenza alguna un pantalón corto en plena ciudad!). Llama la atención la manera directa en que Marías muestra y expresa sus alergias e irritaciones (y, dicho sea de paso, también sus afinidades y pasiones). Se trata de una diferencia llamativa entre el columnista y el novelista: en sus obras periodísticas hay apenas un rastro de la actitud y la manera de formular circunspectas y reservadas tan características de novelas como *Corazón tan blanco* y *Mañana después de la batalla piensa en mí*. En aquéllas no tiene la palabra un narrador distante sino un escritor que busca el contacto con sus lectores.

Marías muestra mayor indignación cuando monta en cólera contra maneras de pensar y proceder intolerantes, como el terror de ETA, o los excesos de la *praxis* del lenguaje políticamente correcto; o bien contra disposiciones de tendencia totalitaria, como la ley aprobada hace algunos años en Alemania, que autoriza al Estado a practicar escuchas telefónicas y vigilancias electrónicas. Las raíces de esta alergia a la intolerancia hay que buscarlas en la época franquista, como queda claro, por ejemplo, en la columna "No los quiero" (en *Mano* 126-28). Marías hace migas de los columnistas y periodistas que se atreven a comparar el régimen franquista y el socialista (todavía en el poder por aquel entonces) y que, además, no dudan en concluir que aquél es de preferir a éste. No es que el autor se ponga a defender al gobierno socialista, pero sí sale en defensa del sistema en que funciona y por el cual en un futuro próximo los socialistas estarán obligados a dar paso a otro gobierno. Es inadmisible, escribe Marías, que la gente con más de treinta y cinco años haya olvidado (o lo finja) que durante el franquismo lo único seguro era que *nunca* iba a haber elecciones y que aquel dictador se marcharía sólo cuando lo decidiera su apacible muerte, como así fue. No era cuestión de esperar uno o dos o tres años, sino indefinidamente, de algunas generaciones se llevó la vida entera. (127)

Después de la Guerra Civil se extinguió de forma sistemática a los adversarios del nuevo régimen, la prensa sólo podía escribir lo que le dictaba el régimen y el sistema era "corrupto desde el primero hasta el último día y desde el Jefe del Estado hasta el más breve de sus ministros, gobernadores o alcaldes […]" (127).

Después de estas comprobaciones sigue un pasaje muy emocional lleno de recuerdos traumáticos de los años del franquismo vividos por el propio Marías (los años sesenta y primeros setenta): la arbitrariedad con que se detenía e interrogaba a la gente, la impunidad con que se retenía a la gente indefinidamente, la retórica cruel, cínica, vulgar y despótica de la que se servía el régimen, la represión de las formas más inocentes de la diversión, "el miedo perpetuo con el que vivíamos y dormíamos" (128).

"Teníamos dieciocho años", dice Marías concluyendo esta letanía, para terminar su artículo con vehemencia:

No me digan que estamos peor que entonces., no me digan que era más leve y honrado el franquismo, no me digan que nada de lo que hoy sucede es más corrupto o criminal que aquello, no me digan que vuelvo a tener dieciocho años. No es verdad, y no los quiero. (128)

Un artículo aparecido en *El País*, "El artículo más iluso", atestigua asimismo una gran indignación moral provocada por la manera en que algunos enfocan el pasado franquista. Característica del clima moral en España es, según Marías, la falta de vergüenza con que algunos españoles prominentes disculpan su actitud y comportamiento durante la época franquista. Ni esconden ni niegan lo que han hecho (o lo que han dejado de hacer) sino que lo admiten abiertamente, convencidos de que, en el fondo, no han hecho nada malo. Como primer ejemplo Marías menciona a un filósofo conocido, que durante un curso de verano dijo que durante años había sido "obligado" a espiar a sus colegas y, llegado el caso, a denunciarlos. El segundo ejemplo se refiere a un columnista que, contestando al descubrimiento de sus elogios del régimen franquista, dijo: "Lo que deseaba, y deseo, es sobrevivir, y a veces hay que cambiar el gesto para seguir adelante, uno tiene que plegarse a ciertas condiciones y personas" (cit. en Marías, "El artículo más iluso" 16). En el tercer caso se trata de un novelista muy conocido que en los años cuarenta trabajó de censor. "Me hice censor para poder comer, para tener un mínimo sueldo… Entonces no había una perra para nadie". Marías no menciona ningún nombre en su artículo pero es obvio que el autor aludía a José Luis L. Aranguren, Eduardo Haro Tecglen y Camilo José Cela.

Por no haber vivido la Guerra Civil y la primera época de la posguerra —la más difícil y la más dura— Marías apenas se considera autorizado para juzgar de lo que entonces se hizo y escribió. "Ninguno podemos saber a ciencia cierta cómo habríamos obrado en aquellas circunstancias, acaso habríamos incurrido en bajezas mayores, quién sabe" (16). Pero más que los propios actos inaceptables, lo que le importa a Marías es la justificación alegada muchos años después por el filósofo, el columnista y el novelista sin mostrar ni una pizca de vergüenza, de arrepentimiento o de remordimiento: no había otra opción, todo el mundo lo hacía. Y eso es absolutamente falso, dice un Marías indignadísimo, reivindicando con una fuerte carga emocional el recuerdo de "los de otra pasta":

> Por mucho que intenten y les convenga olvidarse, también los hubo mejores. O simplemente —y vuelvo a las palabras en desuso, antiguas— más rectos, o más dignos, o más resistentes, o más orgullosos, o más escépticos, o más asqueados, o más derrotados, no sé: aquéllos a los que no quedaron acaso fuerzas ni ánimo para desear más nada, ni sobrevivir. Que sobreviva su memoria al menos, que no se borre su triste y languideciente o pasada existencia, por incómoda que resulte a los vivos o supervivientes que hacia ese espejo mejor, sin azogue y espectral y resquebrajado, nunca quieren ni se dignan mirar. (16)

Hubo muchas reacciones, también desde círculos académicos[2] Se recalcó la necesidad de un debate sobre el pasado comentado por Marías pero se reprochaba al autor una falta de comprensión por las circunstancias en que procedían el filósofo, el columnista y el novelista. El reparo me parece injusto, puesto que la crítica de Marías no concernía su actitud *por aquel entonces* sino su justificación *posterior*. No me parece improbable que el propio autor interprete estas reacciones como otra prueba de la tesis que formuló al principio de "El artículo más iluso": que la moral está muy mal en España.

Antonio Muñoz Molina: la promesa de la novela de una generación

Antonio Muñoz Molina es otro autor/columnista que se pasma y enfada por lo que no vacila en llamar la barbarie de la España contemporánea, donde "[…] con el paso del tiempo, uno se va acostumbrando desengañadamente a que la legalidad y la justicia sean tan dudosas como en un [sic] república tropical regida por caciques y narcotraficantes […]" ("La compasión" 106). No suele haber ironía en las afirmaciones aceradas hechas en las columnas en que el autor andaluz denuncia abusos en la política y la justicia, no dudando en contarlo con pelos y señales.

El compromiso moral de Muñoz Molina se palpa, asimismo, en *Plenilunio* (1997), su última novela propiamente dicha. La intriga se centra en la investigación de una violación y el asesinato de una chica de nueve años y otro intento de repetir estos crímenes poco tiempo después. Con horripilante lujo de detalles se describen los actos y los pensamientos del pervertido autor de los crímenes, lo que no deja de provocar un previsible efecto en el lector. Pero todo ello es de importancia secundaria, puesto que los protagonistas no son las víctimas y el violador/asesino sino la maestra de la chica asesinada y el inspector que dirige la investigación. Ambos, aturdidos por los fuertes golpes que han sufrido en el curso de su vida, recobran su conciencia y sensibilidad a causa de la violación bárbara y fatal del inocente germen de vida que era la chica, y se ven confrontados con sus propios traumas, que habían reprimido durante muchos años.

El inspector, crecido en la ciudad andaluza a la cual acaba de volver, había tenido que trabajar en Bilbao, donde él y su esposa continuamente recibían amenazas de muerte y donde el propio inspector tambien se había pasado de la raya más de una vez. Esta situación esquizofrénica —víctima y verdugo se reúnen en una

149

misma persona— se parece a la de su juventud y adolescencia: por un lado son lastimosas las circunstancias en que creció (un padre preso por sus ideas comunistas, una madre muy enferma y pobre que no podía ocuparse de él), pero por el otro son censurables sus actividades como informante de la Dirección General de Seguridad.

Todo este pasado arrinconado surge durante las intensas conversaciones que el inspector tiene con el padre Orduña, su antiguo maestro y protector al que no había visto por varias décadas. Este cura rojo tampoco tiene la conciencia en paz. Durante la Guerra Civil luchó con los nacionales, y después de la guerra maltrató físicamente y mentalmente a sus alumnos.

No creo que lo más importante sea que el lector llegue a un juicio moral sobre la actitud y los actos de estos dos personajes, sino que se forme una idea del laberinto moral en que el inspector y el cura se encuentran y la lucha que libran consigo mismos. En cualquier caso, la intención ética es considerablemente mayor en *Plenilunio* que en las novelas anteriores de Muñoz Molina. Igual que aquélla, éstas se centran en la presencia del pasado, pero en un marco muy distinto: el contraste (o la falta de él) entre la ficción y la realidad. Así, el diálogo entre pasado y presente en *Beatus Ille* (1986) y *Beltenebros* (1989) no lleva al lector a un laberinto moral sino a un laberinto ontológico. En estas novelas no se pone en juego la conciencia de los personajes sino su percepción de la realidad. Ambas se desarrollan en la época franquista pero remiten más a Eco y Borges que a un periodo histórico concreto.

En *El jinete polaco* (1991) hay más referencias a la Historia. La novela es una amalgama de historias y anécdotas sobre los habitantes de Mágina, una ciudad provinciana que tiene mucho en común con Úbeda, la ciudad donde nació y creció Muñoz Molina. Engloba unos ciento veinticinco años de historia local, incluyendo la dictadura franquista. Pero en esta novela el pasado está al servicio del "presente absoluto" que dos amantes que acaban de conocerse tratan de crear durante el idilio abrumador que viven a miles de kilómetros de su tierra de origen: Mágina, una ciudad provinciana en el interior de Andalucía. En los dieciocho años después de su salida de Mágina, Manuel, el alter ego de Muñoz Molina, se ha convertido en un extranjero, un nómada. También Nadia —hija de un republicano exiliado— lucha con su desarraigo. Las tradiciones y las historias de Mágina, que sus antepasados llevaban en la sangre, ya no son una evidencia para ellos sino más bien un anhelo. Pero no pueden dar marcha atrás al reloj, no sólo porque los dos treintañeros mismos han cambiado, sino también porque su ciudad de origen se ha modernizado. De ahí que recurran a la imaginación y, a base de una vieja colección de fotos, traten de (re)construir el pasado. La abundancia de historias y anécdotas en que resultan sus esfuerzos revela que lo que parece ser un pasado pretérito e irrecuperable puede tener un gran significado e importancia para quienes han llegado a formar parte de la aldea global.

Como ya queda dicho, el pasado (re)construido engloba un periodo mucho mayor que el periodo franquista. En la última fase de este periodo, Manuel —adolescente— soñaba ante todo con un futuro lleno de aventura fuera de España: como escritor en París con una novia del norte de Europa, o como batería en un grupo de rock entre los hippies en San Francisco. Este deseo en sí no era, claro está, típico de la (última fase de la) España franquista, pero la intensidad y el desfase sí lo eran. "We want the world and we want it now," cantaba Jim Morrison. Pero el cantante de los Doors ya había muerto algunos años antes de que estas palabras incitaran la fantasía de Manuel. Lo mismo vale para Jimi Hendrix, Janis Joplin y Otis Redding, mientras que los Beatles ya se habían separado unos años antes. Este desengaño parece valer para toda una generación o incluso todo un país: "Íbamos a llegar tarde al mundo, pero no lo sabíamos, nos preparábamos avariciosamente para asistir a una fiesta que ya había terminado [...]" (346).

Dieciocho años después, Manuel, convertido en un ciudadano del mundo moderno pero frustrado, vuelve a sentir la necesidad de completar su existencia a través de su imaginación, pero esta vez ésta se dirige en sentido contrario —tanto con respecto al tiempo (el pasado en vez del futuro) como al espacio (su tierra natal en vez del extranjero)—, lo cual puede interpretarse como un indicio de que se ha liberado de su tendencia a idealizar lo extranjero y lo moderno.

La novela corta *El dueño del secreto* (1994) se desarrolla en el invierno y la primavera de 1974 y tiene como tema una conspiración para derribar el régimen franquista. Para su asombro, un joven estudiante andaluz que acaba de llegar a Madrid se ve implicado en ella. Con ello, se materializa de la noche a la mañana la existencia apasionante y aventurera que anhelaba. Poco después se descubre la conspiración, porque este "marxista pusilánime y más bien imaginario", lleno de un entusiasmo que quiere compartir, ha hablado más de la cuenta.

Unos veinte años después, el conspirador fracasado, regresado definitivamente a la existencia anodina de donde procedía, recuerda este episodio clave de su vida, comentando el clima gris, represivo y sin perspectiva de aquellos tiempos.

> Nuestra generación [...] fue la última en llegar al antifranquismo, y nos tocó la paradoja de heredar, con dieciocho años, la tradición de la derrota de las generaciones anteriores, de respirar un aire enrarecido por treinta y tantos años de desaliento y de invenciones gloriosas y absurdas de huelgas generales que no fueron vencidas porque nunca llegaron a existir. (95)

Sería exagerado, sin embargo, llamar *El dueño del secreto* la novela de una generación, puesto que el protagonista es más bien atípico. Es el polo opuesto de Manuel de *El jinete polaco*, que en la misma época y a la misma edad cambió lo antiguo por lo moderno, pero que no volvió sobre sus pasos poco tiempo después y que, por consiguiente, es mucho más representativo del desarrollo que vivió España en las últimas décadas del siglo pasado. Además, el yo narrador de *El dueño del secreto* no quiere mantener vivo el recuerdo de su estancia en Madrid por motivos ideológicos o morales —es decir, colectivos— sino por motivos psicológicos, o sea particulares: los meses de la conspiración forman el único episodio de su vida en que al menos parecía haber una *posibilidad* de que su existencia diera un giro aventurado y apasionante. El recuerdo de la conspiración contra Franco ha llegado a ser el único consuelo en su vida anodina.

Conclusiones

Antonio Muñoz Molina es el único de los tres autores comentados aquí que en su obra nunca ha "eludido" el franquismo vivido por él. Es significativo que sea, asimismo, el más joven de los tres y haya empezado a escribir bastante tiempo después de la muerte de Franco. En sentido práctico y programático el periodo franquista apenas puede haber sido un impedimento para él, puesto que la censura ya había sido abolida cuando concibió sus primeros proyectos literarios, mientras que el ajuste de cuentas con el realismo social ya había sido realizado unos diez años antes de que apareciera su primera novela.

A lo sumo, la época franquista puede haber marcado la poética y la temática de su obra en sentido *existencial*, como sugieren, ante todo, los elementos autobiográficos en *El jinete polaco*. Sea como fuere, ninguna de las novelas que Muñoz Molina ha publicado hasta la fecha se *centra* en la vivencia del franquismo, por lo menos no en el sentido autobiográfico a que aludía Mendoza en las afirmaciones antes citadas hablando del "trauma" único de los autores nacidos y crecidos en el franquismo. Pero no me parece improbable que en un futuro próximo Muñoz Molina escriba una novela centrada en el franquismo vivido por él mismo, no sólo porque los años franquistas nunca han sido un problema literario-programático para él sino también porque en *Plenilunio* parece haberse despedido de la manera modernista o postmodernista con que había entablado el diálogo entre pasado y presente en sus novelas anteriores para interesarse más por las implicaciones *morales* de este diálogo o enfrentamiento.

En su narrativa, el propio Mendoza ha mostrado mucho menos interés por esta temática de lo que cabía esperar en vista de sus afirmaciones al respecto, mientras que Marías la considera demasiado poco literaria (¡y demasiado española!) como para elaborarla en su ficción. La poética de Mendoza y la de Marías son muy distintas y casi diría opuestas: anécdota frente a reflexión, aventura frente a (auto)contemplación, discurso leve frente a discurso solemne. Pero tienen en común una cosa: la falta de ganas (o de voluntad o de capacidad) de ficcionalizar las propias vivencias y observaciones en la dictadura.

Considerando la obra de los tres autores comentados aquí, sería apropiado concluir que los pronósticos de Mendoza apenas se han hecho realidad. Sólo en el caso de Muñoz Molina —quien pertenece a la última generación (es decir, la menos traumatizada) de los autores que vivieron el franquismo— parece que tendrá razón Mendoza. Por lo que respecta a las generaciones posteriores, a ellos sólo les queda la posibilidad de ficcionalizar el periodo franquista por vía de la documentación y la imaginación, puesto que no lo conocen por propia experiencia. Parece poco probable, sin embargo, que autores como José Ángel Mañas, Ray Loriga y David Trueba aprovechen esta oportunidad. Están demasiado ocupados con la España hedonista en que viven como para interesarse por el pasado reciente. No sería descabellado, a mi juicio, sospechar que en esta actitud resuena, asimismo, el rechazo o negación de la España franquista tan característico de la narrativa de sus antepasados inmediatos.

Notas

1. Un ejemplo atípico sería la obra de Álvaro Pombo (1939), que merece un estudio aparte. También hay que mencionar aquí a Manuel Vázquez Montalbán (1939), que ya en *El pianista* (1985) había ficcionalizado episodios del franquismo que él mismo había vivido y que luego siguió esta huella en *Galíndez* (1990) y *Autobiografía del general Franco* (1992). Hace falta recordar, empero, que el novelista tardó bastante en acercarse a esa época. Lo mismo vale para Félix de Azúa (1944), que en *Historia de un idiota contada por él mismo* (1986) convirtió en ficción sus vivencias en (y después de) el franquismo. El autor catalán acaba de publicar *Momentos decisivos* (2000), que se desarrolla en un ambiente y época muy bien conocidos por él (la Barcelona de principios de los años sesenta). No son más que algunos ejemplos que más que desmentir la tendencia estudiada aquí la matizan.

2. Ver, entre otras: "Réplicas", carta de Javier Muguerza (*El País* 3 de julio, 1999: 13-14); "Con desagrado respondo", carta de Javier Marías (*El País* 10 de julio, 1999: 13-14); "Que el lector juzgue", carta de Eduardo López-Aranguren y sus hermanos y hermanas (*El País* 17 de julio, 1999: 11-12); "Por alusiones", carta de Javier Muguerza (*El País* 17 de julio, 1999: 12); "Con hastío respondo", carta de Javier Marías (*El País* 24 de julio, 1999: 9-10); Santos Juliá, "Rastros del pasado" (*El País* 25 de julio, 1999: 15); Fernando Vallespín, "Pretérito imperfecto" (*El País* 25 de julio, 1999: 15); "En algo estamos de acuerdo", carta de José Luis López-Aranguren y sus hermanas y hermanos (*El País* 31 de julio, 1999: 11-12); "Con desaliento respondo", carta de Javier Muguerza (*El País* 31 de julio, 1999: 12); Javier Tusell, "La memoria y el encono" (*El País* 11 de septiembre, 1999).

Obras Citadas

Marías, Javier. "El artículo más iluso." *El País* 26 de junio, 1999: 15-16.

——. *Corazón tan blanco*. Barcelona: Anagrama, 1992.

——. *El dominio del lobo*. Barcelona: Anagrama, 1996.

——. *Mano de sombra*. Madrid: Alfaguara, 1997.

——. *Mañana en la batalla piensa en mí*. Barcelona: Anagrama, 1994.

——. *Seré amado cuando falte*. Madrid: Alfaguara, 1999.

——. *Todas las almas*. Barcelona: Anagrama, 1989.

Mendoza, Eduardo. *El año del diluvio*. Barcelona: Seix Barral, 1992.

——. *La ciudad de los prodigios*. Barcelona: Seix Barral, 1986.

——. *Una comedia ligera*. Barcelona: Seix Barral, 1996.

——. *El laberinto de las aceitunas*. Biblioteca de Bolsillo. Barcelona: Seix Barral, 1987.

——. *El misterio de la cripta embrujada*. Biblioteca de Bolsillo. Barcelona: Seix Barral, 1987.

——. "La novela se queda sin épica." *El País* 16 de agosto, 1998: 23-24.

——. *La verdad sobre el caso Savolta*. Biblioteca de Bolsillo. Barcelona: Seix Barral, 1983.

Muñoz Molina, Antonio. *Beatus Ille*. Barcelona: Seix Barral, 1993.

——. *Beltenebros*. Barcelona: Seix Barral, 1993.

——. "La compasión." *El País Semanal* 14 de febrero, 1999: 106.

——. *El dueño del secreto*. Madrid: Ollero y Ramos, 1994.

——. *El jinete polaco*. Barcelona: Planeta, 1991.

——. *Plenilunio*. Madrid: Alfaguara, 1997.

Preston, Paul. *Franco. A Biography*. London: HarperCollins, 1993.

Steenmeijer, Maarten. "Barcelona heeft iets wat andere steden niet hebben. Eduardo Mendoza over zijn boek *De stad der wonderen*." *Vrij Nederland/Boekenbijlage* 18 de junio, 1988: 11-12.

——. "Bedriegen zit in onze natuur. Gesprek met Javier Marías." *Vrij Nederland* 11 de enero, 1997: 74-75.

8

Identidad homosexual y procesamiento del franquismo en el discurso literario de España desde la transición

Dieter Ingenschay

1. Identidad homosexual bajo las condiciones históricas de España

Sólo después de que el féretro de Franco yaciera en su tumba del Valle de los Caídos pudo desarrollarse —según la observación de Gumbrecht (1046)— una nueva actitud hacia el cuerpo. Es un lugar común en la historia cultural española que después de un fundamentalismo católico en el poder durante varios siglos, y después de décadas de dictadura, sólo en el postfranquismo pudo surgir una nueva conciencia del cuerpo. En su forma más extrema, conocida como "destape", la escenificación del cuerpo derivada de este cambio de conciencia se convirtió en una característica propia de la transición y, más aún, del fenómeno social conocido como "la movida". La "emancipación" del cuerpo y la floreciente tematización de la sexualidad produjeron una coyuntura favorable para todas las formas de discurso sexual que hasta entonces habían sido reprimidas por la censura. Además, la homosexualidad como tema literario se puso de moda (cf. Ingenschay 1992, 1995) hasta el punto de dominar gran parte de la producción literaria hispánica del último cuarto del siglo XX.

Esta escritura de la homosexualidad pudo entonces ser leída automáticamente como una escritura contra la represión anterior, como actividad política contra el espíritu del franquismo. Paralelamente a los llamados movimientos de liberación gay en Norteamérica y en la Europa del Norte, ya en los años 70 se habían formado en España varios grupos para la emancipación y aceptación de las formas de vida gay (cf. Perriam, "Gay and Lesbian Culture", Aliaga y Cortés 30s., Ellis 16s.). En diciembre de 1977 se reunieron un millar de personas en un cine de Barcelona con motivo del primer encuentro de homosexuales en la Península Ibérica; Cataluña jugó un papel de pionero en este desarrollo (cf. Mirabet i Mullol).

El encuentro fue organizado por el "Front D'Alliberament Gai de Catalunya" (F.A.G.C.), de orientación izquierdista. Por su parte, el grupo "Dignitat", también fundado en Barcelona por el jesuita Salvador Guasch Figueras, tenía un corte más bien burgués-conservador. Igualmente, en Andalucía ("Unión Democrática de Homosexuales de Málaga", U.D.H.M.), en el País Vasco ("Euskal Herriko Gay Askapen Mugimendua", EHGAM) y en Madrid ("Colectivo de Gais y Lesbianas de Madrid", COGAM) se formaron grupos que combinaban sus preceptos emancipatorios con un decidido ímpetu izquierdista. Más que la solidaridad con la posición política de izquierda del movimiento gay en Francia (encabezado por Guy Hocquenghem, cf. Smith 63-65), fue el pasado español concreto lo que determinó el corte político activista de estas organizaciones. El objetivo era combatir la ley que protegía la persecución de los homosexuales: la Ley de Peligrosidad y Rehabilitación Social (LPRS), sucesora, en su versión del 4 de agosto de 1970, de la Ley de Vagos y Maleantes de 1954 (para más detalles cf. Martínez Expósito 16-19). En ella se incluyó a "los que realicen actos de homosexualidad" en la lista de los "supuestos de estado peligroso". Como consecuencia de esta ley, en vigor hasta 1978, pero cuyos efectos se han podido observar hasta el pasado más reciente,[1] un gran número de homosexuales fue reprimido, perseguido o transportado a un campo de rehabilitación especial en Huelva.

Durante la búsqueda de testimonios para un programa del canal de televisión "Canal +" (transmitido el 27 de junio de 1998) sobre la LPRS y la represión de los homosexuales durante el franquismo, resultó que los periodistas encargados encontraron, principalmente entre los "gays de media edad" de Madrid, a personas que en lugar de quejarse del franquismo se quejaban del liberalismo actual.[2] Sus opiniones parecían una sorprendente nueva versión de la provocadora declaración de Vázquez Montalbán "contra Franco estábamos mejor" (*Crónica sentimental* 151). Los escenarios del documental muestran las ruinas del campo de rehabilitación de Huelva y dan una viva impresión de lo que era la escena homosexual de la antigua ciudad de Barcelona. Uno de los testigos fue localizado en Berlín, adonde se había exiliado. En general el reportaje ofrece un panorama valioso de la situación y recopila documentos contra el olvido. Pero también muestra que la conciencia política del inicio de la transición se perdió durante los años subsiguientes del desencanto y de paulatina despolitización. Si bien en el año 2000 se encuentran todavía movimientos de gays y lesbianas activos que articulan sus reivindicaciones, el interés político de los homosexuales en España ha pasado a un segundo plano (probablemente a consecuencia de la creciente aceptación de la homosexualidad y de los logros considerables, en comparación con otros países, en cuanto una ley de parejas y una ley contra la discriminación a causa de la orientación sexual). En primer plano se observa una escenificación consciente de las formas de vida propias y de una modernidad comercializada (cf. Aliaga y Cortés). Así la transición aparece como una época de cambio, un entreacto histórico en el camino hacia la formación de una conciencia homosexual de grupo y su aceptación política y social. La transición es la época en que por primera vez se forma una "identidad homosexual" con rasgos bien definidos. La problemática noción de identidad homosexual está condicionada no sólo por factores colectivos e históricos sino también por aspectos individuales. Es un gran mérito de Michel Foucault haber estudiado cómo los discursos jurídico y patológico del siglo XIX hicieron del "homosexual" una categoría supraindividual, y es un mérito de los *gay studies* (sobre todo los norteamericanos) haber sondeado la relación entre la construcción social de la homosexualidad, su patologización, su criminalización, su psicologización y sus concreciones individuales. En el contexto español hay que señalar, además, que la marginación de los homosexuales estuvo fuertemente promovida por el machismo mayoritario que hizo del homosexual una otredad prototípica.

A continuación trataré de la relación entre la identidad sexual, la conciencia de grupo, el recuerdo y la experiencia histórica dentro de homotextos literarios, pero primero es necesario analizar los factores externos. Mientras que, por lo general, la literatura de la era postfranquista abordó esporádicamente temas de la historia más reciente, en especial de la guerra civil, pero también la experiencia de la dictadura y la transición, la literatura gay se centró primordialmente (aunque no exclusivamente) en las experiencias individuales del presente, y mucho menos en el procesamiento (histórico) de la dictadura y sus mecanismos de represión. Aquí nos encontramos ante una clara contradicción: por un lado tenemos el corte eminentemente político del movimiento gay (de los 70), por el otro tenemos la falta de politización y la escasa conciencia histórica de la literatura gay. Esta extraña situación se debe a cuatro factores: 1°) a la falta de figuras orientadoras de la "literatura homosexual" que hubieran facilitado la formulación de una posición clara y decidida contra el pasado fascista; 2°) a las posibilidades completamente nuevas de verbalizar el homoerotismo, 3°) a la nueva actitud de la conciencia gay, que se orienta según los paradigmas internacionales, y 4°) a la falta de un trauma colectivo que obligue a enfrentarlo en el discurso (literario o de otra índole).

A continuación quiero hacer algunas acotaciones sobre estos aspectos. Al 1°): La marginación (social y literaria) de los homosexuales en la España católica, tradicionalista y machista impidió el surgimiento de una escritura identitariamente homosexual. Mientras que en otros países la literatura homosexual tenía una tradición canónica y un sentimiento de unidad derivado de dicha tradición —en Inglaterra desde la época victoriana, en Francia desde Proust, Gide y un Genet elevado a la categoría de "santo" por Sartre, en Alemania desde George y los Mann, Thomas y Klaus—, los autores homosexuales españoles tuvieron que permanecer "en el armario". Este hecho dificulta reconocer una "cultura de la homosexualidad" como la que Angel Sahuquillo ha podido reconstruir alrededor de personas como García Lorca, Juan Gil-Albert y Luis Cernuda (cf. Sahuquillo). La mayoría de los autores españoles que se dedican a temas homosexuales después de la derogación de la censura encuentran sus figuras de orientación intelectual e intertextual fuera de España, especialmente en Lautréamont y Rimbaud, Wilde, Proust y Genet, cuando se trata de un discurso de "alta cultura"; cuando se trata de alguna paracultura, encuentran sus referencias en el kitsch de la cultura de masas norteamericana (especialmente en las películas de Hollywood). Luis Antonio de Villena y Terenci Moix son los ejemplos más evidentes de este fenómeno.

Al 2°): Respondiendo a la creciente necesidad social de productos culturales referidos al cuerpo se produjo, durante la transición, una explosión de nuevas posibilidades. Camilo José Cela anuncia su *Enciclopedia del erotismo*, publicada en 1976, con la oración programática: "España se está poniendo cachonda" (cit. Reinstädler 13). Si bien en este contexto Cela se refiere estrictamente al modelo heterosexual,[3] hay que señalar que la homosexualidad se convirtió en una temática preferida no sólo por las formas literarias "tradicionales" sino también por los géneros paraliterarios inexistentes hasta ese momento. Precisamente en estas formas (pornografía, comic, cine de entretenimiento etc.) se observa una presencia exuberante de los temas homoeróticos. Pongamos un ejemplo: en 1978 la Editorial Tusquets lanzó una nueva serie de literatura erótica con el nombre "La sonrisa vertical", donde pululan obras del mundo gay (cf. Reinstädler). Por otra parte, en el terreno del comic destaca sobre todo la figura de Nazario, dibujante barcelonés que desde los 80 publicaba sus transgresores comics en la revista *El Víbora* (cf. Aliaga y Cortés 65-67), y que ha tenido éxito nuevamente en los 90 con *Alí Baba y los 40 maricones*. Además, Paul Julian Smith ha señalado la especial importancia de la temática homosexual en el cine (cf. Smith y también Aliaga y Cortés 81-83). Así, el discurso homotextual del postfranquismo se realiza a través de la celebración de una estética paraliteraria, subcultural e innovadora.

Al 3º): Los primeros movimientos gay españoles no solamente se oponían a la represión franquista, sino que, al igual que todos los movimientos de liberación gay europeos, seguían el modelo norteamericano Post-Stonewall.[4] Si bien la escena gay española se estableció más tarde que en el resto de Europa occidental, el desarrollo de la comunidad gay española desembocó con rapidez en un paradigma internacional de vida social, tomando como modelo las *gay communities* norteamericanas. Como ejemplo concreto podemos mencionar que el poeta Jaime Gil de Biedma, homosexual declarado y catalogado por Luis Antonio de Villena como "un discreto militante por los derechos de gays y lesbianas" (en *El Mundo de la Cultura*, 8 de enero de 2000), mantenía contacto con el movimiento gay norteamericano y con *Gay Sunshine*, la legendaria revista gay de los 70.

Cuando se quiere desplegar la línea principal de la variante española del proceso de emancipación homosexual desde los años 70, se argumenta diciendo que en el mundo hispánico —o sea, tanto en España como en América Latina— primero había que imponer el privilegio de la afeminación, el "derecho a la locura" contra el machismo dominante (cf. Guasch, Martínez Expósito, Ingenschay "Homotextualidad"). Después, durante los 80, se nota un cambio de paradigma cuyo "rasgo más característico [...] es el intento de redefinición viril de la homosexualidad" (Guasch 43). Este es un desarrollo en el cual el objetivo original del movimiento gay español es desplazado por una creciente orientación hacia el modelo

161

(norteamericano y noreuropeo) del gay metropolitano, viril y progresista que, seguro de sí mismo, se apodera de las redes de la infraestructura gay. Por consiguiente, se puede observar una internacionalización o americanización que se extiende hasta las configuraciones del deseo sexual (cf. Guasch).

Al 4°). ¿Por qué motivo las comunidades gay españolas se orientaron según la escena internacional en lugar de acometer el (esperado) procesamiento histórico del fascismo? Las causas de esto serán discutidas a continuación.

2. La ideología fascista, el rechazo homosexual y sus (pocas) huellas en la literatura gay

Este no es el espacio adecuado para examinar el origen y carácter de las ideologías fascistas, ni siquiera en su variante española. Pero hay que decir que el pasado fascista de España aparentemente no provocó traumas colectivos (sino sólo individuales) en el discurso de la transición, y que ciertos mecanismos de represión del pasado han propiciado que la discusión sobre el efecto social de la homofobia franquista raramente se articule en el discurso público. Sólo unos pocos teóricos se han ocupado de esta problemática específica (y las anotaciones que se leen, por ejemplo, en el capítulo "Bajo la dictadura" [Guasch 47-72] no ofrecen una respuesta convincente). En principio la dictadura, el machismo y el catolicismo estatal antisexual darían motivo suficiente para provocar un trauma colectivo. Sin embargo, el fascismo español —a diferencia del nacionalsocialismo alemán— no produjo la experiencia histórica de la ejecución de miles de homosexuales. El "Homocausto" (Consoll) alemán fue una experiencia que los homosexuales españoles no tuvieron que (sobre)vivir (para informaciones sobre los homosexuales en los campos de concentración cf. Müller y Sternweiler). En lo que respecta a la literatura, los escritores españoles no sufrieron el trauma colectivo de la "escritura después de Auschwitz", trauma que determinó la discusión sobre el fascismo en vastos sectores de la literatura alemana de la postguerra (cf. LaCapra). Documentos autobiográficos evidencian que el español profranquista consideraba a Mussolini "más consecuente" que al Caudillo en la cuestión del "ajuste de cuentas con los maricones".[5] Por otro lado el culto fascista al cuerpo viril, característico de la práctica e ideología de Hitler y Mussolini, parece no haber estado tan desarrollado en la variante española, debido a que muchos sectores del fascismo español, sobre todo de orientación católica, no apoyaron este culto. Hechos como el escándalo sobre la homosexualidad del jefe de la SS y supuesto golpista, Ernst Röhm, ejecutado en 1934, dieron muestras de la compleja relación entre la homofobia fascista y el deseo homosexual reprimido en la Alemania de los nazis. El sufrimiento de los homosexuales en los campos de concentración forma parte del trauma colectivo alemán, hecho éste impensable en el contexto del fascismo español. La Segunda República española carece incluso de los movimientos de "amigos de la naturaleza", prohomosexuales (¡y profascistas!), como el grupo encabezado por Adolf Brand en la Alemania de la República de Weimar. Así, entre los iconos del deseo sexual en el contexto español, los símbolos de la virilidad (como soldados, deportistas, después tipos *leather*, etc.) siguen jugando, comparativamente, un papel menor (mientras que en otros contextos sociales, no sólo de connotación fascista —desde las novelas de Genet hasta los dibujos de Tom of Finland— éstos representan ideales gays prototípicos).[6]

Sin embargo, una mirada a la historia de la cultura del fascismo español demuestra que, al menos entre algunos falangistas, el culto a la virilidad de tipo alemán o italiano (cf. Spackman) formaba parte de la autoexaltación. En su investigación sobre la prosa fascista española, Mechthild Albert llama la atención sobre autores como Felipe Ximénez de Sandoval, cuya novela de la guerra civil *Camisa azul. Retrato de un falangista* (1939) muestra, además de un escenario ejemplar de esperanzas heroizadas y romantizadas, una concepción muy concreta de la corporalidad que —al contrario del conservadurismo católico— se regía por la imaginería nazi del héroe ário (y por un difuso socialismo vulgar y antintelectual). La novela despliega en algunas escenas "de hilarante simbolismo" (Mainer 156) una estética sumamente homosocial;[7] por ejemplo, cuando un protagonista habla, con miradas ansiosas, del "cuerpo magnífico de Isidro", su compañero de combate (cit. Albert 290). En la novela se infiltra, además, una dimensión homoerótica cuando dos jóvenes falangistas, de distintas clases sociales, comparten —frente a la muerte— la misma cama: "Sangre azul de blasón. Sangre roja del pueblo. Y un solo sudor, rojo, rojo y negro, en la chavola, bajo la misma manta, sobre el mismo santo suelo de la Patria" (cit.

Albert 290). Mientras que alusiones tan directas como ésta son excepciones, la camisa azul se convierte en el emblema del "progreso" y de la virilidad ("Esta camisa nos igualaba en el servicio a España como un viento ligero que borre las tormentas. Ni clases ni odios, ni parias ni privilegiados", cit. Albert 290). En esta retórica pseudoigualitaria se observa que la Falange siente su posición histórica como tal (acorde con las palabras de José Antonio Primo de Rivera: "así somos, porque así lo fueron siempre en la Historia los señoritos de España", cit. Albert 289). Sin embargo, en el discurso gay postfranquista esta dimensión histórica parece haber sido completamente desplazada por el deseo sexual subjetivo que la supuesta virilidad de la camisa azul pueda producir en ocasiones.

Este deseo sexual, poco típico en el contexto español, ha dejado sus huellas más evidentes en un autor cuyos modelos hay que buscar en la "delicada" cultura francesa del siglo XIX, en Luis Antonio de Villena. En sus novelas aparece repetidamente el joven falangista como icono, como es el caso de su novela polifónica *Divino*, que se propone desplegar varias etapas de la historia española del siglo XX a través del destino de Max, su protagonista (cf. *Divino*, "Nota final" 238). Paquito, uno de los jóvenes amigos de Max, y miembro, como éste, de un grupo de personas extremamente esteticistas, se une a la Falange. El alejamiento político que produce en Max esta decisión de su amigo es transitorio, pues Max acaba por comprender la fascinación estética que ejerce este grupo de hombres. En una carta del protagonista se lee esto de la siguiente manera:

Y Paquito Cortés —llego a lo que te quería contar— se afilia a la Falange Española [...]. De repente, estos fascistas de traza española, con sus cánticos y sus signos imperiales y catoliquísimos han seducido a nuestro Paquito. Y ha acudido a no sé qué concentración vestido con camisa azul, flechas y yugo bordados, en loor de los Reyes Católicos. Sí, nuestro Paquito. El que se travestía de Carmen en los salones de París. [...]

Pero cuando he sabido que Paquito iba vestido de camisa azul... Siempre ocurre lo mismo. Es fácil estar en los ideales de igualdad o fraternidad cuando son sólo una palabra que a nada obliga. [...] Sabes mi credo de que infelicidad, dolor y pena son los hijos de una sociedad hipócrita, imperfecta e injusta. Una sociedad que nos violenta pero nos pide sometimiento. Es posible que tal humillación la haya sabido siempre. Pero sólo en los últimos tiempos he logrado expresarla. [...]

Dicen que Paquito encuentra atractivo a José Antonio, el hijo del dictador. [... E]n nuestro último encuentro [...] no parecía haber cambiado nada. [...] Paquito (muy vestido, con lazo de lunares) iba acompañado de un chico de aire rudo, vendimiador o jornalero del páramo. No era guapo. Pero tenía fuerza y magia. Paquito le celebraba y bailaba en su derredor como una abejita obsesa. Lo que no puede parecerme mal, pues yo le he hecho tantas veces como esa desdichada fascista. (*Divino* 157-59)

Este episodio del texto (de 1993) se desarrolla en la década de los 30, época que el autor, nacido en 1951, no vivió. Junto a esta reconstrucción de perspectivas pasadas econtramos también la perspectiva de la experiencia vivida, como en uno de los cuentos del libro *Chicos*. Aquí el autor narra su afición por el joven Gonzalo ("rubio, de ojos azulados, muy blanco pero levísimamente dorado de piel, según ese modelo germánico que Visconti adoraba como efigie ideal de lo aristócrata" [207]), a quien él conociera en 1976 en "Love", una de las nuevas discotecas de Madrid. El autor se entera de que Gonzalo, de familia burguesa, es la "compañía" de un viejo amigo rico y conservador ("simpatizante de la ultraderecha, franquista de casta" [209]). Algún tiempo después el narrador se cita con el joven para cenar, poco antes de las elecciones de 1977.

Eran los días previos a las primeras elecciones democráticas, tras la muerte del dictador: Fines de mayo de 1977. Un país en ebullición, vitalísimo, contradictorio, fantástico; lleno de presagios negros, pero también —y más— de un inmenso apetito de aurora. La ciudad estaba llena de carteles y pintadas diversas, provocadoras, libérrimas. Y en la puerta de *California-47*, aquel preámbulo nocturno, estaba instalada una gran mesa, con propaganda y símbolos de *Fuerza Nueva*. La custodiaban dos muchachos vestidos con camiseta azul y boina roja, aguiluchos fascistas, llenos de orgullo, apostura y teatralidad macabra. [...] No tardó en llegar. Venía muy hermoso, con una chaqueta azul, tejanos y una camiseta blanca. Delgado, alto, con la dulzura de su esbeltez atlética, espartana. Me dio la mano con una sonrisita entre cordial y fría (indagadora quizá) y le dije, en seguida, que nos fuéramos de allí porque era muy incómoda la presencia de aquel escuadrón de *fachas*, dispuestos siempre como están al cabreo y la pendencia. Entonces Gonzalo, sin decir nada, pero acentuando la gelidez mineral de su sonrisa [...] se desabrochó lentamente la chaqueta azul de botones dorados, y vi que la camiseta blanca llevaba un letrero azul también: *Fuerza nueva*. Al tiempo que me asombraba (no podía ser menos) reí de mi asombro. El tono marcial que había detectado en Gonzalo desde la primera ocasión que le viera en *Love*, su amistad con Claudio Goli, ultraderechista confeso, aquel aura imperante, su propia y física tipología aria, nazi, todo llevaba por la misma senda. Gonzalito era una perla de las nuevas *juventudes hitlerianas* o de los SS de camisas pardas, favorito de un Roehm mucho menos aguerrido y héroe, pero no menos vicioso ni adinerado. Pensé en *El ocaso de los dioses*. Gonzalo pertenecía a esa camada que busca la perfección del vicio, su hondura, el exquisito privilegio de su diferencia, y al tiempo, tralla y fusta para la grey aplebeyada y miserable. Cóndores reales volando, superhombres y majestuosos, sobre misérrimas y adocenadas ovejas. (*Divino* 215 s.)

Para el narrador la presencia del joven falangista evoca la Historia, no sólo detalles del pasado alemán y un difuso "ocaso de los dioses", sino también la figura concreta del jefe homosexual de la SS, Ernst Röhm. A través de la alusión a la Legión Condor el joven, idealizado como nazi alemán, es relacionado con la Guerra Civil española. El texto mismo escenifica la posicion política del bello joven como un escándalo, el cual es anulado cuando el narrador —después de comer juntos y haber tenido contacto sexual— cataloga a su amigo de apolítico: "Gonzalo no era ya el niño facha que había temido. Amaba el elitismo, se creía superior (físicamente lo era) pero la política no le interesaba" (219). No obstante, el narrador no sólo se refiere a Gonzalo —evocando al protagonista de *La muerte en Venecia*, de Thomas Mann— como "Tadzio más germánico y mayor" (221), sino también como "mi duro SS juvenil" (226). En este texto se aprecia claramente cómo la conciencia de una experiencia histórica negativa no ha sido expresada como trauma, sino que ha sido desplazada por una configuración del deseo sexual, de modo que el (¿supuesto?) ultraderechista, paradójicamente, es deseado precisamente por sus atributos exteriores correspondientes. ¿Conlleva esta interpretación subjetiva, esta inversión del procesamiento del pasado fascista en deseo individual, una aceptación o una subversión del fascismo *verdadero*? A pesar de estar lejos de querer atribuirle a Villena una ideología fascistoide, no puedo sumarme a la interpretación de Chris Perriam, quien entiende al autor como un representante de la política contracultural (*Desire and Dissent* 18), aun cuando el mismo Perriam juzga el

episodio tratado como una expresión de incorrección política.[8]
Cuando el narrador del cuento, a pesar de sus convicciones
políticas, se apasiona por su "duro SS juvenil", refleja una posición
que no armoniza con la actividad "izquierdista", sino que busca el
desarrollo del "lado oscuro" de su deseo sexual:

> Buscaba una libertad más íntima o más honda, no desdeñaba la *acción*
> (aunque la entendiese de otra manera) pero sin saber; torpemente, a tientas,
> anhelaba experiencia. No necesitaba las rojas soflamas sociales para sentirme
> libre, precisaba un camino más sutil, más interior, más oscuro, más
> inquietante y de trastorno. (*Ante el espejo* 12 s.)

La fascinación por la virilidad del camisa azul podría ser una
variante de un cierto deseo homosexual que, dada su motivación
masoquista, se dirige al macho, al soldado, al nazi etc. Este
fenómeno ha sido constatado, discutido, atacado, disculpado o
psicologizado frecuentemente por los *gay studies* recientes (en
cuanto a la perspectiva psicológica cf. Bersani; allí se encuentran
más referencias bibliográficas; en cuanto a su cuestionamiento cf.
Sinfield, capítulo 7 "How transgressive do we want to be?"). La
explicación de Bersani demuestra que éste es un fenómeno que se
puede considerar como general y que no tiene ninguna relación con
la vivencia del fascismo o del machismo:

> The gay-macho style [...] is intended to excite others sexually, and the
> only reason that it continues to be adopted is that it frequently succeeds in
> doing so. [...] The dead seriousness of the gay commitment to machismo
> [...] means that gay men run the risk of idealizing and feeling inferior to
> certain representations of masculinity on the basis of which they are in fact
> judged and condemned. The logic of homosexual desire includes the
> potential for loving identification with the gay man's enemies. (Bersani
> 208)

Este aspecto cobra relevancia también para los iconos del deseo
sexual en la obra de Goytisolo (quien admite, por un lado, su
fascinación por el masoquismo, mientras por otro lado logra
canalizar su deseo por el hombre árabe desde una posición fundada
también en motivos historico-políticos). El tratamiento del ideal
machista del fascismo por parte de Villena podría parecer una
prueba de la poca seriedad con que la nueva vida loca del "país en

167

ebullición" del postfranquismo inmediato asumía la ideología fascista, no considerándola un enemigo serio. Sin embargo, esta idea habría sido desenmascarada ya antes del intento de golpe de estado del 23 de febrero de 1981. Durante la transición misma se mantiene el discurso del fascismo en su línea homófoba. La homofobia explícita del fascismo español sobrevivió al dictador. Todavía en 1979 Ernesto Giménez Caballero, probablemente el portavoz más prominente de la propaganda franquista, hace gala de su retórica fascista en una entrevista, mezclando machismo con anticomunismo y homofobia ideologizada, al proclamar la maza de Hércules como símbolo del fascista y estigmatizar la homosexualidad como una enfermedad (curable):

> El fascista es justamente contrario del homosexual en cuanto pretende continuar el gran símbolo de Hércules y de su maza o basta o falo que los mussolinianos llamaban "il manganello". Convertido ahora en barra de hierro no para reprimirse, sino para reprimir un comunismo asiático y antieuropeo. En cuanto a la homosexualidad, es una enfermedad como cualquier otra, un desequilibrio en los genes de la procreación. La genética llegará a corregirlo (*La Bañera*, 2, junio de 1979, cit. Rodríguez Puértolas 693 s.)

Este no es tampoco el espacio pertinente para un análisis detallado de los paralelismos, hasta a nivel lingüístico, entre esta declaración y los discursos homófobos de Hitler y Göring. Pero hay que poner en duda si el narrador de *Chicos*, enamorado de su "duro SS juvenil", hubiera estado de acuerdo con este lado "serio" de la ideología fascista. La búsqueda del "camino oscuro", la confesión de compartir el ideal de belleza de una virilidad nazi triunfa sobre los elementos del conocimiento histórico en un presente en el que la historia —ya antes de la aparición de la "posthistoria"— ha dejado de ser *vitae magistra*. El narrador, dueño de una definida conciencia política, documenta que el dominio de valores privados y deseos personales sobre el conocimiento historiográfico vale también para el discurso gay. El repliegue hacia la zona descomprometida del mítico "ocaso de los dioses" sirve, según las observaciones de Jo Labanyi, para neutralizar la oposición entre la ficción y los hechos (cf. Labanyi). Esta neutralización se nota en la literatura gay con más claridad que en otras formas discursivas, ya que aquí lo nuevo, lo loco, lo sexual del "país en ebullición" de la movida es celebrado de manera más excesiva y más consciente. El "camino oscuro" privado encuentra su correspondencia pública en esta fiesta de la carne que se desata después de la muerte de Franco.

En su estudio *The Hispanic Homograph*, Robert Richmond Ellis enfatiza (como antes Smith; cf. cap. 1 "Writing the Self in Gay and Feminist Autobiography") la importancia del factor autobiográfico en la literatura gay española contemporánea (por cierto, un fenómeno no sólo español). En general su estudio atestigua que en esta literatura el fascismo tampoco es un tema central. Sólo en dos de los siete autores analizados por él (en *Coto vedado*, de Juan Goytisolo, y en *Ante el espejo*, de Luis Antonio de Villena) pueden encontrarse juicios y huellas del franquismo.[9] Ellis interpreta —como Perriam— al Villena de la autobiografía no sólo como un retoño de familia aristocrática sino también como un crítico del franquismo, al referirse a un episodio de *Ante el espejo*, donde el narrador en primera persona cuenta lo ocurrido en un campamento de verano de la juventud falangista. Allí el muchacho llama la atención por su pijama de seda y, sobre todo, porque su abuela le envía delicias con el chófer.[10] Además se ve expuesto a malos tratos por el jefe del grupo, a quien le gusta demostrar públicamente su hombría. Más importante que esto me parece el segundo contexto autobiográfico, al insinuar Villena una oposición entre el padre viril, que sobrevive a la guerra civil, y el tío homosexual y culto, que pierde la vida. Este pasaje me parece interesante porque muestra el efecto sobre una persona abiertamente homosexual de lo que Foucault llamó el dispositivo social de la sexualidad (en breve volveré sobre este tema). Ellis se dedica al análisis de autobiografías de la "alta literatura", en parte líricas (Jaime Gil de Biedma); por mi parte, quiero hacer referencia a una autobiografía más bien "trivial", la del cantante de boleros Miguel de Molina, publicada póstumamente en 1998 por su sobrino bajo el título *Botín de guerra*. El texto proclama su autenticidad enfáticamente al desmentir algunos elementos de la acción de una película que, supuestamente, trata de la vida del cantante. Molina ofrece documentos claros del sufrimiento bajo la homofobia franquista. El refiere cómo en 1939 un grupo de hombres lo estaba esperando después de una actuación para llevarlo a la oficina de la Dirección General de Seguridad; pero en realidad lo llevaron a un barrio apartado y allí lo patearon, le cortaron el pelo y lo obligaron a tomar aceite de ricino (152-54):

Yo sólo atinaba, temblando, a preguntar:
—Pero ¿por qué? ¿Por qué?
Y el sindicalista, a gritos, me contestó:
—¡Por marica y por rojo! Vamos a terminar con todos los maricones y los comunistas. ¡Uno por uno! (153)

En marzo de 1940 se formó un gran alboroto en el Teatro Cómico de Valencia después de la última representación de Molina, que fue interrumpida a gritos:

—¡No queremos maricones!
—¡Hay que prohibir que trabaje ese rojo!
La cadena de gritos e improperios no terminaba y yo, entre cajas, a un costado del escenario, me preguntaba quiénes podían armar ese escándalo. Un tramoyista, que conocía bien los grupos políticos, me dijo:
—Esos no son de Falange. No es su estilo. Deben de ser un grupo de Los Luises.

Luego me aclaró que Los Luises era una rama de la juventud católica, creo que estudiantes de los jesuitas, que se consideraban cruzados, defensores de la moral occidental y cristiana.

El tramoyista no se equivocó, ya que era, efectivamente, ese grupo, y cuando se llamó a la policía pidiendo que restablecieran el orden, un oficial que simplemente les pidió "un poco de calma" nos dijo que no podía deternerlos "porque sólo eran ciudadanos que manifestaban su pensamiento". (164 s.)

¡Y esto le sucede a una persona de una religiosidad casi folclórica! Molina cuenta de paso cómo el gobierno de Franco prohibió el "transformismo" (176) y cómo le prohibieron sus representaciones, acto tras el cual él ve la mano de "cualquier artista envidioso o un político trastornado" (178). En 1942 el cantante se exilió a Argentina. Pero incluso allí no lo dejaban en paz. Molina se enteró de que un importante funcionario de Relaciones Exteriores, secretario de Serrano Suñer y con cargo de jefe de Falange para el exterior, se empeñó en destruirlo. Un amigo le informó que esta persona era "un homosexual retorcido y resentido contra todo" (219). Sólo después de muchos años, en 1953, y bajo circunstancias extrañas, cesa esta persecución. En un club nocturno de Salamanca un funcionario falangista fue agredido por un joven cuando el viejo lo tocó de forma inmoral. Resultó ser que "el enloquecido maricón no era otro que el secretario del ministro, y jefe de la Falange para el Exterior, que durante años me persiguió monstruosamente" (288). Pero con esto no termina la discriminación de Miguel de Molina. Al final de su autobiografía, encontramos dos episodios que muestran las trampas del dispositivo sexual de una sociedad todavía homófoba: "Deseo insistir", escribe Molina en la introducción al pasaje sobre una entrevista falseada, "en que, por lo general, tuve en contra de mí a una especie de mafia internacional de maricones, periodistas, críticos y otras hierbas..." (302). La ofensa mayor para Molina es la película *Las cosas del querer*, que supuestamente toma su vida como modelo —la película trata de un cantante de origen andaluz que canta "Ojos verdes" y otras canciones famosas de Molina—, ya que el protagonista seduce a un tipo en un urinario, "cosa que no me sucedió en mi vida" (311). El hecho de que la película denuncie la homofobia del franquismo de forma "realista" parece ser menos importante para Molina que la conservación de una imagen propia cuyos valores difieren mucho de los que propagan los movimientos gay actuales. En este sentido Miguel de Molina demuestra la inexistencia absoluta del "orgullo gay" de la era franquista y posterior a ella.

Así, demuestra también que los efectos de la homofobia fascista no cesaron con el fin de la dictadura. Sahuquillo hace referencia a una intervención del ministro de cultura de UCD (Unión de Centro Democrático), Iñigo Cavero, en 1981, contra un programa de Radio Nacional que trató el tema de la homosexualidad (cf. Sahuquillo 92). En Alemania Federal no sólo se mantuvo la legislación restrictiva del párrafo 175 del código penal, referido a los homosexuales, sino que ni siquiera se reconoció a los homosexuales sobrevivientes de los campos de concentración como perseguidos políticos; o sea, que siguieron siendo "criminales". Esta es más una cuestión de las estructuras de poder que de mala voluntad. En el primer tomo de su *Histoire de la sexualité* Michel Foucault discute la cuestión del poder, su repartición social y sus efectos sobre el dispositivo de la sexualidad. Según Foucault, el poder no significa solamente la reglamentación estatal, sino el conjunto de las fuerzas que regulan las técnicas y estrategias de las formas de deseo sexual (cf. Foucault, en particular cap. IV, 2). La homofobia siguió formando parte de las fuerzas sociales después del fin del Tercer Reich y después del fin de la dictadura de Franco. En el contexto español esto significa que el catolicismo estatal y el machismo siguieron determinando el dispositivo de la sexualidad y que por tanto la homofobia no pudo desaparecer con la muerte del dictador. El programa de "Canal +" antes mencionado hace referencia a una encuesta sobre la penalización de la homosexualidad, realizada por la revista "Guardiana" en 1975. 80% de los encuestados se manifestó a favor de la persecución penal de la homosexualidad.

En algunas novelas homotextuales del postfranquismo se separa completamente lo nuevo de la transición de su historia precedente. En este contexto cabe mencionar *El joc del mentider* de Lluís Maria Todó, una novela sobre la escena gay juvenil en Barcelona en la época de la formación de una infraestructura gay, con la apertura diaria de nuevos locales de encuentro. La euforia por la nueva libertad hizo olvidar que la Ley de Peligrosidad Social todavía estaba en vigor y que las tendencias homófobas y fascistoides perduraban. El procesamiento literario de la nueva situación tras la muerte de Franco se canalizó en forma de experimentos estéticos y no en reivindicaciones ni reflexiones políticas. El ejemplo más logrado de novela gay experimental es *L'anarquista nu*, una novela epistolar de Lluís Fernàndez (consistente en la correspondencia entre varios gays valencianos y un amigo en el exilio en Amsterdam). Los fragmentos de la acción se refieren al período entre agosto de 1975 y septiembre de 1976, o sea a la primera etapa de la transición. Esta novela, publicada en 1979, puede ser considerada como un ejemplo paradigmático de la movida, debido sobre todo a su experimentación lingüística y estilística, su escenificación del *camp* y del transvestismo (lingüístico y de otros tipos). Al margen son tematizadas las consecuencias de la homofobia social: uno de los "recortes de prensa" incluidos habla de un homosexual asaltado en el lavabo de la Estación de Ferrocarriles del Norte que resulta ser Eugeni, uno de los protagonistas. En esta novela, el discurso prescinde de toda noción de pasado y celebra con exaltación la nueva libertad. Cuando se habla de una de las fiestas orgiásticas, el travesti Lulú Bon da lo que es también la divisa de la novela: "El alcohol, el sexo, la violencia y toda clase de excesos, nos hicieron perder la noción de lugar, espacio y tiempo" (53).

Josep-Anton Fernández interpreta *L'anarquista nu* como documento de una transgresión que justamente no es transgresiva en un sentido político:

> What *L'anarquista nu* shows is the failure of some political discourses....
> [...] My conclusion, then, is that transgression cannot constitute a positive
> basis for a politics, for transgression is nothing in itself. [...] Therefore,
> transgression, rather than the basis of a politics, should be understood as a
> gesture used to perform a strategy... (Fernández 269)

De hecho, las transgresiones de la transición no son inmediatamente
políticas sino "performativas" (y así indirectamente políticas, al
menos en el sentido que da al término Judith Butler [cf. Butler]).
Pero también es posible que el recuerdo del pasado fascista pueda
irrumpir en la escenificación de la locura gay con sus
transgresiones. Esto lo demuestra Eduardo Mendicutti en *Una mala
noche la tiene cualquiera*, novela que tematiza, precisamente, el fin
de la transición. La obra consiste en un largo monólogo interior de
"La Madelón", quien narra su más íntima y personal experiencia de
la noche del 23 de febrero de 1981 (para más detalles cf.
Ingenschay, "Eduardo Mendicutti"). Esta narración de los sucesos
políticos del intento de golpe se lleva a cabo desde el punto de vista
sumamente subjetivo del travesti, en un lenguaje exagerado. Sin
embargo, la experiencia actual del protagonista lleva al recuerdo del
pasado fascista como amenaza de su pequeña y modesta libertad:

> Y si todo aquello seguía adelante y salían las cosas al gusto del Tejero y del
> Milans del Bosch —yo estaba sufriendo horrores por mis amigas de Valencia,
> que son todas el colmo—, si el golpe triunfaba, mi vida se iba a convertir en
> un martirio. (36)

Más concretamente, se acuerda de las crueldades del nazismo
alemán en los campos de concentración:

> ...porque se acuerda de las cosas tan horribles que él escuchaba cuando chico
> sobre los nazis, especialmente de aquello que decían de las mujerones jugando
> al fútbol con las cabezas de bebés judíos, y es una cosa que la deja hecha
> polvo... (94 s.)

La protagonista de Mendicutti muestra que, incluso bajo la estética
del *camp* y una locura gay escenificada, la ficción gay no tiene
necesariamente que asumir un discurso de la desmemoria. *Una mala
noche* relata un suceso que hubiera podido terminar de forma
abrupta con la transición y hubiera podido desembocar en un

desencanto de consecuencias mucho más graves que el desencanto "real" con que termina la transición. Dediquémonos entonces a la novela que trabaja de forma ejemplar el desarrollo desde la pre-transición hasta el desencanto.

3. Manuél Vázquez Montalbán, *Los alegres muchachos de Atzavara* —la conciencia precaria de una naciente identidad gay en el contexto de la transición

De la pluma de un autor heterosexual sale la obra que con más claridad da testimonio de la modificación de la vida gay desde la pre-transición hasta el desencanto. En *Los alegres muchachos de Atzavara* Vázquez Montalbán describe la cotidianidad de los muchachos "alegres", dicho claramente gays, mencionados en el título de la novela, que han comprado viejas granjas a bajo precio en este pueblo aragonés de montaña y las han arreglado con buen gusto "para veranear". Tanto los muchachos como su retahíla de amigas lesbianas, divorciadas o frustradas en su matrimonio son descritos con todos los atributos estereotipados y clichés clásicos (además de pertenecer a la burguesía catalana, todos son estetas ególatras, perfumados y obsesionados con su cuerpo). De acuerdo con sus cuatro partes, la novela polifónica sugiere cuatro narradores(as) que describen las costumbres y reflexiones de estos excéntricos durante el verano de 1974. Ninguna de estas voces narrativas pertenece a alguno de los protagonistas homosexuales. En la tercera parte Millás, escritor de biografías, actúa como narrador. Este reflexiona sobre si un autor heterosexual puede narrar "objetivamente" la vida de los "alegres muchachos", lo que probablemente es el problema del mismo Vázquez Montalbán (cf. *Los alegres muchachos* 187). En todo caso, la novela ofrece un logrado pastiche del "estilo de locas" (107), pero sobre todo muestra, en lo que respecta a los comentarios sobre la transición, el cambio de los contenidos de la vida de los homosexuales españoles, y lo hace de manera más convincente y profunda que ninguna otra novela.

De manera sutil se reconstruyen los ánimos y las expectativas alrededor del año 1974. La España de 1970 es calificada de "sarampión anticultural más que contracultural" (174). En cambio se idealiza el extranjero, sobre todo EEUU y Europa, así como la libertad de fumarse un porro y tomar partido político por Mao o el

Che. Se espera el fin del fascismo, un fin "biológico" con la muerte de Franco (126); uno de los muchachos resume la esperanza general en una oración: "Si Franco muere todo estará permitido" (148).

Los alegres muchachos es ya interesante por dar como un hecho la existencia de una comunidad gay activa en pleno franquismo tardío en un tono realista. El escritor Millás le aclara a un amigo que "aquella abundante floración de homosexualidad, no sólo allí en Atzavara, sino en todos los campos en los que nos movíamos, [era] como un signo cultural de los tiempos" (162). Por esta misma época Marcuse había articulado su tesis de la homosexualización de la sociedad (cf. Marcuse). Naturalmente, no se puede descartar la posibilidad de que la historia que nos cuenta Vázquez Montalbán sea una proyección desde un presente que, siendo posterior a la transición y a la movida, esté influido por las experiencias acumuladas durante estas etapas. Es decisivo que esta novela no sólo constituye un texto paralelo a la *Crónica sentimental de la transición*, sino que además convierte la transición en una cuestión primordial de los homosexuales. Retrospectivamente una de las narradoras constata:

> Sólo dos años después, ya muerto Franco, sabríamos que aquella noche fue el final de una fraternal coexistencia y el principio de una paulatina separación y diáspora final que privó Atzavara de los ingenuos escándalos de sus veraneantes. [...] Vivimos años de una transición declarada que ya había comenzado muchos años antes, aunque quizá no habíamos detectado toda su extensión y profundidad. *La transición nos alcanzó incluso a las personas normales.* (226; subraya D.I.)

La primera característica fundamental de la vida gay en este gueto del pueblo montañés es su incapacidad para articular claramente una conciencia política. Sólo en la televisión, el nuevo medio masivo, como aclara el "ingenuo" narrador heterosexual de la primera parte,

> se habla de todo, y a veces se pasan incluso y eso que yo no soy un carca, pues a veces he visto yo debates a los que acuden de eso que ahora llaman gays y precisamente en uno de esos debates, creo que fue en "La Clave", un chiquito muy normal y con labia, representante de los gays, es decir, de los maricones, catalán creo porque se llamaba Petit, vino a decir que todos somos maricones y que a todos nos iría mucho mejor si nos dejáramos de historias y ancha es Castilla. (74)[11]

De manera más diferenciada, en la tercera parte, la voz del escritor describe el desarrollo político de la comunidad, cuya posición es claramente antifranquista —radical en el plano estético, pero moderada en la vida real:

> ...ya en 1974, después del atentado contra Carrero Blanco, las conversaciones se fueron politizando y nos descubrimos de pronto todos metidos en un esfuerzo de clarificación política que nos alineaba dentro de una clara oposición al régimen, desde posturas ideológicas estéticamente radicales y vitalmente moderadas. Es decir, nada de la estética revolucionaria nos era ajeno y no le hacíamos ascos a ninguna iconografía del santoral revolucionario [...]. Además, junto con la comunión antifranquista, tan lamentablemente oculta y aplazada, se revelaba un sustrato de sentimiento catalanista que con el tiempo se convertiría en el único recurso de radicalismo estético. Es decir, cuando ya decantada la transición política hacia la moderación y la normalidad paneuropea, casi todos los alegres muchachos y muchachas de Atzavara tomaron posiciones sabiamente centristas y centradas, el hecho de ser entonces cada día más catalanistas, más enfrentados al centralismo superviviente en el nuevo estado democrático, les suministraba un gerovital radical, de militantes en una causa aún aplazada, romántica y probablemente perdida. (179)

Con respecto a las esperanzas izquierdistas del "santoral revolucionario", al fin de la transición queda el desencanto. Pero, como se siente en muchos detalles, la posición de izquierdas era sólo una pose exterior y artificial; en tanto que la esperanza de los gays de ser aceptados como tales parecía consumada. Ellos se aburguesarán y dejarán de estar reprimidos para entrar en aquella "marginalidad pasteurizada" internacional que dos gays europeos, "maricas continentales" disfrazados de sultanes árabes, presentan a los muchachos de Atzavara de la novela (189). Una de las lesbianas regresará al campo con su marido, otra propondrá un "pacto de desmemoria" (251). La única posibilidad política que queda es la conciencia de la propia catalanidad ("...Carlos, o mejor dicho Carles, porque decidido a abrirse camino en las filas políticas del nacionalismo catalán, catalanizó su nombre, su habla, incluso su memoria" [154]).

También para Teresa Vilarós *Los alegres muchachos* es un texto "capital" para el problema de la memoria en el franquismo tardío

(Vilarós 70). Para ella, el penúltimo verano franquista no significa más que un punto final: "A pesar del bullicio y la cacofonía sexual y política del grupo de Atzavara, el verano de 1974 es para ellos término final, punto de destino" (73). Además postula: "Una vez muerto Franco los maduros intelectuales caen en el callejón sin salida al que les aboca una debacle ideológica que sólo permite reconocer en el tiempo histórico de la posdictadura que 'contra Franco se vivía mejor'" (73). Yo me sumo a esta conclusión en tanto que en la postdictadura el grupo de muchachos alegres pierde su carácter de "comunidad conjurada" y su necesidad de tener una ideología más o menos uniforme. Pero la novela no dice nada sobre la nostalgia del franquismo atribuida aquí al grupo de veraneantes gays, sólo tematiza su aburguesamiento y su distanciamiento de grupos de homosexuales politizados. Quiero proponer que la nueva libertad, el proceso de emancipación de los homosexuales y su creciente aceptación son las causas de la abstinencia política y que en la literatura gay de la memoria no se encuentran sólo esporádicamente claros ecos del franquismo y de un pasado traumático. Esto contradice el argumento de Vilarós de la despolitización esencial de la transición.

Los alegres muchachos se vuelve particularmente interesante si se lee como complemento de la *Crónica sentimental de la transición*. La novela traduce con éxito la transformación histórica de la situación de los homosexuales en un discurso de la memoria, ya que Vázquez Montalbán parte de que la comunidad gay de esta época, más allá de su vida hedonista, posee competencia política. En la *Crónica sentimental de la transición* no sucede esto; allí el único papel que le corresponde al homosexual es el de desconcertar en sus valores, más todavía, a la desconcertada sociedad del postfranquismo. El único mérito cultural de los homosexuales que Vázquez Montalbán menciona es el desconcierto que Bibi Anderson (antes de volverse famosa por sus papeles en las películas de Almodóvar) pudo provocar como representante de una cultura *transgender*. Vázquez Montalbán menciona, irónicamente, que el cliente de la prostitución —ante la innumerable cantidad de prostitutas travestis o transexuales en Madrid— tenía que asegurarse del sexo "biológico" de la persona deseada. Y esta situación, que según las teorías de Judith Buttler representa un cambio epocal en las concepciones esencialistas del género y por tanto un progreso, es presentada en esta crónica con un tono negativo:

> Película de travestis *Un hombre llamado Flor de Otoño*, basada en la obra de Valle-Inclán interpretada por José Sacristán. Travestis en los escenarios y un nombre de leyenda sobre la transustanciación de los sexos: Manolo o Bibi Anderson, como ustedes prefieran, símbolo sexual ¿y moral? de la transición. Travestis en las calles de tolerancia de las ciudades, donde el automovilista cazador de muchachas con o sin flor ha de preguntar ¿chico o chica? a la supuesta meretriz que le ofrece su rimmel y su sonrisa de cartón anochecido. (Vázquez Montalbán, *Crónica* 150).

Que el juicio de Vázquez Montalbán de la transición gay sea tan difuso e inconsecuente subraya el discutido carácter de este cambio. Parte de los críticos de la cultura hispánica opinan que las décadas de la transición significan una frustración de las posibilidades históricas que podrían haber resultado de la tradición de izquierdas, o sea anarquista y socialista, de España. Vilarós resume este desarrollo con las siguientes palabras:

> Durante los casi cuarenta años de gobierno dictatorial de Francisco Franco el pensamiento de una parte importante de la intelectualidad española de izquierda se estructuró alrededor de un proyecto utópico de recuperación. Parecería que la muerte del dictador en 1975 debería de haber dejado en principio vía libre a una práctica de realización de signo más o menos marxista pero, como bien sabemos, no ocurrió así. [...E]n el periodo de la transición política de la dictadura a la democracia la sociedad española, aun votando masivamente al partido socialista, rechazó los presupuestos ideológicos dolorosa y pacientemente incubados en la era franquista por los sectores izquierdistas. (8)

Sobre la base de un cambio que parte de un "pacto del olvido" en lugar de una reconsideración de los valores "de izquierda", la transición no puede ser más, en la opinión de Vilarós, que una mancha en el devenir histórico ("El momento de la transición es el espacio donde se procesa el olvido, agujero negro que chupa, hace caer y encripta los desechos de nuestro pasado histórico..." [11]). En consecuencia, la estética de la movida le parece sospechosa por ser apolítica. En este punto ella no toma en cuenta que la dimensión política de la movida puede resultar de factores completamente

178

diferentes de la tradición de la izquierda. Sus argumentos se fundan en un modelo que permite para España la oposición única entre ruptura y transición, la alternativa entre un "saldo de cuentas" con la historia y un "distanciamiento" (supuestamente descomprometido) de ella. Esta alternativa me parece en general históricamente falsa, y problemática en el caso especial de España, precisamente porque la estética de la movida sí tiene contorno político, aun cuando no se defina como tal. Lo nuevo de la situación, la innovación de una estética loca, se entiende como un contraproyecto a una tradición que no es olvidada ni negada en cuanto se va contra ella. Si bien la ridiculización de la España eterna —aspecto determinate en la estética de la generación de Almodóvar— no conlleva la memoria, tampoco se puede decir que proponga la amnesia (para la discusión de la dimension política en Almodóvar, cf. Smith 166s., quien niega el carácter comprometido del cineasta). Esto vale, en particular, para la literatura gay, para la que la alternativa entre ruptura y transición apenas tiene cabida por tener tan pocos antecedentes que asumir o con los que romper. No obstante, la conciencia de una singularidad muy distinta de la tradición hace referencia de forma implícita (y no pocas veces de forma explícita) al anterior estadio social superado. Precisamente esto se ajusta al modelo de "rupture" de Michel de Certeau:

> Le discours historique explicite une identité sociale, non pas en tant qu'elle est "donnée" ou stable, mais en tant qu'elle se differencie d'une époque antérieure ou d'une autre société. Il suppose la rupture qui change une tradition en un objet passé, à la manière dont l'histoire de "l'Ancien Regime" implique la Révolution. Mais cette relation à l'origine proche ou lointaine dont une société se sépare sans pouvoir l'éliminer, l'historien l'analyse. (Certeau 59)

La oposición entre ruptura y transición son las dos caras de la misma moneda. Pero mientras que los alegres muchachos viven la transición (y con ella la pérdida paulatina de sus ideales políticos), los protagonistas homosexuales de Todó, Fernàndez, Mendicutti y Villena, así como los héroes de las primeras películas de Almodóvar ven el franquismo como un "objet passé", como la encarnación de un espacio angustiante que se intenta negar con el "glamour" de un mundo nuevo, bello y gay. El discurso loco de la movida, con su proyecto de instaurar un estilo de vida gay extremo e impúdico, contiene un potencial contracultural (cf. Ellis y Perriam) que —y esto importa en este contexto— subvierte el dispositivo de la sexualidad de una sociedad todavía machista y católica. Hay que admitir, sin embargo, que en la innovación estética del discurso gay surge con frecuencia un espacio de la desmemoria (lo que para mí —contrariamente a Vilarós— no es razón para negarle un potencial contracultural). La memoria sobrevive explícitamente en la autobiografía, allí donde la experiencia individual toma la forma de trauma.

Durante el postfranquismo los homosexuales sufrieron una experiencia mucho más traumática que la del franquismo, el trauma del SIDA. A pesar de ser tan diferente del holocausto, muchos críticos (y autores como Hervé Guibert) comparan ambas experiencias, a veces de manera rápida y poco reflexiva. Salvo algunas excepciones, no se tiene en España un discurso literario y cultural del SIDA.[12] La novela *Las virtudes del pájaro solitario* de Juan Goytisolo combina la experiencia de la marginación, el significado histórico, los traumas personales de los gays (entre ellos el miedo al SIDA) y experimentos del lenguaje en un mismo discurso; ello merece una atención especial.

4. Goytisolo, SIDA y la posmovida

La obra autobiográfica de Juan Goytisolo, recientemente analizada por Ellis, tematiza una memoria que asocia la historia privada y la pública. Esta obra trata de superar, en primer lugar, el trauma provocado por el franquismo, trauma doble en el que confluyen las memorias personales (la muerte de la madre, el rechazo del padre que no acepta al hijo homosexual, y la experiencia de la homosexualidad del abuelo Ricardo) con la memoria de la guerra civil y de la dictadura. Bajo la influencia de esta combinación, Franco se vuelve una figura paternal, "ese otro Padre castrador y tiránico" (Goytisolo *Coto vedado* 250; cf. Ellis 43). La solución (provisional) para escapar a este trauma consiste en encontrar una nueva "familia", una genealogía particular:

> *forjar una genealogía a tu aire e incluir en ella a los que acusados de patria renuncia eludieron el modelo común y su conminatoria fuerza centrípeta: dibujar las constelaciones literarias en torno a las que*

orbitas y dotar a tu nuevo tronco de arborescencia y frondosidad: la
galería de retratos que ventajosamente sustituye a la antigua incluye a
ladrones y prófugos, herejes, sodomitas, proscritos [...]. (Goytisolo *En*
los reinos 121)

Este repliegue a una genealogía literaria es provisional, porque no
consigue solucionar el problema que consiste en representar él, al
mismo tiempo, "both the prisoner of Francoism and the repressed
homosexual within the heterosexual hegemony" (Ellis 45). La
muerte de Franco es, por tanto, la condición y la base de una
escritura explícitamente autobiográfica que a la vez puede referirse
a Genet, al "padre literario".[13] Moreiras Menor interpreta el
proyecto autobiográfico psicológicamente como trabajo de duelo:
"La intención oculta tras ese parricidio no es otra que resistirse ante
el poder ejercido por la autoridad y ante un discurso que pregona la
homogeneidad y la similaridad." (Moreiras Menor 333). Sólo
después de este "parricidio" una subjetividad puede determinar el
discurso de Goytisolo, que, al menos, es capaz de nombrar y
analizar la experiencia del pasado. También la configuración del
deseo sexual de Goytisolo se orienta hacia el hombre superior y
fuerte; se fundamenta en tres aspectos: en la experiencia infantil
(estimulación sexual a través de la violencia), en la búsqueda de una
genealogía literaria (Genet) y en el tratamiento de la historia
española (influido por Américo Castro).[14] Por tanto, las obras de
Goytisolo están determinadas por el doble trauma de la sexualidad
marginada y la experiencia histórica del fascismo. En *Las virtudes
del pájaro solitario* se suma un nuevo tema a su obra: el miedo al
SIDA. Goytisolo no articula este miedo con una voz "realista" o una
forma discursiva representativa de la experiencia gay, sino que lo
traduce a un texto idiosincrático, una compilación de poemas
experimentales en prosa, donde no se reconoce ningún eje narrativo.
Los intertextos los encontramos, sobre todo, en la reconstrucción
del desaparecido *Tratado de las propiedades del pájaro solitario* de
San Juan de la Cruz, quien, según la leyenda, se comió el
manuscrito en la cárcel. Al mismo tiempo el texto despliega una red
de referencias, donde encontramos al místico en su prisión, a un
enfermo en un hospital, contagios, y a través del intertexto de San
Juan "En una noche oscura" se codifica la experiencia de una
corporalidad y una sexualidad marginadas y tabuizadas. Las
referencias explícitas al SIDA son sutiles pero claras: el joven

maestro de árabe nombrado "Ben Sida", la inequívoca escena de cuarto oscuro, de lenguaje barroco,[15] o la mención del "Vel d´Hiv" sin explicarse de qué se trata.[16] (Para más detalles sobre la temática del SIDA en *Las virtudes*, cf. el excelente análisis de Epps, quien también ha destacado la relación entre la "impureza de la sangre" [como elemento "árabe" en la mentalidad tradicional española de la limpieza de la sangre] y los traumas de una enfermedad supuestamente de gays.)

La oscuridad del texto da testimonio de lo subjetivo del trauma; por tanto me parece mucho más sorprendente que Vilarós interprete *Las virtudes* como expresión de la subcultura homosexual. Sus argumentos no tienen en cuenta que esta obra está determinada por la apropiación particular de sus intertextos líricos; más bien Vilarós ve en ella parte de un "discurso invisible" contra lo que llama la amnesia de la movida. Contra esta interpretación hay que decir que en el centro de la obra no se encuentra la historia de la represión de la corporalidad (recordemos la escena en el cuarto oscuro, cf. nota 15). Se trata de lo contrario: de realizar una fiesta orgiástica (lo que a su vez es una fiesta barroca del lenguaje) contra el trauma del miedo al SIDA. La forma de Goytisolo de tratar el SIDA es muy idiosincrática, así como su reflexión sobre el tema del franquismo. Su obra completa ocupa un lugar especial dentro de los discursos homotextuales, ya que relaciona claramente la historia privada con la tradición de la "España negra" como ninguna otra. No obstante, el deseo de dar voz a los marginados es, en su intención, idéntico al proyecto gay de un Lluís Fernàndez, de un Mendicutti, de un Nazario o de un Villena. Pero Vilarós utiliza la temática del SIDA para convertir a la odiada España del postfranquismo en un cuerpo "infectado". También los discursos gay que no tocan el tema del SIDA son calificados por Vilarós de "sectores de riesgo",[17] probablemente sin tomar en cuenta hasta qué punto tiene que resultar homófoba esta denominación para los seropositivos y los homosexuales en general. También desde la perspectiva de la teoría del discurso se puede preguntar qué significado tiene hablar de un "discurso de la infección" en el caso de Goytisolo o de otros autores homosexuales. De hecho, sólo se intenta omitir los aspectos reflexivos y subversivos del discurso homosexual con el fin de reforzar una imagen "ideológica" negativa de la transición, lo que la lleva a declarar el discurso de la infección como único lugar de la memoria histórica. (Al margen sea dicho que Vilarós malinterpreta en extremo el desarrollo del discurso del SIDA y la política en España y EEUU al poner a la política norteamericana como modelo ante los errores de la política española [cf. Vilarós 249 y 252]. Remito a los comentarios al respecto en la literatura norteamericana sobre el SIDA, sobre todo la del grupo ACT-UP y su difícil y tenaz lucha para poder manifestarse políticamente; cf. Llamas.)

En el esbozo de una concepción de la historia homosexual, John Champagne plantea: "the discontinous discursivities we designate as race, class, gender, and sexuality do not cast their subjects identically. Or, to state this another way, cultural othering works along a variety of axes" (Champagne 133). Tampoco el procesamiento del franquismo en la literatura gay española sigue una línea unitaria. Gran parte de la literatura homotexual escenifica superficialmente un discurso al que muchas veces se le puede acusar de practicar la desmemoria. Pero estos textos "ahistoricos", que con la estética loca de la movida sondean lo nuevo de una sociedad cambiante, tienen un carácter subversivo inmanente, que indirectamente saca a flote la época del fascismo, con cuyas premisas estéticas e ideológicas ha roto. Este discurso no es incapaz de procesar sistemáticamente el pasado, sino que se niega a hacerlo. Por tanto el discurso homosexual literario desde la transición suma otra variante a las tesis de David Herzberger: "History in the post-Franco novel is therefore reinvigorated through the liberating admixture of fact and imagination, free now of censorship and myth, rather than through the more narrowly focused design of historiographic dissidence" (Herzberger 155). El espacio de la memoria se constituye más bien en las autobiografías y los documentos personales; éste es el lugar para procesar los traumas de un pasado como horizontes individuales de la experiencia. Probablemente el mejor ejemplo de todo ello sea la obra de Juan Goytisolo.

Notas

1. La revista gay madrileña *Entiendes?*, no. 59, junio/julio (1999): 7, reporta bajo el título "Destruida una ficha policial por 'peligrosidad social'", sobre un homosexual valenciano, cuya ficha policial se encontraba en manos de la policía todavía en 1995. Este hombre había conseguido, tras pasar por muchas instancias, la destrucción de su expediente de "peligrosidad social" abierto en el año 1976.
2. Entre las personas entrevistadas figuran no solamente las "víctimas", sino también los "culpables". Aparecen los escritores Antonio Roig y Enrique Miret Magdalena, el director de cine Eloy de la Iglesia, y también un ex-jefe de la Asistencia Social de Prisiones, un inspector jefe de la Policía Nacional y un ex-director general de prisiones. Este último confirmó: "todos somos culpables". Agradezco mucho a Line Franco, una de las encargadas de la documentación, por su información y por haberme facilitado los vídeos del programa.
3. La homofobia de Cela se hizo evidente durante la celebración del centenario de Lorca en 1998, cuando el Nobel español buscaba distanciarse de "los que toman por el culo".
4. La noción de Post-Stonewall se refiere a los acontecimientos del 28 de junio de 1969 en el bar "Stonewall Inn" de la calle Christopher Street, frecuentado por la "comunidad loca" de Nueva York. Después de una redada policial, algunos de los homosexuales intentaron liberar a otros detenidos por la policía. Se considera el inicio del movimiento de "Orgullo Gay" ("Gay Pride"), que organiza en muchísimas ciudades manifestaciones anuales en conmemoración del "Christopher Street Day".
5. Cf. Goytisolo, *Coto vedado*: "La fobia visceral de mi padre a los homosexuales [...] alcanzaba a veces extremos morbosos: había referido con gran satisfacción a José Agustín —y éste se había apresurado a repetírmelo— que Mussolini mandaba fusilar sin contemplaciones 'a todos los maricones'" (105).
6. En la literatura gay española predominan los iconos del adolescente, del efebo, del joven "normal"; en el contexto de los iconos viriles, el árabe juega un papel importante (Goytisolo, Mendicutti; para más detalles cf. Ingenschay "Homotextualidad"). La primera novela que habla de una escena con tipos *leather* (para tratarla inmediatamente con ironía) es *Yo no tengo la culpa de haber nacido tan sexy* (1997), de Mendicutti. Para más detalles sobre las escenas *leather* cf.

también "Ecos de la comunidad gay en España. Mesa redonda celebrada en Madrid en 1996" en Aliaga y Cortés, 199-237.

7. En cuanto a la diferencia entre un deseo homosexual y otro homosocial y su relación a partir de la sociedad inglesa del siglo XIX, cf. Sedgwick.

8. Perriam: "However, just as the parenthetical detail of Gonzalo's smile [...] so tellingly interrupts and eroticises the revelaton of Gonzalo's affiliation, so too is the probity of the narrator's counter-cultural discourse in *Boys* disrupted by the presence of Gonzalo. In his effort to assimilate Gonzalo into the drama (and get him into bed) the narrator half leaves aside and half accepts the macabre element in this part of the story. [... I]n doing so he reveals a political incorrectness and a personal instability brought about by the combination of desire for absolute change and desire for absolute male beauty" (110). Antes ya, Perriam muestra una perspectiva diferenciada cuando describe el proyecto total de Villena: "Some of Villena's prose narratives look back on the final years of Franco's dictatorship to construct what to many of us is an unfamiliar reading of the period. Villena does not offer the view which is in common circulation and which sees the whole period of the dictatorship as a unitary dark age of sexual and cultural politics awaiting the kiss of democracy [...], nor does he attempt an objectivist chronicle of the times; instead he prefers to engage with the spectre of opresion more equivocally" (17).

9. Otro autor tratado en el estudio de Ellis, Antonio Roig, relata sus experiencias de la homofobia franquista en el programa de "Canal +" antes mencionado (ver nota 2).

10. El toque aristocrático, que hace que la abuela del autor no reciba al supuesto falangista "plebeyo" (cf. *Ante el espejo* 77s.) forma parte integral de la identidad de Villena y es en mucho menor grado una expresión *camp*, como interpreta Ellis. En el caso de la autobiografía de Terenci Moix, concuerdo completamente con Ellis en que *camp* es la técnica discursiva principal en esta obra; sin embargo, no hay en ella ningún reflejo del franquismo.

11. Se trata justamente de Jordi Petit, una de las figuras claves de los inicios del "Front d'Alliberament Gai de Catalunya", miembro del partido comunista catalán y persona de gran resonancia pública.

12. Entre las excepciones cuentan —además de *Las virtudes del pájaro solitario* de Goytisolo— *Todas las almas* de Javier Marías (Barcelona 1989). Otro ejemplo (aunque de estilo y técnica narrativa muy modestos) de novela sobre el SIDA es *O yacoi* de Augustín Muñoz Sanz. Sobre la cultura del SIDA ver también Llamas.

13. Sigo aquí la interpretación de Moreiras Menor 1996 333. Existen, sin embargo, huellas autobiográficas ya desde *Señas de identidad*. El encuentro con

el albañil marroquí en el cap. 8 de *Señas*, por ejemplo, reaparece en el contexto autobiográfico de *Coto vedado* (105 s.).

14. En *Coto vedado* Goytisolo declara: "Como en muchos españoles de mi generación, el término 'moro' se asoció en mí [...] a unas vagas e inquietantes imágenes de violencia y terror. Sería preciso el lapso de veinte años para que [...] alcanzara a establecer una fecunda relación personal con el mundo árabe en su triple dimensión de espacio, cuerpo y cultura, relación que pronto se trocaría en un eje fundamental de mi vida" (74).

15. "[P]ara percibir el olor inconfundible de sus cuerpos lubrificados, brazos sarmentosos, músculos de suave y tersa dureza, presentir la acechante vecindad de sus presas, ruda trabazón de abrazo, sinuosa coyunda de enamorados y abandonarte a la visión interior de sus espaldas recias, omóplatos lucientes y combados, textura suntuosa de miembros enlazados, mutua devoración lenta, dos jayanes ungidos hasta el borde de los robustos calzones de cuero, óleo y sudor entremezclados, humo anhelando quien no exuda fuego, enardecedora concreción de tu sueño, anhelo de posesión compartida, lenitiva fricción del tórax maltrecho con aceite vertido por los alcuceros, difusa quietud transmutada en dicha, alquimia, dilatación, calor, goce, luz, anonadamiento (81).

16. "Vel d'Hiv" es una abreviatura de "Vélodrome d'Hiver", el estadio donde reunían a los judíos franceses antes de transportarlos a los campos de concentración nazis. De esta manera Goytisolo establece, aunque de forma indirecta, una relación entre el SIDA y el Holocausto.

17. "Eduardo Haro Ibars, [...] Leopoldo Maria Panero o Nazario que aunque no se refieren nunca al sida en sus textos están claramente situados (sitiados) en el sector de riesgo" (254).

Obras Citadas

Alas, Leopoldo. *De la acera de enfrente. Todo lo que se debe saber de los gays y nadie se ha atrevido a contar*. S.l.: El Papagayo, Ediciones Temas de hoy, 1994.

Albert, Mechthild. *Avantgarde und Faschismus. Spanische Erzählprosa 1925-1940*. Tübingen: Niemeyer, 1996.

Aliaga, Juan Vicente y José Miguel Cortés. *Identidad y diferencia. Sobre la cultura gay en España*. Barcelona/Madrid: Editorial Gay y Lesbiana, 1997.

Bersani, Leo. "Is the Rectum a Grave?" En Douglas Crimp (ed.). *AIDS: Cultural Analysis, Cultural Activism*. Cambridge, Mass: The MIT Press, 1988: 197-222.

Butler, Judith. *Gender Trouble: Feminism and Subversion of Identity*. New York/London: Routledge, 1990.

Certeau, Michel de. *L'écriture de l'histoire*. Paris: Gallimard, 1975.

Consoll, Massimo. *Homocaust*. Milano: Kaos Edizioni, 1991.

Champagne, John. *The Ethics of Marginality: A New Approach to Gay Studies*. Minneapolis: Univ. of Minnesota Press, 1995.

Ellis, Robert Richmond. *The Hispanic Homograph: Gay Self-Representation in Contemporary Spanish Autobiography*. Urbana/Chicago: Univ. of Illinois Press, 1997.

Epps, Bradley. "The Ecstasy of Disease: Mysticism, Metaphor, and AIDS in *Las virtudes del pájaro solitario*", en David Foster and Roberto Reis (eds.) *Bodies and Biases: Representations of Sexualities in Hispanic Literatures and Cultures*. Minneapolis: Univ. of Minnesota Press, 1996: 359-96.

Fernández, Josep-Anton. "Death and the Angel in Lluís Fernàndez's *L'anarquista nu.*" *Neophilologus*. 79 (1995): 263-71.

Fernàndez, Lluís. *El anarquista desnudo*. Barcelona: Anagrama, 1979. Primera ed. catalana: *L'anarquista nu*. Barcelona: Edicions 62, 1979.

Foucault, Michel. *Histoire de la sexualité I. La volonté de savoir*. París: Gallimard, 1976.

Goytisolo, Juan. *Coto vedado*. Barcelona: Seix Barral, 1985.

——. *En los reinos de Taifa*. Barcelona: Seix Barral, 1986.

——. *Las virtudes del pájaro solitario*. 1988. Madrid: Alfaguara, 1994.

Guasch, Oscar. *La sociedad rosa*. Barcelona: Anagrama, 1991.

Gumbrecht, Hans-Ulrich. *«Eine» Geschichte der spanischen Literatur*. 2 vol. Frankfurt/M.: Suhrkamp, 1990.

Herzberger, David. *Narrating the Past: Fiction and Historiography in Postwar Spain*. Durham/London: Duke UP, 1995.

Hesse, Silke. "Fascism and the Hypertrophy of Male Adolescence." En John Milfull (ed.). *The Attractions of Fascism: Social Psychology and Aesthetics of the "Triumph of the Right"*. London/New York: Berg, 1990: 157-75.

187

Ingenschay, Dieter. "Das kommt mir spanisch vor. Homosexualität in der modernen spanischen Literatur." *Forum Homosexualität und Literatur.* 16 (1992): 25-52.

——. "Eduardo Mendicutti, *Una mala noche la tiene cualquiera.* Narración de maricas o la irrupción de un discurso del travestismo." En Dieter Ingenschay y Hans-Jörg Neuschäfer (eds.). *Abriendo caminos. La literatura española desde 1975.* Barcelona: Lumen, 1994: 157-65.

——. "Die Thematisierung von Körperlichkeit im postfrankistischen Roman Spaniens." En Rudolf Behrens y Roland Galle (eds.). *Menschengestalten. Zur Kodierung des Kreatürlichen im modernen Roman.* Würzburg: Königshausen und Neumann, 1995: 251-68.

——. "Homotextualidad. Imágenes homosexuales en la novela española contemporánea." *Antípodas.* 11 (2000) (en prensa).

Labanyi, Jo. *Myth and History in the Contemporary Spanish Novel.* Cambridge UP, 1989.

LaCapra, Dominick. *History and Memory after Auschwitz.* Ithaca/London: Cornell UP, 1998.

Llamas, Ricardo (ed.). *Construyendo sidentidades. Estudios desde el corazón de una pandemia.* Madrid: Siglo XXI, 1995.

Mainer, José-Carlos. *La corona hecha trizas (1930-1960).* Barcelona: PPUU, 1989.

Marcuse, Herbert. *Triebstruktur und Gesellschaft. Ein philosophischer Beitrag zu Sigmund Freud.* Frankfurt/M.: Suhrkamp, 1968.

Martínez-Expósito, Alfredo. *Los escribas furiosos. Configuraciones homoeróticas en la narrativa española.* New Orleans: UP of the South, 1998.

Mendicutti, Eduardo. *Una mala noche la tiene cualquiera.* Barcelona: Tusquets, 1988.

——. *Yo no tengo la culpa de haber nacido tan sexy.* Barcelona: Tusquets, 1997.

Mirabet i Mullol, Antoni. *Homosexualitat avui.* Barcelona: Edhasa-Institut Lamda, 1984.

Moix, Terenci. *El beso de Peter Pan.* Barcelona: Plaza y Janés, 1993.

——. *Extraño en el paraíso.* Barcelona: Planeta, 1998.

Molina, Miguel de. *Botín de guerra. Autobiografía.* (Coordinación de las memorias de Salvador Valverde. Investigación de Alejandro Salade). Barcelona: Planeta, 1998.

188

Moreiras-Menor, Cristina. "Juan Goytisolo, F.F.B. y la fundación fantasmal del proyecto autobiográfico contemporáneo español." *Modern Language Notes*. 11 (1996): 327-45.

Müller, Joachim y Andreas Sternweiler. *Homosexuelle Männer im KZ Sachsenhausen*. Berlin: Rosa Winkel, 2000.

Muñoz Sanz, Agustín. *O Yacoi*. Badajoz: Publicaciones de la Diputación Provincial, 1994.

Nazario. *Alí Babá y los 40 maricones*. Barcelona: La Cúpula, 1993.

Perriam, Chris. *Desire and Dissent: An Introduction to Luis Antonio de Villena*. Oxford/Washington: Berg, 1995.

———. "Gay and Lesbian Culture." En Helen Graham y Jo Labanyi (eds.). *Spanish Cultural Studies. An Introduction: The Struggle for Modernity*. Oxford UP, 1995: 393-95.

Reinstädler, Janett. *Stellungsspiele: Geschlechterkonzeptionen in der zeitgenössischen erotischen Prosa Spaniens (1978-1995)*. Bonn: Erich Schmidt, 1996.

Rodríguez Puértolas, Julio. *Literatura fascista española*. Madrid: Akal, 1986.

Sahuquillo, Angel. *Federico García Lorca y la cultura de la homosexualidad masculina. Lorca, Dalí, Cernuda, Gil-Albert, Prados y la voz silenciada del amor homosexual*. Alicante: Instituto de Cultura "Juan Gil-Albert", 1991.

Sedgwick, Eve Kosofsky. *Between Men: English Literature and Male Homosexual Desire*, New York: Columbia UP, 1985.

Sinfield, Alan. *Gay and After*. London: Serpent's Tail, 1998.

Smith, Paul Julian. *Laws of Desire: Questions of Homosexuality in Spanish Writing and Film 1960-1990*. Oxford: Clarendon Press, 1992.

Spackman, Barbara. *Fascist Virilities: Rhetoric, Ideology, and Social Fantasy in Italy*. Univ. of Minnesota Press, 1996.

Todó, Lluís Maria. *El juego mentiroso*, Barcelona:Anagrama(1995. Primera ed. catalana: *El joc del mentider*. Barcelona: Columna, 1994.

Vázquez Montalbán, Manuel. *Los alegres muchachos de Atzavara*. Barcelona: Seix Barral, 1987.

———. *Crónica sentimental de la transición*. Barcelona: Planeta, 1985.

Vilarós, Teresa. *El mono del desencanto. Una crítica cultural de la transición española (1973-1993)*. Madrid: Siglo XXI, 1998.

Villena, Luis Antonio de. *Ante el espejo*. Madrid: Mondadori, 1988.

———. *Chicos*. Barcelona: Planeta, 1998.

———. *Divino*. Barcelona: Planeta, 1994.

9

Memory and Forgetting, Resistance and Noise in the Spanish Transition:
Semprún and Vázquez Montalbán

Ofelia Ferrán

> It is the loss of memory, not the cult of memory, that will make us prisoners of the past.
> Paolo Portoghesi (111)

> Todos sabemos que la democracia que nos gobierna ha sido edificada sobre la losa que sepulta nuestra memoria colectiva.
> José Vidal-Beneyto (33)

What Transition?

"La transición," "la postransición," "la pretransición," "la doble transición," "la segunda transición," "la tercera transición," etc., etc., etc. All these terms have been used, at one time or another, to place a label on a historical process whose diffuse temporal borders defy any easy labeling attempts.[1] One can always go back and find social, political, economic, or cultural conditions that predetermined the nature and evolution of the transition that Spain underwent in the mid-seventies from the Franco dictatorship to a democracy. One can equally consider that the effects of that transitional process continue to be felt beyond its supposed end. Any historical dates one may try to set for the beginning and end of this variously defined epoch of recent Spanish history are therefore arbitrary and, more importantly, depend on what one is thinking of as having "transitioned." What has come to be called "la transición" in fact involves a number of related processes taking place in Spain after Franco's demise. These range from the change in the formal trappings of a system of governance to the redefinition of a broader set of social institutions and practices in the country, from the shift in a broader societal attitude towards power, government and politics in general to the changing views regarding Spain's past and its status as a multi-nation state.

The temporal markers for the beginning and end of the period called "the transition" have been variously defined by different scholars. Gregorio Morán, for example, clearly affirms that the end of the transition should be 1982, the year the socialist government headed by Felipe González won the national elections, while he admits that different dates can be ascribed to the beginning of the period (23). The most commonly used is that of the death of Franco on November 20, 1975, although many people believe that the transition truly began when, on December 20, 1973, his appointed successor, Admiral Luis Carrero Blanco, was killed by a bomb planted by the Basque terrorist group ETA.

However, the date of the end of the transition is not as uncontroversial as Morán would have it. Many consider the end of the transition to be, strictly speaking, December 27, 1978, the date the new Constitution officially declared Spain to be a constitutional monarchy governed by a parliamentary democracy, while others believe it to be February 23, 1981, when an attempted coup by a group of military generals ultimately proved unsuccessful, thus reinforcing the sense that the parliamentary democracy that was being established was truly viable despite much opposition from right-wing forces, predominantly in the military. Of course, these demarcations serve to delimit the transition only in terms of a change in the formal system of government, which, indeed, is no small matter.

Some, however, take a broader view of what the transition involved and thus also inscribe it in a wider time-frame. Teresa Vilarós, for example, sets the framework for her study of the culture of the transition between the dates of 1973, Carrero Blanco's death, and 1993, the year of the signing of the treaty of Maastricht, an event that, in Vilarós's mind, signifies the full and effective integration of Spain within the European political and economic systems and the definitive abandonment of the isolationist tendencies that had marked much of the Franco regime.

Of course, Spain's integration within Europe had had various important landmarks, among them the joining of the EEC in 1986.

Furthermore, the process of international integration began already during the Franco years: a case in point is Spain's joining the United Nations in 1955, an event seen by many as a betrayal of the Spanish people on the part of the United Nations, which for many years had declared that it would not allow Franco's fascist dictatorship to join its ranks and then received it with open arms. In exchange for the international legitimacy afforded by this entrance to the United Nations, the Franco regime was pressed to make some changes in the country to give the appearance of more openness and freedom in what, nevertheless, was still unquestionably a repressive dictatorship. Certain measures, such as the Ley de Convenios Colectivos of 1958, which allowed some degree of collective bargaining and worker representation in industry, or the later Ley de Prensa e Imprenta of 1966, which slightly loosened government censorship of published material, were undoubtedly only cosmetic and superficial changes to a system that still incarcerated, tortured, and killed people whom it deemed too openly and actively in dissent. Some observers, however, see these measures as marking a change in the later years of the regime, a shift Raúl Morodo, for example, calls a "pretransición." Along this line of thought, Ramón Buckley suggests that there was really a double transition, "la doble transición," in which the emblematic year of 1968 served as a marker for a social process of change that preceded, and thus set the stage for, the narrowly defined political transition of the mid-seventies.

The argument that there existed a "pretransición" during the later years of the Franco regime is a tricky one. To be sure, in the sixties Spain slowly developed economically, abandoning the isolationist dream of an autarchy in favor of a gradual integration into the international capitalist system and experienced, at the hands of the famed "technocrats" in charge of the economy, some level of modernization. These economic changes were accompanied by a certain loosening of official censorship in cultural matters. In certain revisionist views of the Franco regime that have become all too common, this is taken to mean that Franco should, in fact, be credited with preparing Spain for democracy.[2] Such a belief is ludicrous, given the fact, among many others, that the general was signing death sentences for opponents to his regime virtually on his death-bed. The fact that such a belief exists does, however, raise important issues: first, the need to reflect about *what* exactly it is that we think "transitioned," or changed, when we set about trying to define such a period or process, and, second, the need to acknowledge that any effort to delimit and define the transition period will be arbitrary, and subject to ideological constraints.

If I have begun this essay by enumerating some of the ways in which the transition has been historically demarcated by different scholars, it is not because of any belief in the importance of dates as such, or even in the real *need* to set dates for the transition. On the contrary, it seems to me that if there is so much discrepancy in people's efforts to date this period, to mark exactly when the process of change began and ended, it might just be because it is *not* so clear when the change occurred, or even, with respect to certain aspects of the transition, if it occurred to any significant degree. The measures by means of which the Franco regime, in its later years, became somewhat more flexible in order to appease international opinion were enacted in the name of change but with the intention of fundamentally maintaining the regime intact. As the French adage states, "plus ça change, plus c'est la même chose" (the more things change, the more they remain the same). In many ways, something similar could be said about certain elements of the transition, in particular, the one I will explore in this study: the manner in which the transition failed to create a space for a true critical reflection about the past, about the experience of the civil war and the long years of repression suffered under Franco, despite the new political freedoms gained. In this sense, it is important to recognize that, alongside the obvious important changes secured within Spanish politics during the transition, there were also certain elements of Spain's social reality that did not change enough.

Under Franco, no one was allowed to question the official version of Spain's recent past which portrayed the general's National Crusade as having saved Spain from the hands of those bent on destroying its sacred Catholic destiny and unity. In a somewhat parallel fashion, during the transition a similar repression of reflection about the past was subtly imposed on the Spanish people. All too often, attempts to discuss and think through the experiences of the Second Republic, of the Civil War, or of the suffering under Franco were quelled in the name of a generalized attitude, imposed from the top political levels down through the rest of society, that the past had to be laid to rest in the name of the "reconciliación nacional" that the politicians of the transition were so carefully

194

orchestrating. It was a repression of the past imposed by means very different from those used by Franco, to be sure. In no way do I mean to diminish the importance of the difference in formal political governance enacted by the transition. The creation of a viable democracy is unquestionably an enormous achievement of this time period. However, to use Gregorio Morán's expression, that achievement came at a price. "El precio de la transición," as he refers to it, was the loss of an opportunity to reflect deeply on the nature and legacy of the Franco regime and of the recent Spanish past in general.

Morán claims that, with the fundamental democratic right of equality before the law that was recovered with the transition, a more problematic "equality before the past" was implicitly assumed (75). As he claims: "Desde los primeros días de diciembre de 1975 se inicia un proceso de desmemorización colectiva. No de olvido, sino de algo más preciso y voluntario, la capacidad de volverse desmemoriado" (75). Morán claims that the transition created a "Reino de desmemoriados" (75) in which everyone was expected to give up any serious and concrete re-evaluation of their past during the Franco regime, either as part of it or as part of the opposition to it, because of the supposedly destabilizing effects such a re-evaluation would have: "la ingenua convención de igualdad ante la ley fue sustituida por la retorcida presunción de que todos los pasados eran igualmente perjudiciales y por tanto convenía instalarlos en el armario de los cadáveres" (77). That is to say, all pasts were equally to be forgotten, those of the people who had been on the side of the victors during the war and those of the vanquished, the pasts of those who had been part and parcel of the Franco regime and the pasts of those who had suffered its consequences in the form of repression of all kinds, incarceration, or exile, whether exterior or interior. In this "retórica de la desmemoria," as it could be called, the time of the Second Republic and the Civil War were particularly taboo, for fear, supposedly, that the incipient democracy might suffer the same fate as that last experience of democratic freedom Spain had seen.[3] Everyone was in the same boat, without distinctions. All were equally served, supposedly, by not evoking the ugly past of the war or of the Franco regime. Of course, this lack of memory of the past was particularly helpful to all the right-wing politicians who conveniently changed hats during the transition, suddenly becoming fervent democrats after having worked for the Franco regime. This lack of memory was also helpful to many members of the opposition parties, such as the Partido Comunista Español, who, in exchange for being incorporated into the process of negotiating the return to democracy, could conveniently forget many of the excesses of power committed by the party in its work against the regime. The great losers in this process were, of course, the majority of the Spanish people, who had had their past completely erased or rewritten for them by Franco and now saw it swept under the carpet of the "reconciliación nacional" upon which the transition was supposedly being built.

With this implicit silencing of the past, with this erasing of Spain's collective memory, or memories, what was also denied was a much-needed critique of the authoritarian practices that had characterized the Franco regime, many of which, in disguised form, were to persist throughout, and perhaps beyond, the transition. Again, it was the Spanish people that had the most to lose. An authoritarian, top-down approach to politics was one of the legacies of the Franco regime. In large measure, this top-down approach characterized much of the transition. The manner in which the "Pactos de la Moncloa" were developed, by a select group of political leaders behind closed doors, is an example. It is significant that in a poll organized by the magazine *Cambio 16* in November 1977, the month that the "Pactos" were signed, it was shown that, although a majority of people polled supported the pacts, only one in every four could name any of the economic measures implemented by them, though the measures were to affect deeply the lives of all Spaniards ("El Pacto, un desconocido" 20). The article presenting the poll highlighted the lack of the people's involvement in this crucial event of the transition by claiming: "No se sabe si el tan mentado Pacto es un convidado de piedra entre los españoles, o los españoles un convidado de piedra al Pacto" (20). Such a vision of the Spanish people as silent guests at the table of power, where an active role is reserved for a chosen few, is certainly one of the "legacies" of the Franco regime, to use Raymond Carr's expression.[4]

The survival of such Francoist legacies was based precisely on that silencing of the past, on that slow but steady creation of a "Reino de desmemoriados," which guaranteed that no one should engage in any serious critique of the authoritarian practices that were being inherited from the past. Another Spanish thinker who highlights the damaging effects of this lack of historical memory during the transition is Eduardo Subirats, who goes so far as to state that, until such a critical recuperation and re-evaluation of the past is undertaken, no real transition will have taken place. As he claims: "es ilusoria toda pretensión de reforma social y cultural que no asuma al mismo tiempo una reforma de la memoria histórica" (209). He further argues:

> Ahora ya podemos comprender, sin embargo, el sentido último de este olvido y de las complejas estrategias políticas y mediáticas que han contribuido a él: el retorno de lo reprimido. La degradación de nuestra memoria histórica . . . [h]a sido, al mismo tiempo, una consigna clara y explícitamente formulada por aquellos sucesores de la tradición totalitaria española (y no española ciertamente) que han visto en las estrategias del olvido, y en la suplantación de la memoria histórica por sus simulacros técnicos y políticos, la clave última de la destrucción de una verdadera democracia social. . . . (128)

For Subirats, therefore, a true democracy will have been established only once such a confrontation with the past is undertaken, for only a recuperation of Spain's historical memory will lead to the overcoming of many of the dangerous "legacies" of the Franco regime that the transition simply perpetuated.

It is significant that Subirats uses the Freudian concept of the return of the repressed to explain the dangers of this "desmemoria" that characterizes the transition. This same concept is evoked by Michel de Certeau in his study *The Writing of History*, in which he examines the way any new historical time period tries to see itself in contrast to that which came before and in this process selectively remembers some things from that past and forgets others. Inevitably, however, those forgotten, repressed aspects of the past return. As he explains:

> But whatever this new understanding of the past holds to be irrelevant— shards created by the selection of materials, remainders left aside by an explication—comes back, despite everything, on the edges of discourse or in its rifts and crannies: "resistances," "survivals," or delays discreetly perturb the pretty order of a line of "progress" or a system of interpretation. These are lapses in syntax constructed by the law of a place.

> Therein they symbolize a return of the repressed, that is, a return of what, at a given moment has *become* unthinkable in order for a new identity to *become* thinkable. (4)

Those aspects of Spain's past that had tried to be forgotten, repressed, will inevitably return, and they will function as "lapses in syntax," "resistances" to the official historical narrative of the transition that explains the past away while trying to enshrine the present in an unquestionable plot of historical progress and development.[5]

At two important moments of recent Spanish history, two writers, both with long-standing records of "resistance" to the Franco dictatorship, publish novels that embody a "resistance," a return of the repressed, similar to that which de Certeau mentions. They are novels that do, indeed, become important lapses in the syntax of the transition that was turning Spain into a "Reino de desmemoriados." Both *Autobiografía de Federico Sánchez* (1977), by Jorge Semprún, and *Autobiografía del general Franco* (1992), by Manuel Vázquez Montalbán, thematize the recuperation of that historical memory that many were trying to make "unthinkable" so that the transition's identity as radical departure from the past could "become thinkable." Both novels, furthermore, do so by means of a similar narrative strategy, the creation of a real/fictitious autobiography in which an individual's memory is refracted into multiple memories, all of them working to deconstruct a unitary, monolithic, repressive view of history: that of the Spanish Communist Party in its most fervent Stalinist epoch in the case of Semprún's text, and that of Franco's mythifying discourse in the case of Montalbán's. Each novel recuperates the memory of suffering and oppression, from either side of the political spectrum, that the official discourse of the transition was trying to repress. Thus, these novels try to engage in a difficult dialogue with the past by openly critiquing the authoritarian legacies of that past. These texts, therefore, embody major resistances, important exceptions to that "retórica de la desmemoria" of the transition that is to blame for the fact that, as Subirats claims, in general, "Los valores autoritarios que políticamente representaron tanto a la derecha franquista como a la izquierda leninista, a lo largo de un amplio periodo histórico de represión hosca y de agitación clandestina, nunca fueron realmente cuestionados" (30).

198

Jorge Semprún: Memory as Resistance

In *Autobiografía de Federico Sánchez*, Semprún revives one of the *noms de guerre*, Federico Sánchez, that he had used during his many years of clandestine work as a member of the Spanish Communist Party. The text is structured around two main time periods: that of 1976-77, the years in which Semprún wrote the book, and 1964, the year in which he, or rather Federico Sánchez, was expelled, along with Fernando Claudín, from the Executive Committee of the Spanish Communist Party for dissenting on fundamental issues of how the party should organize its opposition to the Franco regime, as well as for criticizing the increasingly hierarchical, authoritarian practices within the party. Moving constantly between these two periods, the text further shifts vertiginously back and forth in time by always evoking an earlier memory when recounting some incident of the past. The text incorporates memories from Semprún's last summer vacation, as a child, in the Spain of 1936 when the civil war began, his exile in France, his work with the French Resistance, his deportation to the concentration camp of Buchenwald, his subsequent involvement with the Spanish Communist Party, and his work, political and literary, since his expulsion from the party. Throughout this kaleidoscopic recuperation of memory, the work is overtly self-reflexive, highlighting at every turn the process of its own writing. This de-naturalizing, relativizing self-reflexivity will ultimately stand in sharp contrast with the discourse of the Communist Party that Semprún had critiqued in 1964 and that he continues to critique in 1977, an intransigent, mythifying discourse completely closed to any form of questioning, much less dissent.

One of the themes recurrently raised by the self-reflexive comments in the text is the ambiguity surrounding its very genre. At one point, the narrator, aware of how he could embellish a certain historical anecdote being related, exclaims: "Si estuviera escribiendo una novela, en lugar de hacer un relato meramente testimonial, con tan sólo los hechos y los dichos, los pelos y las señas, la cara y la cruz de la verdad escueta, sin duda aprovecharía esta ocasión de lucimiento literario" (194). Despite the narrator's disclaimer that he is not writing a novel but a strictly historical testimony, the original edition published in 1977 had the word "novela" on the cover, thus implying that, in spite of the accumulation of verifiable historical facts and recognizable historical characters, the book is Semprún's literary reworking of this historical material. It is interesting to note, however, that in later editions, such as that of 1982, the Planeta "edición de bolsillo" of 1995, and the English translation of the text, the word "novel" is dropped from the cover. The issue of the relationship between writing and reality, of the inextricable connection between history and narrative, is thus raised as a problem from the very cover of the book.

The title further exacerbates this ambiguous relationship between fact and fiction as it claims to be the real autobiography of a fictional character, Federico Sánchez, who, nevertheless, was the persona behind which a very real person, Jorge Semprún, existed. This ambiguity is explicitly and self-consciously exploited in the text itself. There are numerous occasions in which the narrative voice finds itself split between these two identities. At one point, while retelling an event, the narrator stops and clarifies: "y yo mismo: bueno no yo: yo no existía apenas por aquel entonces: no yo por tanto sino tú: Federico Sánchez" (7). At another point, he continues: "Y estabas tú

(bueno no tú Federico: estaba yo: tú Sánchez no existías todavía: y a ninguno de los presentes sin duda podía ocurrírsele que existieras algún día . . ." (16). The break in the spacing of the text in this quotation serves to highlight the deep rift between these two identities, Federico Sánchez and Jorge Semprún, which belong to the past and to the present, respectively, but are embodied by the same person. Both of these issues, that of the genre of the text and that of the identity of its protagonist, issues in which the relationship between fiction and reality is problematized, will be raised recurrently throughout the narrative.[6]

The book begins and ends with the same scene. It is the moment, during the meeting of the Executive Committee of the Spanish Communist Party in 1964, in which Dolores Ibárruri, "La Pasionaria," is about to speak up and officially expel Semprún and Claudín from the party. "Pasionaria ha pedido la palabra" is the name of the first and last sections of the book, which therefore has a circular structure. The text is thus framed by the scene of Semprún's expulsion from the party after he has, in a sense, been framed

200

himself, misrepresented as a traitor to the communist cause. The book in its entirety will be an attempt to correct that misrepresentation, to demonstrate that, as time has shown, it was he and Claudín who were right about the strategies that the party should follow. Ironically enough, at the time of the book's writing, in the midst of the transition, the party was indeed taking up many of the strategies proposed by Semprún and Claudín in the sixties.

However, the book attempts much more than a clearing of Semprún's name, a denouncing of the unfair treatment he had received. It is a deconstruction of the mythic, alienated and alienating discourse and mentality that the Spanish Communist Party had developed. It is an effort to make known the dark, authoritarian past of the party, which was being repressed during the transition. It recovers the memory of that problematic past in the belief that only through such a confrontation with its past could the party truly hope to make a viable contribution to the democratic process being forged in Spain. Therefore, the book quite literally enacts that return of the repressed mentioned, in different contexts, by both Subirats and de Certeau.

At the beginning of the book, when Pasionaria is about to "take up the word" and expel Semprún/Sánchez from the party, the narrator takes up *his* word and, in the only act of resistance left to him, postpones Pasionaria's sentence (in every sense of the word) by interjecting the thoughts that occur to him at that very moment. The mnemonic voyage that becomes the novel thus begins. By means of that voyage, Semprún/Sánchez is able to present *his* version of the story, *his* memory of what had happened, before he is forever exiled from the party when Pasionaria finally does speak at the end of the text. In part, the thoughts that occur to the narrator will revolve around the kind of narrative that he is constructing:

> Si estuvieras en una novela, si fueras un personaje novelesco, seguro que ahora te acordarías, mirando a Dolores Ibárruri, de otros encuentros con ella. En las novelas hábilmente construidas, las iluminaciones de la memoria quedan muy bien, resultan muy vistosas. Además, permiten dar al relato una densidad que no se consigue con un desarrollo narrativo meramente lineal. Si estuvieras en una novela, en lugar de estar en una reunión del Comité Ejecutivo del partido comunista, ahora mismo te acordarías de tu primer encuentro con Pasionaria. Es lógico: en los

> momentos decisivos, la memoria siempre se remonta a los orígenes, incluso remotos, de la vivencia en que uno se encuentra sumergido. (9)

Although the narrator implies that he is *not* part of a novel, the next thing recounted in the text is precisely that which, he claims, would appear in a well-crafted novel: the memory of his first encounter with Pasionaria. There is a curious "lapse in syntax" here, as the narrator goes on to present in his narration the kind of novelistic strategy he was carefully excluding from his discourse by the use of the subjunctive ("si estuvieras en una novela. . ."). A certain lack of choice is implied in that subjunctive tense (if he *were* in a novel he could write things as he wants to, but he is *not* in an novel, so he *can't*). However, that lack of choice is then undermined, just as syntactical coherence is undermined, by his appropriation, at the moment of writing, of his right to choose. The narrator subverts the hypothetical nature of the subjunctive by making it a real possibility in his text, by writing a novel when he was supposedly writing a strictly historical account instead. This passage illustrates how the repressed can emerge through a kind of "lapse in syntax," as de Certeau claimed. It further points to the possibility of uncovering a "syntax of remembering" in Semprún's text, one that involves issues of freedom of choice, of both a political and narrative nature, as well as issues of the relationship of history and fiction. In fact, through this playful manipulation of the subjunctive the ambiguity as to the nature of the text we are reading is raised once again. It is definitely true, definitely historical, but it is also a fiction, or, at least, a fictional recreation of real events.

There is another ambiguity that hovers over this passage, however. When the narrator refers to the way in which this story *could* be constructed, the moment of its writing is implicitly evoked. Although the narrator affirms he is present at the meeting in 1964 that is being recounted, the moment of the *recounting*, the moment in which the text is being written, in 1976-77, haunts the passage. In this sense, the final sentence takes on added importance. At decisive moments, memory always goes back to the origins, the history, of the present situation. Here, the decisive moment is a double one. It is the moment, in 1964, in which Semprún is facing Pasionaria and in which he is thinking of the importance of going back and recalling the history of his relationship with her. The decisive moment, however, can also be seen to be that of the text's *writing*,

1976-77, a time in which all of Spain is facing the transition, a time in which it is equally important to go back and recall the history of the Communist Party, particularly because the party is about to be legalized and will have to rethink its strategies to better deal with the new political reality in Spain. Of course, the issue of how to find the best strategy to deal with changing realities in Spain was precisely one of those that led to Semprún's distancing from the official party line in the sixties and to his ultimate expulsion in the meeting of 1964. As the narrator elsewhere evokes: "una de las cuestiones esenciales de la discusión de 1964 que habíamos estado evocando todo el día [era] la cuestión de las formas de transición del franquismo a la democracia, de la liquidación del franquismo" (203).

Throughout the novel, Semprún/Sánchez recalls the process whereby he slowly grew to question, and later openly disagree with, the official party doctrine regarding the best means to oppose the Franco regime in Spain. This distancing intensified after 1958, the year that the party helped to organize the much-awaited Huelga Nacional Pacífica, which was supposedly going to show that there was a powerful mass oppositional movement arising in Spain, organized by the communists, that would, eventually, manage to topple the regime.

Since 1953, Semprún had been working clandestinely in Spain, acting as liaison with other oppositional groups, as well as with the intellectual elite. He was therefore one of the members of the Executive Committee of the Spanish Communist Party most in contact with the internal situation in Spain. The radical failure of the strike of 1958, the lack of popular support it experienced, surprised even him. Nevertheless, at that time, Semprún was still willing to follow the party blindly and participated in the Executive Committee's effort to manipulate the information so as to make it seem that the strike had been a success. However, his continued contact with Spain, his first-hand experience of the changes in the Spanish society and economy, the country's modernization and slow incorporation into the international capitalist system, all eventually made him see that the party could not continue to work as it had until then. He came to believe, as Claudín would too, that the party needed to work *within* the new economic framework that was developing in Spain. To the rest of the Executive Committee this was heresy, an abandonment of the fundamental precepts of communist doctrine. Ironically, some of those precepts were abandoned later, and many of the suggestions made in 1964 by Semprún and Claudín appeared in the new approach to politics that Carrillo dubbed Eurocommunism and which, significantly, he passed on as being his own original initiative. As Régis Debray would later remark to Carrillo himself, the only "sin" that Semprún and Claudín seemed to have committed was that of being right before their time (qtd. in Buckley 48).

Yet this disagreement as to the best oppositional strategy to follow in the work against the Franco regime was not the only element in Semprún's gradual distancing from the rest of the Executive Committee. It must be remembered that the sixties were years in which the international communist movement still suffered from the legacy of Stalin's influence. It was this authoritarianism, as it was being felt in the Spanish Communist Party and in the communist movement at large, that Semprún began to question. He began to disagree with the communist movement's labeling of any critical thinking on the part of its members as heresy and betrayal. He criticized the way the movement stifled such critical reflection either by eliminating the bothersome members from its ranks, as was to happen to him later, or sometimes by simply eliminating them altogether. Above all, he became disillusioned with the way the movement covered up these authoritarian practices, later pretending they had not happened, conveniently "forgetting" any abuses of power. It was the party's suppression of memory as well as its abusive authoritarianism that Semprún began to critique, and for which he was expelled from its ranks.

In *Autobiografía de Federico Sánchez*, Semprún/Sánchez not only critiques the abuses of power committed by the Communist Party under its Stalinist influence, but he performs his own self-criticism, the "autocrítica" of the self-alienation he himself had reached within the party. One event that comes back to haunt him is his failure to speak up, in 1952 , about the innocence of a communist from Czechoslovakia, Josef Frank, who had been condemned to death in a major Stalinist trial because he allegedly had worked for the Gestapo while he had been in the concentration camp of Buchenwald. Semprún, who had organized clandestine activities with Frank in the camp, knew he could not possibly have belonged to the Gestapo, or he would have denounced Semprún. Nevertheless, in 1952, Semprún/Sánchez was still, as he confesses, "un intelectual estalinizado" (115), and he did not speak up to defend Frank, who was unjustly killed. Semprún/Sánchez recalls the incident with guilt:

> No proclamaste en ningún sitio la inocencia de Frank, la falsedad de la acusación que se hacía. Sin duda, de haber proclamado esa inocencia habrías terminado siendo expulsado del partido. Decidiste permanecer en el partido. Preferiste vivir, dentro del partido, la mentira de la acusación contra Frank que vivir, fuera del partido, la verdad de su inocencia. (114)

Later on, in 1964, in the meeting in which he will be expelled from the Spanish Communist Party, he will publicly evoke this guilty memory, accompanied by a newly found resolution:

> Me había callado, sacrificando la verdad en aras del Espíritu Absoluto, que entre nosotros se llamaba Espíritu-de-Partido. Y esa herida del estalinismo en mi propia piel seguía quemándome. Nunca más, cualquiera que fuese la circunstancia, cualquiera el precio a pagar, volvería a sacrificar la verdad en aras de la pragmática Razón de Estado o de Partido. (124)

That is why, years later, during the transition, when many were arguing that it was better not to dig up the past of the party so that it could easily become integrated into the process of negotiating the return of democracy in Spain, Semprún felt that all the deaths and suffering caused by communism's authoritarian past had to be confronted. And that is what the book does—confront the party with its past, recover the memory of the suffering it had caused. In the face of the official party line that denies that past, Semprún/Sánchez claims: "el peor enemigo de ese sistema es el testimonio verídico. Una memoria lúcida y crítica es la peor enemiga de esa pragmática y arbitraria historia de los desmemoriados" (173-74). That is why his memory becomes his most powerful form of resistance: "Sería muy fácil olvidarse de su propio pasado, desmemorizarse. . . . Sería demasiado fácil. No me olvido de mi propio pasado" (17). Semprún further exclaims: "No voy a hacer lo mismo que los demás, que casi todos los demás dirigentes comunistas formados en la época de Stalin. No voy a cerrar a cal y canto mi memoria" (129). If a machine gun had been his weapon for fighting oppression when working for the French Resistance, this new form of resistance

Semprún undertakes calls for a different kind of weapon: an open and uncompromising memory.

Since the effort to revive his own memory is also the attempt to revive the party's memory of its past, as well as the effort to make all of Spain, at the time of the transition, revive its memory of one of its main oppositional parties during the long Franco years, Semprún/Sánchez goes beyond his own personal testimony in the book and incorporates many other texts and documents, a strategy that transforms *Autobiografía de Federico Sánchez* into a text made of texts, a memory made of multiple memories. Official party documents, articles published in various magazines, excerpts from books, letters, poems, even the file that the Franco police had created about his political activism appear. Many of these texts are his own: poems, a play, a part of an unfinished novel. By rereading many of these texts, Semprún/Sánchez can trace, and critique, his own political and ideological development. For example, poems that he wrote in his youth manifesting his fervent glorification of the Communist Party appear recurrently. Semprún/Sánchez criticizes the blind adherence to the party and its discourse that these poems reflect: "como lo reprimido que retorna bruscamente a la clara conciencia o a la memoria claroscura, este legajo de papeles amarillentos y mecanografiados, hace surgir de nuevo el fantasma de lo que yo era en aquellos años" (23).

Within *Autobiografía de Federico Sánchez,* therefore, Semprún/Sánchez faces the return of the repressed—a confrontation with his own past— just as the book itself, at the time of its publication, becomes an embodiment of the return of the repressed for the Spanish Communist Party and for Spanish society at large.

The focus on the re-evaluation of all these written texts underscores a significant aspect of this book's critical reflection about the past: the recognition of the importance of language in any construction, or reconstruction, of history. In fact, it was, in part, a critique of the language and discourse used by the Communist Party that led Semprún/Sánchez to distance himself from it. He reflects on his increasingly critical view and questioning attitude towards the party:

> Te llevaron, sobre todo a rebasar las fronteras de un discurso político monolítico y monologante, monoteísta y monomaníaco, de una

logomaquia autosuficiente y autosatisfecha, para comenzar a situarte en una posición que te permitiera escuchar las voces de la realidad. (116-17)

Semprún/Sánchez's critique of the "discurso monologante" of the party, and his desire to hear "las voces de la realidad," reveal the need for a dialogical view of reality, an open stance, ready to accept the many voices of the world, even if those voices make one change one's own discourse. Explaining how it was that the increasing tension between the multidimensional reality that he saw within Spain and the unchanging, monolithic discourse of the party led him to question the official party line, he further states:

> Las voces y los rumores de la realidad fueron amplificándose para mí, hasta hacerse ensordecedoras, hasta acallar el runruneo beatífico de nuestro discurso ideológico, cada vez más desfasado de la realidad. Había que elegir entre la realidad del discurso y el discurso de la realidad. Elegí este último, naturalmente. . . . (181)

The dialogical relationship to the world, the incorporation of the many voices emanating from it that Semprún/Sánchez here affirms is reflected in the very form of his autobiography. The many different texts that appear, from different sources, are an example of Bakhtin's concepts of dialogism and heteroglossia in the novel, where the text becomes a composite of the many voices in society, not only a particular author's voice. Bakhtin's explanation of the function of this heteroglossia is particularly relevant to *Autobiografía de Federico Sánchez*: "It is necessary that heteroglossia wash over a culture's awareness of itself and its language, penetrate its core, relativize the primary language system underlying its ideology and literature and deprive it of its naive absence of conflict" (368).

This relativizing of a primary language system, that of the "discurso monologante" of the Spanish Communist Party, and the desire to "deprive it of its naive absence of conflict" are precisely what this book seeks. Not only does the book intend, by means of what it recalls, to question the forced absence of conflict that had been imposed within the Spanish Communist Party, it further seeks, with its publication in 1977, to challenge the absence of conflict that was also being subtly enforced during the transition.[7]

In fact, when the book appeared in 1977, and won the Premio Planeta for that year, it sparked a sometimes acrimonious debate within and beyond the Communist Party. Accusations flew, personal pasts were evoked, and many were offended not only by the critical content of the book, but also by its often excessively heavy-handed accusatory tone.[8] If Semprún sought to generate debate, to create dialogue at that crucial moment of the transition when oppositional parties were being legalized, he certainly managed to do so. The heated debate caused by the book shows that, oftentimes, when the repressed returns, it does so with a vengeance. As Semprún explains in an interview:

> El libro tiene ese tono agresivo y polémico precisamente para provocar una cierta reacción, porque yo tenía una impresión de cómo iba a ser la situación en la transición, de cómo iba a ser el "consenso" —aunque todavía no tenía vocablo, nombre, ya establecido—, de cuál iba a ser la situación del poder y de los poderes para ocultar, para no hablar de ciertas cosas del pasado, igual del pasado franquista que del pasado comunista, porque uno de los aspectos esenciales del consenso es eso, no recordar. Eso es lo que permite que Conesa siga siendo el comisario general de Gobernación, cuando es, como todo el mundo sabe, uno de los mayores torturadores de la Policía franquista. (Sinnigen 68)

Again, for Semprún, his memory is the best form of resistance, and his book becomes a major act of rebellion against the erasure of the past being enacted during the transition. It is precisely as an act that one of its reviewers characterizes the book. José Angel Valente states that "la *Autobiografía* tiene más condición de acto que de libro . . . acto de brusca, súbita y escandalosa presencia" (qtd. in Buckley 51). Valente further asserts the same thing Semprún himself says of the intention behind the book when he affirms that it was presented to the Spanish people "en busca de una reacción" (qtd. in Buckley 52).

Semprún's book can be thought of as a powerful "speech act," one that hoped to generate a strong reaction in its reading public. The recuperation of memory enacted in the book was not meant to discredit the Communist Party and make voters turn away from it. As Vargas Llosa claimed about the book:

El propósito de Semprún al dirigirse a ese público particular, con la ayuda inesperada del Premio Planeta, no es alertarlo contra el Partido Comunista y su líder, sino, más bien, contra la ingenuidad de aceptar cualquier "imagen" política sin someterla a la prueba de fuego, que no consiste en escuchar lo que los dirigentes y los partidos políticos dicen, sino relacionar lo que han hecho y lo que hacen con lo que dicen. (60)

Indeed, the discrepancy between what political parties and leaders were saying and what they had done was a major problem during the transition. *Autobiografía de Federico Sánchez* is an attempt to introduce some measure of accountability from a political party Semprún knew well and, by extension, from all parties into the new democratic process being forged in Spain. Despite some problematic aspects of the book, the recuperation of memory that *Autobiografía de Federico Sánchez* represents is the most powerful form of resistance Semprún could engage in against the "retórica de la desmemoria," both the one that he had encountered within the Spanish Communist Party in the fifties and sixties and the one that Spanish society at large was facing during the transition in the seventies.[9]

Manuel Vázquez Montalbán: Memory as Noise

Manuel Vázquez Montalbán, like Semprún, was an active opponent of the Franco regime, also a member of the Spanish Communist Party for a time, and an equally strong critic of the "desmemoria" that characterized the transition. Explaining in an interview how the different political parties all had their reasons to suppress their individual history during the transition, he presents a critique of the Communist Party that echoes Semprún's criticism in *Autobiografía de Federico Sánchez*:

Los interesados [en rescatar la memoria histórica] podrían ser los comunistas, pero sobre ellos también gravita el hecho de que quienes ocupan la dirección del PC después de la muerte de Franco eran gentes poco interesadas en reconstruir la memoria y consideraban que era un ruido, algo molesto para la formación de la democracia. Así se fraguó una conspiración no escrita para que la gente olvidara y no reivindicara la memoria, y eso a mí me parece sencillamente terrible. (Padura Fuentes 49)

Like Semprún, Vázquez Montalbán in much of his work explicitly thematizes the issue of memory, its loss and its needed recuperation during the transition. If the memory Semprún was recovering in *Autobiografía de Federico Sánchez* was a form of resistance to the "retórica de la desmemoria" of the transition, Vázquez Montalbán will see memory as a noise, an interference in the transition's message of the benefits of silencing the past for the good of the present. Much of his literary work will be an attempt to register that noise, to tune into its wavelength, to give a voice to the repressed past, and thus, as in Semprún's work, to provide an avenue for the return of the repressed. Vázquez Montalbán describes his work in an interview:

> One of my obsessions is the use of memory as a source for knowledge, but a falsified or distorted source. One's memory is never the same as the memory of someone else who has gone through the same experience. In the case of Spain particularly, memory plays an important part in our own present, because it is the only link with a dramatic period in our history— the hidden memory of the Spain of the wounded, those who were defeated in the Civil War. Those of us who were children of the defeated have had to struggle to recover that concealed past. (Gazarian Gautier 304)

Autobiografía del general Franco is a work in which the "struggle to recover that concealed past" of the defeated in Spain is explicitly thematized. Ironically, it is presented as part of the attempt to re-create the history of the victor himself, Franco, the great repressor of the past of those he defeated.

In Vázquez Montalbán's novel, Marcial Pombo is commissioned by a young editor, Ernesto Amescua, the son of an old friend of Pombo's, to write an autobiography of Franco. Pombo is an old, second-rate writer of pseudoautobiographies of famous cultural figures and author of abridged history books for children. The book Amescua asks him to write is scheduled to appear that year, 1992, the anniversary of Franco's birth, as the first of a new collection of autobiographies of important political figures. The idea for the book arose when Amescua's young son asked him who Franco was, and the editor realized how important it was to tell the life of the dictator to the Spanish children who had not lived the Franco years and were growing up not even knowing who he had been.

210

At first, Pombo complains that it would be too difficult for him to write the story of Franco, since his father, a member of the Communist Party, had fought for the Republic, had been a prisoner for years, almost being executed several times, and had then worked as a forced laborer for the nationalists after the war until he came back home a withered, broken man. Pombo himself had been a member of the Spanish Communist Party and an active opponent of the regime. As he complains: "Me atreví a decirle que desde niño Franco ha sido una sombra que ha modificado mi vida, la de mi familia y que algo de sarcasmo tiene que yo sea ahora su autobiógrafo, secreto, de cámara" (20). The editor replies that he will not be a ghost writer but will sign the autobiography himself. He will get two million pesetas as an advance payment, another three million upon handing in the manuscript, and the guarantee of a first edition of twenty thousand copies. It is a difficult deal to reject. What finally convinces Pombo to take the project, however, aside from his dire economic condition, is the realization that, despite the cruel irony in his having to give a voice to the person that had silenced so many Spaniards, among them his own father, he has, with this book, the opportunity to fulfill the dream that millions of Spaniards shared but were never able to realize, that of killing off the dictator: "Resucitarle para matarle. ¿No estoy en condiciones de cumplir el sueño de media España vencida?" (22). Pombo's task of "killing off" Franco will take shape through an interesting literary strategy.

Most of the novel is comprised of the pseudoautobiography of Franco that Pombo writes, with the supposed voice of the general telling his life in the most minute historical detail. As Franco's autobiography progresses, however, Pombo begins to interject his own and his family's story, thus incorporating into the discourse of the victor the voices of the defeated: "Permítame que irrumpa con mi vida privada, general, por primera vez en este largo viaje autobiográfico que compartimos" (64). Interrupting the general's narrative, therefore, and set off from it by a different character type (Franco's discourse appears in italics, while Pombo's does not), Pombo's narration of his family's life begins to "correct" the general's memory, to fill in the gaps, the blanks, the silences of the general's story. Pombo's interjections represent the return of the repressed "on the edges" and in the "rifts and crannies," to use de Certeau's expression, of Franco's discourse. By incorporating "the other side of the story" into Franco's self-aggrandizing discourse, the novel is effectively recovering the concealed past of the defeated, the past of suffering and repression that Franco was responsible for, but which he is careful to leave out of his own version of his life. If, as Pombo had complained to Amescua, Franco had modified the writer's whole life, now Pombo's life was modifying the general's, or, at least, the narrative of the general's life.

The text thus enacts a dialogue, a dialogical reconstruction of the past. It becomes, in Bakhtin's terms, a "double-voiced discourse" (324), a text confronting different social and ideological currents in a manner that shows how the past is always constructed out of the confrontation of these different voices. Yet Pombo's text does not just oppose his personal narrative to that of Franco. It also incorporates into Franco's voice a myriad of other voices, dozens of historical texts by people who knew, or have studied, the figure of Franco and who also challenge many of the general's assertions. These texts range from autobiographies of members of the Franco family, such as that of his niece, Pilar Bahamonde, *Historia de una disidencia*, to biographies of Franco or accounts of recent Spanish history written by historians, such as Gerald Brenan's *El laberinto español*. They include citations of newspaper and magazine articles, letters from various family members or important political figures, as well as excerpts from texts written by Franco himself, such as *Raza* or *Diario de una bandera*. The incorporation of all these often contradictory texts into Franco's narrative reflects the "heteroglossia" in this reconstruction of the past, which, as Bakhtin states, serves to "deprive it of its naive absence of conflict" (368). This "multi-voiced" narrative slowly overpowers what was supposed to be Franco's own story told only by himself. The "heteroglossia" of the text completely undermines "the one language of truth" (Bakhtin 271) that had characterized the discourse of Franco's regime and that the narrative voice of Franco was trying to re-create in his autobiography. By having Franco face all these opposing voices, by not allowing him complete control of the narrative of the past in his autobiography, as he had tried to do during his life, Pombo's autobiography of the general manages to "kill him off," in a way. What is killed off, also, is any illusion of objective truth, any pretense to be able to narrate history from one

212

and only one vantage point, repressing all dissenting views in the process.

In this sense, Vázquez Montalbán's novel echoes Semprún's, as the heteroglossia that characterizes it relativizes all claims to a single historical truth and raises the issue of how we know the past. In both cases, the dialogical nature of the text completely undermines the unitary, monolithic, hegemonic representation of the past put forth by an authoritarian force, be it the Spanish Communist Party in the case of Semprún, or Franco and his regime in the case of Vázquez Montalbán. Both novels can be seen to share many of the characteristics of what David Herzberger has called the "novel of memory," in which the recuperation of the past through memory "strips history of its structured one-ness, of its mythical enactment of progression, and most importantly, of its discourse that disaffirms dissent in the narrative capturing of the past (67).

If Franco had brutally repressed any dissent to his regime during his lifetime, his autobiographical narrative is forced to coexist with the memory of the dissenting forces he so ardently tried to silence. As one example among many, at one point of the text Franco is recounting the end of the Civil War, expressing the pride he felt while watching, from a massive platform, "el primer desfile de la victoria entre aclamaciones de vencedores y vencidos, liberada toda España del yugo rojo" (350). Interrupting this triumphalistic view of the end of the war, Pombo interjects his personal memory of the same event:

> No quiero aburrirle, general, con el inventario de su propia barbarie. Le diré que nos daba miedo salir a la calle por donde desfilaban los retoños de la Falange con sus camisas azules, sus pantalones cortos, su boina en la cabeza o al hombro, cantando cosas épicas que me estremecían y me desidentificaban, como si me deshabitaran. Tuve suficiente edad y suficiente vivencia como para sentirme ya un topo entonces, un exiliado interior y comprender que en el censo de sus exterminios había que incorporar el de los desidentificados, los miles y miles de españoles obligados a perder la identidad, obligados incluso a perder la memoria. . . . (353-54)

By telling, within Franco's version of the past, his family history; by recounting how his father's suffering in the Franco jails after the war and his withering away in the forced labor groups constructing the

213

"Valle de los Caídos" turned his father into a frightened and frail shadow of a man; by describing his own work in opposition to the regime, for which he was incarcerated and tortured several times, Pombo is making a place, in the narrative of recent Spanish history that Franco's autobiography represents, for all those thousands and thousands of Spaniards forced to lose their identities, and their memories, by the regime's imposed discourse of triumphalistic "truth." In this double-voiced discourse that Franco's narration becomes under Pombo's influence, all the defeated of the recent Spanish past can find a space to be "reidentificados" and "rehabitados."

In the end, however, these voices of the defeated will once again be silenced, their memory once again erased. The repressed voices that had returned in Franco/Pombo's narrative will once again be suppressed. When Pombo finally delivers the finished manuscript to Amescua, he is not prepared for the editor's reaction. Amescua praises the way Pombo has managed to make Franco's speech credible, although, as the editor remarks, Pombo's influence over the general's words is noticeable, if expected. What the editor cannot accept are all the "noises" interrupting the general's discourse. He goes on, in an ironically paternalistic tone, to explain the technical definition of "noise" to an expectant Pombo:

> un ruido es todo aquel fenómeno que al producirse una comunicación no pertenece al mensaje intencionalmente emitido. . . . Todo lo que en ese canal obstaculiza la correcta, la natural finalidad de ese mensaje, ir directamente del emisor al receptor, es un ruido. Pues bien, yo te propuse un mensaje: que Franco explique a las generaciones del futuro quién fue y por qué fue lo que fue y eso está explicado muy bien, pero constantemente ese mensaje aparece obstaculizado por tus ruidos. (650-51)

Amescua tells Pombo that the interruptions, in which he tells his own family's life, which he imposes on the general's discourse, as well as the many critical notes from texts that contradict what Franco says, are all mere noises, not part of the original message. When Pombo tries to defend those interruptions, and in fact claims that "El franquismo fue un ruido, eso sí fue un ruido que interrumpió el mensaje de la democracia . . . de la libertad . . ." (651), Amescua cuts him off impatiently, basically saying that history is written by the winners, and that's that:

La historia sólo puede tener un sentido fáctico, lo que está hecho, hecho está y sólo interesa resaltar lo curioso de su causalidad, no la moral de su causalidad. . . . En definitiva, Franco es el que hizo la historia y vosotros la sufristeis. Mala suerte. Eso es todo. Dentro de cien años vuestras sensaciones de odio, impotencia, fracaso, miedo no estarán en parte alguna y Franco al menos será siempre, para siempre una voz de diccionario enciclopédico, unas líneas en los manuales o en los vídeos o en los disquets, en cualquier soporte de memoria seleccionada para el futuro. Y en esas pocas líneas no cabrá vuestro sufrimiento, vuestra rabia, vuestro resentimiento. (652)

The supposedly objective view of history that Amescua is espousing is precisely the one that was radically undermined by Pombo's incorporation of many dissident historical memories into Franco's discourse. It is significant that the main forces at work in excluding the supposed "noises" from the text are economic and market considerations. Amescua has timed and organized the presentation of the book perfectly in order to maximize its market visibility and economic viability. It is to come out close enough in time to the anniversary of Franco's birth to be helped by the publicity but not so close as to be seen as an opportunistic endeavor. It will be promoted during the "Feria del Libro," and it will be launched as part of a series of new school books that will guarantee it a secure and stable market. Amescua reassures the unhappy Pombo that, with the elimination of all the "noises," the book will do very well given this marketing plan. He further hands Pombo a check with a million more pesetas than agreed upon, to appease the writer, who is not happy to see all the "noises" he has so carefully orchestrated removed from the text. Despite his objections to the elimination of those "noises" that represented his last gesture of resistance to Franco, Pombo ultimately surrenders to the forces of the market and the economy, or, more specifically, to the appeal of the check he has already pocketed. In an ironic twist on the technical discourse on "noise" that Amescua had bombarded him with earlier, he thinks:

El cheque ya estaba doblado en el bolsillo interior de mi chaqueta, es decir, habría mucho que hablar sobre la teoría del ruido, porque mientras mis labios tratan de oponer algún ruido al mensaje del cheque, mis dedos lo habían doblado casi sin que yo me diera cuenta y me lo había metido en

215

el bolsillo desde donde enviaba señales, mensajes por lo tanto, de seguridad. (653)

This power of the market, of the economy, is an ironic comment on Montalbán's part about the new forces of repression in the capitalist society of the transition. In an interview, Montalbán mentions this fact explicitly:

> Sin embargo, cuando desaparece el franquismo—al menos en lo que se refiere a Franco y al aparato más directo de represión—, la sociedad que se instaura es la que se ha venido preparando desde Franco y nos queda una cierta sensación de que ha cambiado algo, pero nada esencial. Ha cambiado, por ejemplo, que ya no hay represión ideológica directa y la única que existe es la de una economía de mercado y una cultura de mercado. (Padura Fuentes 47)

Autobiografía del general Franco demonstrates the way these market forces and culture of the market that have come to rule in the transition become a new form of repression. Pombo's book will, unfortunately, become one more of a slew of texts appearing in 1992 which, although perhaps presenting infinite new amounts of information about the figure of Franco, the man, will leave out, as his own text will ultimately leave out, all the voices of the defeated, erased from collective memory once again. Pombo can imagine the books that historians, following that supposedly objective view of their work that Amescua described, will present in the market-friendly year of 1992. He describes them to Franco in a dialogue he continues to have with the general even after he has finished his book:

> Los historiadores insistirán algo más pero le objetivarán y nos objetivarán: guerra de crueldades equivalentes, posguerra de autoritarismo a cambio de desarrollo . . . en fin, la historia es biplana y en ella no caben los ruidos, sean gemidos o gritos de rabia y terror. Y cada vez que un ciudadano del futuro lea la historia objetivada o presencie esos vídeos, será como si usted emergiera del horizonte conduciendo un fantasmal bulldozer negro dispuesto a cubrir con una capa más de tierra a todas sus víctimas de pensamiento, palabra, obra y omisión. (663)

Pombo is afraid that most of the books about Franco that will appear along with his will try to present a sanitized image of Franco and his regime. However, he harbors the hope that, in his book, even without the "noises," the dissenting voices and memories that he had included in the text, Franco will condemn himself through his own discourse, thanks to the contrast between his words and the reality around him: "Mientras volvía a casa pensaba que tal vez sin las notas críticas sin duda, ya que por la boca muere el pez, [Franco] se bastaba y sobraba para autocondenarse al infierno de la memoria del futuro" (653). Indeed, despite their physical elimination, the echoes of those "ruidos," of those "gemidos o gritos de rabia y terror" that Pombo had incorporated into the text will linger over the general's words, haunting them as much as the general's figure and legacy haunt the Spanish people.

In the real world, of course, those noises, those memories of the defeated, have not been completely silenced again, for they are part and parcel of Vázquez Montalbán's book. Appearing, as Pombo's was supposed to, in 1992, Vázquez Montalbán's novel, in some measure, has prevented that year from becoming yet another victory on Franco's part. Among the many history books that inevitably came out with a sanitized, revisionist view of the Franco years, Vázquez Montalbán's text, with its wide array of "ruidos," is making sure that the dictator has not been allowed, once more, to "cubrir con una capa más de tierra a todas sus víctimas de pensamiento, palabra, obra y omisión." Because of this, in a review of the book, Eduardo Haro Tecglen praises it as "un monumento antifranquista" (9).[10]

Not only has this novel salvaged from oblivion the cries of suffering and dissent of the defeated in Spain, but, as an example of what Linda Hutcheon calls historiographic metafiction, the text questions the very possibility of any objective, monolithic reconstruction of the past. As José Colmeiro claims, in studying this aspect of the novel, "*Autobiografía del general Franco* obliges us to examine the dissonant discourses of historiography and memory and to ascertain the political function of writing as counter-discourse" (338). Colmeiro further sees Vázquez Montalbán's novel as "a site of counter-memory, a massive memorial of resistance" (338).[11] In the definition given by Natalie Zemon Davis and Randolph Starn of Foucault's notion of counter-memory, this term implies "the residual or resistant strains that withstand official versions of historical continuity" (2). The noises that interrupted Franco's text within Montalbán's novel, as well as the noise that the novel itself represents in a historical time that would have preferred to put the more disturbing aspects of the memory of Franco and Francoism to rest, are elements that make of this novel a site of counter-memory. These noises guarantee that Vázquez Montalbán's novel becomes a massive memorial of resistance, as they embody the recuperation of the past of suffering and dissent that had been concealed by Francoism and that, unfortunately, in large part continued to be concealed during the transition.

A Noisy Resistance and a Resistant Noise

Memory is, in fact, the protagonist of both *Autobiografía de Federico Sánchez* and *Autobiografía del general Franco*. Both novels employ a similar narrative strategy: a supposedly autobiographical account by an individual is refracted into multiple memories that ultimately create a collective reconstruction of a concealed past of repression. In this sense, both novels become embodiments of a much needed return of the repressed.

Not only is the remembering self split in each case, but the autobiographical recuperation of the past is in turn refracted into a plural, often discordant chorus of multiple voices based on the integration into the work of a plethora of historical documents and texts. These novels do not just recover a history of repression. By underscoring their own process of construction and incorporating extraneous texts, they question any and all reconstructions of the past, showing them all to be based on textual interpretations, therefore never fully complete and always open to reinterpretation and dissent. These texts point to the past but also to the way the past is written, and rewritten, constantly. They reflect David Herzberger's characterization of certain postmodern texts:

> The double referencing by postmodern texts of other texts and of the powerful meanings that those texts are given in our lives, constitutes the principal reference of postmodern narrations. Double referencing therefore makes the postmodern emphasis on words more than a playful game of literary manipulation. It makes it, in fact, a political act of dissent. (143)

Indeed, each of these texts becomes a "political act of dissent," dissent from the implicit silencing of the past imposed during the transition. While Semprún's memory of the authoritarian legacy of the Spanish Communist Party becomes a noisy resistance to that process of silencing the past, Vázquez Montalbán's memory of the repression and suffering caused by Franco becomes a resistant noise interrupting that same process. Both texts are powerful and political acts of dissent, acts that, at least in some small measure, try to prevent the Spain of the transition from becoming a "Reino de desmemoriados."

Notes

1. I would like to express my gratitude to the Office of the Vice President for Research of the University of Minnesota for granting me a McKnight Summer Fellowship and a University of Minnesota Faculty Summer Fellowship in 1998 that made part of the research for this study possible. I would further like to thank Joan Ramon Resina for his continued support with this project, as well as John Kronik for his help, editorial and otherwise, in this and other projects, and Joanna Oconnell for her helpful comments on a first version of the essay.
2. Neither Morodo's nor Buckley's arguments present this revisionist interpretation. For a summary of one recent book that does, and a detailed rebuke of the revisionist rescue of Franco and his regime presented in its introduction, see Santos Juliá's "Un Fascismo bajo Palio, en Uniforme Militar."
3. For an interesting account of the way the memory of the Second Republic and the Civil War were constantly present, although continually repressed, during the transition, see Paloma Aguilar Fernández's *Memoria y olvido de la Guerra Civil española*.
4. The expression "el legado franquista" is the title of Carr's 1982 study in which he highlights, among other "legacies" of the Franco regime, this lack of popular involvement in politics: "persiste la sensación de que la política es algo de cierta manera remoto para el hombre de la calle" (133). For an in-depth look at some of these problematic "legacies" of the past that affect Spanish politics much more recently, through the time of the socialist governments, see Víctor Pérez-Díaz's well-documented study *The Return of Civil Society*. Another scholar who has

traced the legacies of the Franco regime through the years of the socialist governments is Joan Ramon Resina. Resina sees in the socialist government's gesture of winning the elections of 1982 on a promise to keep Spain out of NATO and then, once in power, forgetting that promise and negotiating Spain's entry into the alliance one more sign of the transition syndrome of conveniently forgetting the past when it serves one's interest to do so. In *El cadáver en la cocina: la novela criminal en la cultura del desencanto*, Resina explains the pernicious effects of this attitude: "Se olvidaban las promesas con que se había llegado al poder y se olvidaba la voluntad de transformarlo. En medio de la euforia democrática se olvidaba también lo poco que había conseguido la lucha antifranquista, el escaso apoyo que había tenido en la población española y lo insuficientemente democráticos que habían sido su organización y procedimientos. Se olvidaba que el franquismo había penetrado en el tejido social mucho más allá de las instituciones. Y esta capacidad de olvido alimentaba el desencanto. El régimen no había desaparecido, simplemente había recibido un baño de cal: la Constitución de 1978 (58-59)."

5. Although it does not address either of the two novels discussed here, Teresa Vilarós's book *El mono del desencanto: una crítica cultural de la transición española* is relevant to the present study. She incorporates de Certeau's use of the return of the repressed into her main argument, which is that the transition was characterized by a problematic, and unconscious, series of withdrawal symptoms left behind by the disappearance of the Franco regime.

6. These issues have significantly more importance in the text than I can develop in this study. For a more detailed analysis of these aspects of the text, see Nöel M. Valis's "Reader Exile and the Text: Jorge Semprún's *Autobiografía de Federico Sánchez*."

7. One of the reviewers of the book, upon its publication, stressed the dialogical dimension of the text: "La dialecticidad o diálogo entre los textos pasados y presentes es uno de los principios que caracterizan el proceso de desacralización ideológico-literaria de *Autobiografía de Federico Sánchez*" (Ortega 197).

8. The reproaches hurled at Semprún were many. Some claimed that the book inadvertently helped the right-wing campaign to delegitimize the Communist Party at the moment of its legal re-incorporation into Spanish politics (see José Vidal-Beneyto). Others criticized Semprún for displaying a partial and self-interested recuperation of memory, forgetting some of his own questionable actions in the past (see Javier Pradera). Others have highlighted the fact that, although Semprún criticizes the authoritarian methods of the Communist Party, he sometimes reproduces them in his own discourse, for example when he

220

accuses people not so much on the basis of facts but of speculation (see Sinnigen). This last observation is important and shows just how much the "legacies from the past" can come back to haunt one, even when one is explicitly trying to undo them.

9. In the nineties, Semprún will publish a sequel of sorts to *Autobiografía de Federico Sánchez*: *Federico Sánchez se despide de ustedes*. In this book he condemns the corruption and despotism he saw within the Socialist Party while he served, from 1988 to 1991, as its minister of culture. The need to combat the "desmemoria" of the transition and the issue of the "return of the repressed" remain important themes: "La transición democrática, en efecto—vuelvo a repetirlo: es un dato histórico fundamental—habrá sido un periodo de amnesia colectiva, espontánea o deliberada, henchida de mala conciencia tanto como de positiva y lúcida voluntad de reconciliación (294-95)." "¿No es precisamente la democracia el sistema que se nutre y se desarrolla en función de sus conflictos internos, asumidos y gestionados en la transparencia social de una participación ciudadana? ¿No habrá llegado el momento de dominar colectivamente el "retorno de lo reprimido", de salir de nuestra amnesia voluntaria de los contenidos de la guerra civil, para abordarlos en fin—sin espíritu de retorno, de revancha o de rencor, naturalmente—con la voluntad de un avance social que no tenga en cuenta ni los mitos del pasado ni los silencios u olvidos del presente? (111)."

10. In his review, Haro Tecglen mentions some of the most blatantly revisionist books about Franco to appear in 1992.

11. I recommend Colmeiro's "Dissonant Voices: Memory and Counter-Memory in Manuel Vázquez Montalbán's *Autobiografía del general Franco*" for an in-depth reading of the fascinating way in which this novel problematizes such issues as authorship, the nature of autobiography, and historical referentiality. Colmeiro mentions a review by Michael Ugarte of Paul Preston's book *Franco: A Biography*. In "Still Seriously Dead," Ugarte critiques the sanitized historical approach to Franco that Preston's book presents. It is precisely the approach to Franco and his regime that Pombo, in *Autobiografía del general Franco*, is afraid will ultimately prevail.

Works Cited

Aguilar Fernández, Paloma. *Memoria y olvido de la Guerra Civil española.* Madrid: Alianza, 1996.

Bakhtin, M.M. *The Dialogic Imagination.* Ed. Michael Holquist. Trans. Caryl Emerson and Michael Holquist. Austin: U of Texas P, 1981.

Buckley, Ramón. *La doble transición: política y literatura en la España de los años setenta.* Madrid: Siglo Veintiuno de España, 1996.

Carr, Raymond. "El legado franquista." *España: 1975-1980: conflictos y logros de la democracia.* Ed. José L. Cagigao, John Crispin, and Enrique Pupo-Walker. Madrid: José Porrúa Turanzas, 1982: 129-40.

Certeau, Michel de. *The Writing of History.* Trans. Tom Conley. New York: Columbia UP, 1988.

Colmeiro, José F. "Dissonant Voices: Memory and Counter-Memory in Manuel Vázquez Montalbán's *Autobiografía del general Franco.*" *Studies in Twentieth Century Literature* 21.2 (1997): 337-59.

Davis, Natalie Zemon and Randolph Starn. "Introduction." *Representations* 26 (1989): 1-6.

Gazarian Gautier, Marie-Lise. *Interviews with Spanish Writers.* Elmwood Park: Dalkey Archive P, 1991.

González Cabezas, José Ramón. "¿Hacia la tercera transición?" *La Vanguardia,* Suplemento Revista 2 Aug. 1998: 8.

Haro Tecglen, Eduardo. "Un monumento antifranquista: El desdoblamiento de Manuel Vázquez Montalbán." *El País,* Suplemento Libros 31 Oct. 1992: 9-10.

Herzberger, David. *Narrating the Past: Fiction and Historiography in Postwar Spain.* Durham: Duke UP, 1995.

Hutcheon, Linda. *A Poetics of Postmodernism: History, Theory, Fiction.* New York: Routledge, 1988.

Isaia, Nino, and Edgardo Sogno. *Due fronti: la grande polemica sulla guerra di Spagna.* Florence: Liberal Libri, 1998.

Juliá, Santos. "Un Fascismo bajo Palio, en Uniforme Militar." *El País,* Suplemento Babelia 18 July 1998: 12-13.

Morán, Gregorio. *El precio de la transición.* Barcelona: Planeta, 1991.

Morodo, Raúl. *La transición política.* Madrid: Tecnos, 1984.

Ortega, José. Rev. of *Autobiografía de Federico Sánchez* by Jorge Semprún. *Cuadernos Hispanoamericanos* 340 (1978): 192-98.

"El Pacto, un desconocido." *Cambio 16* 15 Jan. 1978: 20-21.

Padura Fuentes, Leonardo. "Reivindicación de la memoria: entrevista con Manuel Vázquez Montalbán." *Quimera* 106-107 (1991): 47-53.

Pérez-Díaz, Víctor. *The Return of Civil Society: The Emergence of Democratic Spain.* Cambridge: Harvard UP, 1993.

Portoghesi, Paolo. *After Modern Architecture.* Trans. Meg Shore. New York: Rizzoli, 1992.

Pradera, Javier. "Las verdades parciales de Semprún." *Cambio 16* 8 Jan. 1978: 16.

Resina, Joan Ramon. *El cadáver en la cocina: la novela criminal en la cultura del desencanto.* Barcelona: Anthropos, 1997.

Semprún, Jorge. *Autobiografía de Federico Sánchez.* Barcelona: Planeta, 1977.

———. *Federico Sánchez se despide de ustedes.* Barcelona: Tusquets, 1993.

Sinnigen, Jack. *Narrativa e ideología.* Madrid: Nuestra Cultura, 1982.

Subirats, Eduardo. *Después de la Lluvia: Sobre la ambigua modernidad española.* Madrid: Temas de Hoy, 1993.

Ugarte, Michael. "Still Seriously Dead." Rev. of *Franco: a Biography* by Paul Preston. *The Nation* 2 Jan. 1995: 24-26.

Valis, Nöel M. "Reader Exile and the Text: Jorge Semprún's *Autobiografía de Federico Sánchez.*" *Monographic Review/ Revista Monográfica* 2 (1986): 174-87.

Vargas Llosa, Mario. *Contra viento y marea (1972-1983).* Vol. 2. Barcelona: Seix Barral, 1983.

Vázquez Montalbán, Manuel. *Autobiografía del general Franco.* Barcelona: Planeta, 1992.

Vidal-Beneyto, José. *Diario de una ocasión perdida: materiales para un principio.* Barcelona: Kairós, 1981.

Vilarós, Teresa. *El mono del desencanto: una crítica cultural de la transición española (1973-1993).* Madrid: Siglo Veintiuno, 1998.

10

Autobiografía del General Franco: un problema lingüístico

Manuel Vázquez Montalbán

Cuando en 1998 el escritor chileno Miguel Rojas Mix me pidió un artículo sobre el franquismo y sus orígenes, se me ocurrió un título que traducía mi punto de partida analítico de las raíces del franquismo: "1898-1936: el huevo de la serpiente"; es decir, el noventayochismo como ideología difuminada que había llevado a la coartada del regeneracionismo militarista. Cuando escribí *Autobiografía del general Franco* viajé a su ciudad de origen, El Ferrol, y no sólo físicamente sino desde la memoria histórica traté de reconstruir la atmósfera que constituyó el gaseoso *país de la infancia* del futuro dictador. Franco dejó un nítido autorretrato psicológico en el guión de la película *Raza*, que firmó con el seudónimo Jaime de Andrade y que reflejó en positivo todos los traumas en negativo de su infancia de hijo de un padre librepensador, masón, mujeriego, que tan mal vivir dio a su mujer, Doña Pilar, idealizada por Franco como la madre natural y como la madre España, sufridora y vejada por la masonería y el marxismo internacional. Cuando se produjo la derrota de 1898, Franco tenía seis años y estaba siendo educado en un colegio de su propio barrio con la formación típica de un hijo de oficial de la Armada en una ciudad cerrada, ensimismada, cuyo nivel económico y cultural dependía del Arsenal Militar, de la construcción de barcos de guerra y de la instalación de oficiales y marinos de la Armada. El padre de Franco, Nicolás, era un hombre de cierto nivel cultural, muy viajado, con pasados destinos en Filipinas y Cuba, dedicado a dar una información cosmogónica y fantasiosa a sus hijos y al sobrino huérfano, Franco Salgado Araujo. La educación espiritual, emocional, patriótica, Franco la recibió sobre todo de su madre, apostólica dama de la Adoración Nocturna, evidencia misma de que la *Imitación de Cristo* no erraba y que la vida es dolor. La memoria histórica de la ciudad estaba controlada por la filosofía militarista y patriotera de la vida y de la Historia, desde la conciencia de ciudad fundamental para el sistema defensivo de España y que había sufrido asaltos ingleses en tiempos de zozobra, asaltos no siempre rechazados, pero que dejaron una memoria épica convencional.

> ¿Qué es aquello que aparece
> en lo alto de la Graña?
> Son los ingleses que quieren
> separar Ferrol de España.

En las lecturas familiares dirigidas por Doña Pilar, el hermano mayor, Nicolás, ya manifestaba su espíritu burlón como el de su padre y desafecto a la disciplina, pero Franco era un niño obediente que expresaba con una vocecita gangosa la concepción de España que le trasmitían su madre y la escuela.

> España es la patria mía
> y la patria de mi raza
> miras hacia el Nuevo Mundo
> al Viejo vuelves la espalda.

Tal era el estado de falsa conciencia que habitaba en la sabiduría convencional de la España de final de siglo, y aunque los intelectuales regeneracionistas habían presagiado la catástrofe y los políticos conocían lo suficiente la situación como para pensar que Filipinas, Cuba y Puerto Rico no eran conservables, circulaba la castiza ideología de la majeza que menospreciaba cuanto ignoraba, por ejemplo el poderío real de los Estados Unidos y el grado de complicidad en Cuba entre criollismo y capas populares para sacudirse el dominio político español. Según me reveló la sobrina socialista de Franco, Pilar Jaray Franco, uno de los poemas recitados en el hogar de su tío y su madre, y que habían llegado a ella desde la tradición familiar, era una declaración de tópicos e intenciones sobre la relación idealizada entre España y lo que le quedaba de las colonias:

> Al occidente de Europa
> Se halla la fértil España,
> Por altos montes y mares
> En contorno resguardada.

226

Al norte los Pirineos
La dividen de la Francia;
Sirviendo sus altas cumbres
De límite y muralla.

Dos mares, al mediodía,
Sus costas en torno bañan;
Y un estrecho las divide
De las costas africanas.

Galicia yace al ocaso,
Al Portugal apegada,
Y el Atlántico es el foso
Que defiende aquellas playas.

En tanto que por Oriente
El Mediterráneo aguarda
A las naves que algún día
Fueron a Grecia y a Italia.

No lejos las Baleares
Recuerdan su antigua fama,
Por los célebres honderos,
Terribles en las batallas.

Mientras a extremo opuesto
Descúbrense las Canarias,
Como descanso y refugio
En navegaciones largas.

Por aquella nueva senda
Fueron los hijos de España
A conquistar otro mundo
Con una cruz y una espada.
....

De modo que donde quiera
Se ven las señales claras

De que el sol a todas horas
Tierra española alumbraba.

Cuando Franco era niño jugaba a capitanes y a matar *mambises*, los odiados guerrilleros que se habían enfrentado a las tropas españolas de ocupación. Franco en *Raza* se inventa una situación familiar idealizada en la que su secretamente ansiada *muerte del padre* se traduce en la heroica muerte en el 98, en aguas cubanas, del padre literaturizado y elevado a la categoría de noble marino, Churruca. El padre real, grandote, de ojos caídos, estrecho de hombros, excesivamente amplio de caderas para su contextura, locuaz, bebedor y mujeriego, era muy crítico con la estrategia política y militar seguida por el Estado español en las antiguas colonias y algunas de sus afirmaciones sonaban a blasfemia librepensadora y masónica. La falsa conciencia sobre la situación real provocó desencanto en las masas víctimas del tópico e irritación entre los militares que acusaron al poder civil de entreguismo y de incompetencia. Hay que recordar que buena parte de los profesores que Franco encontraría en la Academia militar de Toledo, habían vivido el desastre como oficiales y conservado un gran resentimiento contra políticos, intelectuales y civiles en general, que al día siguiente de la derrota consideraron que la corrupción político-militar había sido la causante fundamental del descalabro y los más jóvenes intelectuales, como ha demostrado Blanco Aguinaga en *Juventud del 98*, preconizaban por aquellas fechas un radicalismo panrevolucionario. Las grandes potencias reales y una potencia en decadencia total como España, construyen en el tránsito del XIX al XX una ideología militarista y anticivil, a la vista de que la expansión imperialista tenía en los militares su principal sujeto agente y de que en situaciones de crisis social condicionadas por la lucha de clases, eran finalmente los militares quienes reestablecían el orden. En la memoria de Franco quedó el agravio del 98 asumido en plena infancia, como en la memoria del cadete de quince años quedaría el susto de la Semana Trágica de Barcelona y el agravio de la conjura internacional propagandística de descrédito del Estado español que siguió a la ejecución asesinato de Ferrer i Guardia. Unamos a estos dos tumores cerebrales el generado por el expediente Picazo tras el desastre del Anual y tendremos las tres patas del rearme ideológico militarista de los cuatro generales que se alzaron en 1936 contra la legalidad republicana. Uno de ellos, el tantas veces descerebrado Queipo de LLano, había participado, tan intempestivo e imprevisible como siempre, en las últimas luchas imperiales, así como el sanguinario Millán Astray, modelo épico de Franco durante la constitución de la Legión Extranjera. Aquellos militares colonialistas, luego llamados africanistas porque trataron de acrecentar sus carreras en las guerras de Africa, tenían en sus cerebros más el vejamen abstracto sufrido por España en el 98 como entidad metafísica o los problemas que sus carreras habían experimentado como consecuencia de la definitiva pérdida del imperio, que los sufrimientos de las tropas enfrentadas a una apabullante logística militar norteamericana y al irreversible impulso emancipador de los cubanos o filipinos. Las clases populares españolas sí extrajeron de la derrota la conclusión de que habían entregado a sus hijos a una carnicería sin sentido y conservaron esta memoria para enfrentarse a las levas para las guerras africanas, enfrentamiento que culmina en la Semana Trágica de Barcelona de 1909. La carnicería sufrida por los soldados españoles fue testimoniada, y a veces con complejo de culpa, por los propios memorialistas norteamericanos, como refleja Sebastian Balfour en *El fin del Imperio español*. El historiador inglés describe una de las situaciones de exterminio padecidas por los soldados españoles y cita como testimonio una fuente norteamericana, el cronista Feuer, autor de *The Santiago Campaign*:

> No obstante, también es verdad que muchos soldados españoles habían llegado hacía muy poco y eran jóvenes y bisoños. Vestidos con sombreros de paja, uniformes blancos de algodón y alpargatas, muchos fueron barridos por las ametralladoras Gatling y el fuego artillero de los norteamericanos. Un soldado raso de los Rough Riders describió el lastimero cuadro de las posiciones defensivas españolas después de la batalla por las colinas de San Juan: "Cuando llegamos a las trincheras españolas, en la vertiente norte de las colinas de San Juan, vimos la obra de las ametralladoras Gatling. La mayor parte de los españoles habían sido heridos en la cabeza, algunos dos y tres veces. Así que, válgame Dios, parecían niños de unos doce años de edad. Cientos de ellos yacían allí muertos. Era un espectáculo lastimoso. Todos nosotros nos sentimos avergonzados de nosotros mismos".

Por otra parte, el corte de relación con las colonias significó la decadencia económica de El Ferrol, la aparición de malestar social ante la pérdida de puestos de trabajo, protestas, aparición de formas orgánicas del movimiento obrero, la escisión ideológica en una ciudad que se regía por la hegemonía de la aristocracia militar, pero también contaba entre sus hijos a Pablo Iglesias, fundador del PSOE y de UGT. Franco detestó desde la infancia el desorden social y sustentó en aquellos años su convicción de que los civiles no daban garantías para el mantenimiento del orden, según las tesis militaristas que llegaron posteriormente a las academias militares siguiendo el análisis del general Fanjul, autor de *Misión social del Ejército*, inspirada en el estudio del general francés Lyautey sobre la importancia del poder militar.

Franco, Franco, Franco

No obstante, se suele hablar mucho más de las causas psicológicas del voluntarismo autoritario de Franco, tal vez porque los historiadores que así hacen, al culpar a Franco como exclusivo culpable del franquismo, exculpan a los sectores sociales que lo hicieron posible, le respaldaron durante la guerra y durante la larga postguerra. Los argumentos psicologistas no son despreciables. Desde que nació, Franco comprobó que cuantos le rodeadan tendían a llamarle Paquito y al ingresar en la Academia de Infantería le bautizaron Franquito. Su estatura empezó a agigantarse a partir de su primera misión en Africa. Años después fue tres veces Franco, porque en los resúmenes de prensa de sus discursos siempre *trascendentales*, se concretaba así la explosión espontánea de las masas: Franco, Franco, Franco, que evoca la eufonía de Sanctus, Sanctus, Sanctus.

Para entonces ya el cardenal primado Plá y Deniel había decretado: "Mandamos a todos los sacerdotes que desde el día de la ratificación del Concordato, en el curso de la santa misa, rezada o cantada, exceptuando las misas de difuntos, en las primeras oraciones, en las secretas y en las poscomuniones añadan a la oración *Et formulas* las palabras *Ducem nostrum Franciscum.*" Entre el Franquito y el Caudillo por la Gracia de Dios hubiera sido correcto un injusto término medio para una persona que fue bautizada el 17 de diciembre de 1892 en la parroquia castrense de

230

San Francisco, en El Ferrol, como Francisco Hermenegildo Paulino Teódulo más un montón de apellidos paternos y maternos, según la costumbre de la época y de la gente de posibles. Los Franco no tenían demasiado dinero, pero en El Ferrol los oficiales de Marina eran como una casta aristocrática y endogámica. Paquito, para los niños de su edad, para su familia, diminutivo con el que nunca se sentiría a gusto, sobre todo porque a su primo Francisco Franco Salgado Araujo, más alto, le llamaban Pacón, a pesar de que era huérfano y tenía en la familia Franco Bahamonde el trato de ahijado del padre, don Nicolás. Además, según reveló su hermana Pilar, a Franco, de pequeño, los otros niños le llamaban cerillita por la poca cosa que era en comparación su primo. Paquito y Pacón. Así se relacionaron durante años, hasta que, compañeros de carrera militar, el huérfano Pacón se convirtió en el perpetuo actor secundario en el reparto, *el amigo del chico*, el hombre que ya a punto de morir dejaría escrita su amargura por lo mucho que le había dado a su primo y lo poco que había recibido.

Se le empezó a llamar Franquito en la Academia de Infantería de Toledo, donde ingresó en 1907, tras un viaje desde El Ferrol acompañado por su padre, del que hay testimonio directo redactado por el propio Franco, según consta en el libro de su último médico de cabecera, el doctor Pozuelo, que le incitó a recordar y redactar unas memorias para reactivar al alicaído Franco posterior a la crisis de la flebitis. Una página interesante por lo que revela de constantes de su vida: relación con el padre, retórica en los ojos y en la comprensión de la historia.

> He de confesar que este primer viaje con mi padre, rígido y adusto, no resultara divertido, pues te faltaba la confianza y la solicitud que le hicieran cordial. ¡Qué diferencia con los futuros viajes con los compañeros! Entrando en la dilatada llanura de Castilla, el tren parece precipitarse, con propósito, sin duda, de ganarse el retraso acumulado en la parte montañosa del recorrido. Bajo ese traqueteo del tren, necesitábamos pasar la noche, para amanecer en el cruce de la sierra. Allí quedaba Ávila, recoleta tras sus viejas murallas. Y más abajo, El Escorial, desde donde Felipe II gobernaba el mundo. Y, enseguida, el llano de Madrid, con sus modestos pueblos y diminutas colonias veraniegas. Y, tras una dilatada parada, para conceder la entrada, la llegada a la estación del Norte, donde esperaba la algarabía de los mozos de cuerda y la salida a la espera de los

coches de punto y los ómnibus de los hoteles. Ya estamos en el Madrid feliz de los 500.000 habitantes. El paso por Madrid no pudo ser más rápido. Unas horas para asearse, visitar a unos parientes y recoger una carta de recomendación, para volver, a la tarde, a tomar el tren para Toledo. Así, salvo el paso a través de las avenidas y calles principales, quedaba para mí, inestimable, la capital de España. Esto de la carta de recomendación era cosa que yo no alcanzaba a entender. Me parecía un vicio que arrastraba la sociedad, que no podría tener influencia en el ingreso en un establecimiento militar y que podría alcanzar efectos contrarios a los pretendidos. Así se lo expresé a mi padre, que acabó por comprenderlo. Por otra parte, las cartas en sí carecían de valor. ¡Quién iba a decirme entonces que, 21 años después, me iba a corresponder, como director de la Academia General Militar, el corregir estos abusos!... Mediada la tarde, en un viaje en tren de dos horas, salimos para Toledo. Próximos a la llegada, al cruzar la vega, se nos presentó la vista magnífica de la ciudad, coronada sobre la cumbre por su alcázar y, más abajo, la catedral y los principales monumentos asomándose sobre las casas de la vieja urbe. Frente a la estación, nos esperaban las típicas galeras tiradas por seis caballos que, cruzando el Tajo por el viejo puente de Alcántara iban a enfrentarse con la dura faena de remontar la cuesta del Miradero, que da acceso a la típica plaza de Zocodover, mentidero y centro comercial de la población, y en donde se dislocaba el tráfico, para tomar por el laberinto de las estrechas y sombreadas callejuelas, que imprimieron su carácter a esta antigua población dormida en el tiempo. Allí nos esperaba el que había de ser mi apoderado durante mi futura estancia en la academia, quien nos pilotó hasta la calle del Horno de Bizcochos, en la que estaba el alojamiento que nos había buscado para nuestra estancia en la ciudad. El día siguiente había sido señalado para mi presentación en el alcázar. La impresión que me produjo la entrada, la grandeza de su patio de armas, presidida por la estatua de Carlos V, con aquella leyenda de su base: "Quedaré muerto en África o entraré vencedor en Túnez", fue inenarrable. La emoción que me producían esos lugares gloriosos, con sus piedras seculares, embargaba mi ánimo y desbordaba mis ilusiones.

Es curioso que en *Raza*, el personaje positivo, José, él mismo, también lance un canto a lo que se puede aprender en las piedras frente al conocimiento frío de los libros. También aprovechó *Raza* para hacer un ajuste de cuentas a los *primeros de la clase*. Él nunca lo fue. Al contrario, un estudiante del montón, situado en el escalafón de notas muy por detrás de don Camilo Alonso Vega, amigo de infancia y futuro ministro de la Gobernación. Y es que Franco, Franquito, lo pasó muy mal en sus primeros meses de estancia en aquella academia. Casi un niño, frágil, con una voz retenida por el frenillo, le llamaban Franquito y le ofrecían los mosquetones más pequeñitos, a la medida del diminutivo. Hasta que un día, harto de aguantar novatadas, cogió una lámpara y se la tiró a la cabeza al cabecilla de los provocadores... Dejaron de importunarle, pero siguieron llamándole Franquito. Sus compañeros de promoción le recordaron años después según sus afinidades ideológicas pero poco hablaban sobre el período de la academia y empezaban a agigantarle la estatura a partir de su primera misión en Africa. Del Franquito de la academia, Vicente Guarner, militar republicano que vivió un largo exilio, lo recuerda como un gallego poco culto, tímido, receloso, y se compromete a decir que de haber hecho una encuesta en la Academia de Toledo sobre cuál de aquellos aspirantes a oficial podría llegar a caudillo, Franco no hubiera estado en las listas. ¿Despecho del vencido? Es posible; pero no deja de ser cierto que la biografía gloriosa de los franquistas suele vitaminizarse y cargarse de proteínas a partir de la primera misión en África, y sobre todo tras la gravísima herida que recibió en El Biutz en junio de 1916. Pero a pesar de su buen comportamiento durante las batallas, demostrando un desprecio de vida propia y ajena que sorprendía por su frialdad calculada, siguió siendo Franquito para los altos oficiales, y todavía Sanjurjo en 1936, cada vez que dudaba si Franco se decidía o no a intervenir en el Alzamiento, preguntaba: "¿Qué va a hacer Franquito?"

El estudiante tímido, ordenancista, mirón de piedras, receptor de una historia y una filosofía de la vida filtrada por la endogamia cultural de la academia, callejeante por un Toledo que sólo le ofrecía barberos callejeros, mentideros y poca cosa más para su asignación de dos pesetas para gastos, cambió de psicología cuando se hizo soldado en guerra, pero en función de ese escenario y de los reflejos que le despertaba la convivencia con gente militar. En la vida privada seguía siendo un muchacho inseguro en los ambientes donde no podía aplicar las ordenanzas de Carlos III o los reglamentos militares particulares. En Melilla se enamoró de una muchacha, Sofía Subirán, hija de un coronel, y ya muerto Franco, la anciana ex cortejada de Franquito se confesaba a Vicente Gracia:

¿Que cómo era Franco? Fino, muy fino. Atento, todo un caballero. Si se enfadaba tenía un poco de genio, pero en plan fino. Tenía mucho carácter y era muy amable. Entonces era delgadísimo. Parece mentira cómo cambió luego. Conmigo era exageradamente atento. A veces te fatigaba. Me trataba como a una persona mayor y eso que yo era casi una niña... Estaba en la plaza de Melilla casi todos los días, el paseo por las tardes o por las mañanas en el parque de Hernández... No, no me contaba chistes, no tenía ocurrencias... Tal vez creo que era demasiado serio para lo joven que era. Tal vez por eso no me gustaba, me aburría un poco.

Y más adelante, doña Sofía sanciona: "Debió ser un buen marido, sí. Aburridito el pobre, sí, pero bueno...".

Toda la inseguridad de Franco en la vida privada, entre civiles, se convertía en su contrario cuando entraba en el cuartel o en campaña. Tenía fama de reglamentista, duro, implacable, exageradamente implacable hasta la crueldad, pero también exigente consigo mismo y concienzudo en sus movimientos de liturgia militar o de guerra. Y allí se construyó la base de su pedestal de oficial africanista, muy diferente a los otros militares *echaos palante*, puteros, jugadores de la soldada, de valor caliente. Él antes de atacar ponía los prismáticos entre él y el enemigo. Los otros oficiales solían echarle muchos testículos al asunto... Franco examinaba, calculaba y luego sacaba de su frenillo toda la voz que podía para anunciar la carga. Esta diferencia de talante le creó admiradores entre sus compañeros de mando más cabestros y entre la alta oficialidad (Berenguer o Sanjurjo), que enseguida reconocieron en él a un oficial con porvenir. Los moros decían que tenía *baraka*, algo así como buena suerte, y que *sabía manera*, es decir, que sabía mandar. La oficialidad africanista era muy dada al autobombo propiciador de ascensos, hasta el punto de que los oficiales de la Península se sintieron molestos y acusaban a sus compañeros en campaña africana de exagerar hazañas para acumular méritos y ascensos. Pero aquella oficialidad africana joven, respaldada por veteranos como Millán Astray o Sanjurjo o los mismísimos Berenguer, Queipo de Llano, Silvestre, ya empezaba a ser un grupo de presión dentro del Ejército, un *lobby* como diríamos ahora, que tenía acceso directo al rey. Y el propio rey bien pronto preguntaría por Franquito, y le llamaba Franquito años después, cuando ya era general, y no por la estatura, sino porque le hacía gracia lo grave que se ponía aunque hablara de las plagas del cerezo, y el tonillo de gallego con las palabras justas y la prudencia en el gatillo.

Abc fue un diario muy importante en la historia de España, lo sigue siendo, y en la de Franco. De hecho el futuro generalísimo era seguidor de *Abc* porque era el diario de su madre y porque le emocionó aquella carta de Luca de Tena protestando contra la conjura internacional antiespañola a raíz del ajusticiamiento de Ferrer i Guardia tras la Semana Trágica de 1909. Pero también debería a *Abc* buena parte de su prestigio militar en la Península, cimentado por los corresponsales del diario en la guerra de África y muy especialmente por *Tebib Arrumi*, seudónimo de Ruiz Gallardón, abuelo del actual antagonista de Leguina en el Gobierno de la comunidad autónoma de Madrid. Entre los biógrafos laudatorios de Franco aparece otro abuelo de un nieto hoy importante, don Manuel Aznar, pretérita semilla del actual José María Aznar, cabeza del PP. También fue *Abc* quien utilizara por primera vez la calificación de *caudillo* aplicada a Franco. A raíz de su boda con doña Carmen Polo Meléndez Valdés, le llamaba *el joven caudillo,* y con razón, porque era joven y había llegado a jefe de la Legión y a emparentar con una rica familia de Oviedo, muy por encima de los niveles de pequeñísima burguesía militar ferrolana de los Franco.

Dos testimonios complementarios señalan ese salto de mando y estado de los años veinte como la clave del progresivo acercamiento de Franquito a ¡Franco, Franco, Franco! Otra vez Guarner señala ese tiempo de glorioso herido de guerra, destinado a Oviedo y prometido a doña Carmen, como el arranque de su definitivo complejo de excelencia:

Desde entonces se despertaron en él ambiciones ilimitadas y un inmenso complejo *señoritil* de vanidad v presunción, rayando el narcisismo. Incluso había cambiado su aspecto, adelgazando y ostentando fino bigotito. Medía prudentemente todos sus pasos y acciones, y en Oviedo, en un destino poco militar, como era la zona de reclutamiento, podía aguardar tranquilamente ascensos sucesivos y el acceso al generalato, figurando en la *sociedad* local, tan admirablemente retratada por Clarín en *La Regenta,* con aspiraciones a la mano de una señorita adinerada (con disminuida fortuna, de origen indiano), sin mucho éxito inicial. Cuando el inconmensurable histrión que era Millán Astray organizó, bajo el patrocinio regio, la Legión Extranjera, imitada de Francia, escribió a los tres comandantes de Infantería más jóvenes para mandar *banderas,* pequeños batallones, y Franco mandó la primera de ellas, con imposición de una disciplina que rayaba en la crueldad. El *pelotón de castigo* trabajaba duramente, con las mochilas rellenas de piedras, y eran fusilados sistemáticamente los legionarios indisciplinados. Franco no tuvo nunca prejuicios humanitarios. La compasión y la piedad ante los sufrimientos de sus semejantes no entraban en su mentalidad. Se cubrió, desde entonces, con una falsa máscara impasible y severa.

La boda de una Polo Meléndez Valdés no era un trueque desigual. Ella aportaba posibles y apellidos sonoros, pero Franco ya era gentilhombre del rey. A la boda asiste la familia del novio, menos el padre, desde 1907 residente en Madrid, donde hacía vida marital con una buena mujer que tenía estudios de maestra de escuela, aunque los Franco, menos Pilar Jaraiz, siempre dijeron de ella que era una "chacha" que se había aprovechado del viejo. La sobrina de Francisco Franco, Pilar Jaraiz, era una niña que formó parte del cortejo de la novia y años después comentaría que, a partir de aquel enlace, Franco se había ido distanciando de su familia ferrolana paulatinamente, entre 1923 y 1939; distanciamiento acentuado cuando los Franco Polo emparentaron con los Martínez Bordiu, altos, bronceados, con título nobiliario, frente a la gordura y la escasa estatura y la drogadicción por el lacón grelos de los Franco. A Francisco Franco le gustaba el lacón, pero a doña Carmen la ponía nerviosa. En *Historia de una disidencia,* la sobrina socialista de Pilar Jaraiz, hija de doña Pilar y reinstauradora del PSOE en Barcelona en los años del tardofranquismo, escribe:

> Nostalgia del tiempo pasado, sí, y desencanto del tiempo que había de venir. Porque, recordando ahora todo lo que allí pasó, pienso en los cambios que experimentan las personas. ¿Por qué los protagonistas de aquellos acontecimientos llegaron a convertirse en unos seres extraños a mí, ajenos? Y no lo digo como es natural por mi abuela, que siguió siendo la misma hasta su muerte. Pero ¿y los demás? ¿Qué se hizo del cariño, intimidad que nos unía? ¿Qué de la confianza y de la llaneza en el trato? ¿A qué vino más tarde tanta sequedad y dureza? Porque es lo cierto que hasta a mi madre se la recibía a veces a regañadientes. A mi madre, la única hermana del jefe del Estado y en cuya casa habían pasado tantas temporadas e incluso durante una de sus estancias se había operado mi tía

236

Carmen de las amígdalas y mis padres les habían cedido su propio cuarto. Dígase lo que se diga, la actitud de despego no partió de mí cuando empecé a concienciarme. Tampoco yo era entonces la misma. Pero el cambio de posición hizo de aquella familia unos seres llenos de despego, inamistosos, altaneros. ¿Por qué? ¿Les parecíamos poco? ¿Ambicionaban alternar con personas de mayor alcurnia? ¿Tanto había cambiado Franco desde que asumió la jefatura del Estado? ¿Y la familia Polo? ¿Qué se hizo de su trato cortés y amable? ¿Dónde quedaba su cariño? Y mirándolo desde otro punto de vista, ¿cuál había sido nuestro delito?, ¿les habíamos hecho algún daño? o ¿es que nuestra posición social les parecía poco?

Complementa la impresión de Guarner o la de Pilar Jaraiz el testimonio de Hidalgo de Cisneros, oficial aviador, piloto de hidroaviones durante la guerra de África:

También hice varios viajes con Francisco Franco, que había ascendido aquellos días a teniente coronel, y por el cual nunca sentí la menor simpatía. En la base de Mar Chica lo detestábamos, empezando por su hermano Ramón, con el que casi no se hablaba. Cuando pedían un *hidro* para el teniente coronel Francisco Franco, todos procurábamos eludir el servicio, pues nos molestaba su actitud. Llegaba a la base siempre puntualísimo y siempre serio. Muy estirado, para parecer más alto y disimular su tripita ya incipiente. Según nos decía su hermano, siempre tuvo el complejo de su pequeña estatura y de su tendencia a engordar. Nos saludaba muy reglamentario, ponía mala cara o decía algo desagradable si el *hidro* no estaba listo. Montaba al lado del piloto y no soltaba palabra hasta llegar al sitio de destino. Allí se despedía también muy militarmente, sin haber abandonado un solo instante su aspecto antipático de persona perfecta.

No recuerdo nunca haberlo visto sonreír ni tener un gesto amable o humano. Con sus compañeros del Tercio era igual o quizá más seco; se veía que lo respetaban y temían, pues como militar tenía mucho prestigio, pero sin la menor muestra de amistad o de afecto. Franco es antipático desde que era célula.

Pero la hagiografía franquista opone a estas *apariencias*, posiblemente interesadas, comentarios como el de Petain, que conoció a Franco en las campañas africanas y que, después de la batalla de Alhucemas, dijo de él: "Es la espada más limpia de Europa".

Tras la batalla de Alhucemas, que compensaba el desastre de El Annual e iniciaba el principio del fin de las guerras africanas, Franco asciende a general. Ya es el general más joven de Europa y, con Goded, el militar joven más valorado por los entendidos. De ahí que no sorprendiera a nadie que, mientras Goded se llevaba con el general Primo de Rivera las glorias de ultimar la pacificación en Marruecos, a Franco se le encargara la Academia Militar de Zaragoza. Ya pocos le llamaban Franquito; sólo los más viejos de la milicia. El personaje ha cambiado. En Madrid se codea con la oligarquía asturiana (su mujer), la Casa Real, la alta oficialidad, y hasta asiste a una tertulia política en casa del ex-ministro Natalio Rivas. Allí aparece por primera vez un Franco locuaz, que no siempre calla ante lo que no entiende. Es el mismo Franco locuaz que tratará de dar una lección de economía a Calvo Sotelo, dejándole perplejo ante una exhibición de nacionalismo económico autárquico que desbordaba el talante no excesivamente abierto del señor ministro. También salió de actor de cine en una sobremesa de casa de Natalio Rivas y presumía de ser un buen filmador de escenas de lo cotidiano, coincidente con Lenin en la importancia propagandística que iba a adquirir el aún llamado séptimo arte. Como director de la academia persiguió las novatadas y la sífilis, dos de sus cuatro obsesiones persecutorias. Las otras dos, el comunismo y la masonería. Las novatadas, porque las había padecido; la sífilis, porque la temía como una consecuencia de los desórdenes de la sexualidad. El comunismo, porque leía una revista francesa dedicada a impedir que la Tercera Internacional penetrara en los ejércitos de Europa, revista a la que le había suscrito Primo de Rivera. Su odio a la masonería es consecuencia de lo que aprendió en los libros de devoción y desinformación histórica de su infancia y del espectáculo de la masonería influyendo en carreras militares y en la ruina del imperio español. Pero la masonería siempre le siguió como una sombra. Su hermano Ramón fue masón. Su padre admiraba a los masones y despreciaba a Paquito como político. Uno de los más importantes jefes sindicales fraguados en la Cruzada, Salvador Merino, resultó ser masón. Su fotógrafo particular, Campúa, había sido masón, y tanto doña Carmen como su hija siempre desconfiaron de que hubiera dejado de serlo. En cuanto a la sífilis, también se burló alguna vez de sus terrores. Paul

Preston, autor de una biografía de Franco, me contaba que altísimos cargos del franquismo de después de la guerra fueron contagiados por la misma espía del Intelligence Service.

Durante su etapa al frente de la Academia Militar de Zaragoza se convierte en un punto de referencia social en la ciudad. Se codea con lo mejorcito, aunque de vez en cuando vaya en coche hasta Valencia a ver a Nicolás, que trabaja como ingeniero naval en una empresa de Juan March, o a Madrid, a comerse el lacón con grelos que tan excelentemente hacía su hermana Pilar. Su sobrina Pilar Jaraiz Franco sigue haciéndolo estupendamente. En Zaragoza, Franco es una figura social y militar, consultado mediante los rudimentarios teléfonos de la época por los altos oficiales que desde Madrid asistían nerviosos a la caída de la dictadura, el desgaste del rey: "¿Tú qué harías si se provoca la caída del rey?" le preguntan Berenguer y Millán Astray. Y él contesta con otra pregunta: "¿Qué haría Sanjurjo?" Le contestan: "Nada". Pues si Sanjurjo, que es el jefe de la Guardia Civil, no haría nada, Franquito tampoco.

Y cae el rey y llega la República, y Azaña le cierra la academia. Pobre Azaña, Franco no le cazó nunca para hacerle pagar esta agresión a su ilusión y su soberbia, pero sí cazó a su cuñado Rivas Cheriff, en el mismo lote de Companys, Joan Peiró y Julián Zugazagoitia, devueltos por la Gestapo alemana a la *gestapo* franquista. Los tres políticos fueron fusilados. Rivas Cheriff, sin otras responsabilidades que haber sido hombre de teatro y secretario de su cuñado Azaña, pasó largos, larguísimos años en el penal del Dueso. Azaña y Prieto sabían que Franco era el militar más peligroso, mal compensado por el republicanismo de su hermano Ramón, autor de una de las exposiciones más insultantes que jamás nadie se atreviera a hacer a ¡Franco, Franco, Franco!: "Si desciendes de tu tronito de general y te das un paseo por el estado llano de capitanes y tenientes, verás que pocos piensan como tú y cuán cerca estamos de la República", y tras este toque lo deja para el arrastre:

Como estoy profundamente convencido de que los males de España no se curan con la monarquía, por eso soy republicano, ¿está bien claro? Creo sería una gran desdicha para España que perdurase la monarquía. Hoy se es más patriota siendo republicano que siendo monárquico, pero claro es, esto es incomprensible cuando la vida que se ha creado uno le lleva a tratarse con las clases aristocráticas y más acomodadas del país, como te pasa a ti.

Todavía es tiempo de que rectifiques tu conducta y no pierdas el tuyo en vanos consejos de burgués. Tu figura, al lado de la República, se agigantaría; al lado de la monarquía, pierdes los laureles tan bien ganados en Marruecos. Si te gusta una postura más cómoda, más de cuco, siéntete constitucionalista como han hecho muchos políticos viejos y conviértete en censor de la pureza de las nuevas elecciones, y no olvides que se puede ser amigo de la persona del rey —aunque el monarca no lo sea tuyo— y ser un buen republicano. A la República no debe irse por odios, solamente por ideales, y cuanto más amigo se fuere del rey y más favores se hayan alcanzado de él, más mérito tiene ser republicano.

Ni caso. Pero por si acaso, cuando Ramón tuvo que exilarse, Paquito le mandó 2.000 pesetas, porque un Franco no debe hacer el ridículo en el extranjero, aunque sea republicano, masón y anarquista, futuro diputado de Esquerra Republicana y colaborador de Blas Infante en el renacimiento de Al Andalus. Tampoco se subleva Franco con Sanjurjo en 1932, pero ayuda a reprimir salvajemente la revuelta asturiana de 1934, la Legión por delante, la misma Legión a la que había permitido cortar orejas y cabezas de los moros muertos o acribillarlos *in situ* si se ponían plañideramente pesados (lean, si quieren comprobarlo, la primera edición de *Diario de una bandera*).

Así como Kindelán, Mola, Orgaz, Galera, Barba... estuvieron conspirando contra la República desde que fue proclamada, Franco se dejaba querer y ayudaba indirectamente, devolviendo posiciones claves a militares antirrepublicanos durante su etapa de jefe de Estado Mayor a las órdenes del ministro Gil-Robles. Se dejaba querer y tardó en subirse a la conspiración del 36, hasta el punto de que sus compañeros de conjura llegaron a llamarle Miss Canarias por lo mucho que se dejaba cortejar, y Queipo, cuando supo que Franco se había cortado el bigote para subir al *Dragon Rapide* y así poder encabezar la Cruzada desde África, comentó: "Ese bigote es lo único que Franco ha sacrificado por el Alzamiento". No era cierto. Se jugaba una carrera militar, aunque don Juan March ya le había prometido cubrirle las espaldas en caso de fracaso y exilio. Se suma al Alzamiento a las órdenes de Sanjurjo, porque Goded no hubiera tolerado que lo encabezara Franco, y las simpatías de Franco por Goded eran equivalentes. "No hay mal que por bien no venga", es una frase constante en boca y pluma de Franco y la pronuncia cuando se le mueren Sanjurjo, Mola, o le matan, muchos años después, a su mano derecha, Carrero Blanco. Tiene algo de síndrome de viuda, desconsolada en un primer momento, pero consciente de que la desaparición del marido le va a dejar un espacio libre que podrá recuperar.

La muerte de Sanjurjo, el fracaso y fusilamiento de Goded en Barcelona y la poca ambición de Mola le convierten en el jefe *in pectore* del bando rebelde, por más que, necesitado siempre de poseer la razón jurídica, llamara rebeldes a los otros, a los que defendían el Gobierno legítimo de la República. Esta curiosa contradicción la observó el mismísimo Serrano Súñer, su cuñado, quien junto a Nicolás Franco y Matilde Fuset componen la tríada de pigmaliones que hicieron de aquel caudillo militar un caudillo político. Al recibir el mando único de los ejércitos y posteriormente del conglomerado político que respaldaba la Cruzada, Franco deja de ser responsable ante los hombres y ya sólo lo será ante Dios y ante la historia. La jerarquía católica española le pone bajo palio, cerrando los ojos a los horrores que está causando la Cruzada y a los que causará en una de las posguerras más largas de la historia de la humanidad. Franco ya ha dejado de ser, para siempre, Franquito, y cuando él lo olvide momentáneamente, la señora, es decir, doña Carmen Polo, se lo recordará. Es un rey sin corona, que juega con el aspirante a rey, don Juan, entre 1939 y 1946: Franco de ratón y don Juan de gato; pero a partir del encuentro de 1948 en el Azor y del respaldo norteamericano y vaticanista de los primeros años cincuenta, Franco será el gato y don Juan el ratón. Por eso alguna vez Franco dijo: "Yo no seré nunca una reina madre".

¿Cómo iba a ser una reina madre un hombre cuya estatura personal, militar, providencial sería jaleada como si se tratara de un dios o a lo sumo la estatua de Dios en una perpetua procesión de Semana Santa?

> Oh, ruina del Alcázar. / Yo mirarte no puedo, / convulsa flor de otoño, sin asombro. / Vivero de esforzados capitanes, / Nido de gavilanes. / Huevo de águila: Franco es el que nombro.

De momento Gerardo Diego ya le ha confesado su amor. Pero atiendan al rosario de declaraciones: "El Caudillo es como la encarnación de la patria y tiene el poder recibido por Dios para gobernarnos..." (del *Catecismo patriótico español*, publicado en Salamanca en 1939). Ridruejo tampoco se había quedado corto: "Padre de paz en armas, tu bravura / ya en Occidente extrema la sorpresa, / en Levante dilata la hermosura..." *La Estafeta Literaria* lo compara con Cervantes, sin duda tras haber leído *Diario de una bandera* o *Raza*. Manuel Aznar, abuelo del actual jefe del gobierno español y un galápago de mucho cuidado, proclama que Franco era arquitecto de capitanes de la historia y que su espada estaba por encima de la que había vencido a los sarracenos en las Navas de Tolosa. Cunqueiro, Álvaro, tuvo un orgasmo y, tras sostener que Franco era el Sol, añadía que la mirada del Señor le escogió entre los soldados: "De ella está ungido. El Señor bruñó su espada y el santo Uriel arcángel le enseñó a pasearse entre las llamas..." Laín Entralgo afirma que al burgués y al empresario hay que oponerle el modelo de jefe, "más acorde con nuestro concepto militar de la vida". Pero quizá nadie como Pemán y Ernesto Jiménez Caballero para poner las cosas en su sitio. Empecemos por Jiménez Caballero, el partidario de casar a Pilar Primo de Rivera con Hitler y de masculinizar la Falange hasta el punto de llamarla Falanjo: "Nosotros hemos visto caer lágrimas de Franco sobre el cuerpo de esta madre, de esta mujer, de esta hija suya que es España, mientras en las manos le corría la sangre y el dolor del sacro cuerpo en estertores. ¿Quién se ha metido en las entrañas de España como Franco, hasta el punto de no saber ya si Franco es España o España es Franco? ¡Oh, Franco, caudillo nuestro, padre de España! ¡Adelante! ¡Atrás, canallas y sabandijas del mundo!"

En cuanto a Pemán, a él se debe uno de los botafumeiros más impresionantes que perfumaron de incienso la efigie del Caudillo y avalaron aquel ¡Franco, Franco, Franco!:

Sabe marchar bajo palio con ese paso natural y exacto que parece que va sometiéndose por España y disculpándose por él. Se le transparenta en el gesto paternal la clara conciencia de lo que tiene de ancha totalidad nacional la obra que él resume y preside. Parece que lleva consigo a todas las ceremonias y liturgias protocolarias el honor de los caídos. Parece que lleva, sobre su pecho, la laureada como ofreciéndosela, un poco, a todos. Éste era el caudillo que necesitaba esta hora de España, difícil, delicada y de frágil tratamiento, como toda contienda civil. Todo, la guerra o la integración, el avance cotidiano o el cotidiano gobierno, había que manipularlo con mano firme y suave. Se necesitaba un hombre cuya imparcialidad fuera absoluta, cuya energía fuese serena, cuya paciencia fuese total. Había que tener un pulso exacto para combatir sin odio y atraer sin remordimiento. Había que escuchar a todos y no transigir con nadie. Había que llevar hacia allí, en dosis exactas, el perdón, el castigo y la catequesis, como hacia aquí, en exactas paridades, la camisa azul, la boina roja y la estrella de capitán general. Conquistó la zona roja como si la acariciara: ahorrando vidas, limitando bombardeos. No se dejó arrebatar nunca porque estaba seguro de España y de sí mismo. Éste es Francisco Franco, Caudillo de España. Concedámosle, españoles, el ancho y silencioso crédito que se tiene ganado. En Viñuelas hay un hombre que sabe dónde va. Que lo supo siempre. Y que, gracias a su paso inalterable sobre toda impaciencia, nos devolvió a España a su tiempo y nos rescató intactas muchas cosas que estuvieron en gran peligro. Lo que hizo en la guerra, lo hará en la paz.

Enriquecido por la aportación política de Serrano, Franco, a medida que crecía bajo el palio, buscaba colaboradores aduladores, militantes en aquella *cruzada de la adulación* a la que se refirió su propio cuñado. Pacón, el teniente general Francisco Franco Salgado Araujo, en sus memorias póstumas, se hace cruces sobre la insensibilidad de su primo para darse cuenta de tanto pelotilleo. No hay que olvidar que a lo largo de su caudillaje, ya no Franquito, ya definitivamente ¡Franco. Franco, Franco!, fue comparado con Napoleón, Fernando el Católico, el Gran Capitán, Agamenón (difícil de entender), César, Almanzor, Federico II de Prusia, Recaredo... El cardenal Plá y Deniel aprovechó el sermón de bodas dirigido a Carmen Franco y el marqués de Villaverde para equiparar la pareja de la Virgen María y San José con la de Franco y doña Carmen. La lista de metáforas da que pensar sobre la poesía como laboratorio del lenguaje: desde "padre adoptivo de la provincia" hasta "la figura más importante del siglo XX", pasando por "espiga de la paz", "vencedor del dragón de siete colas", "el cirujano necesario", "el gran arquitecto", "el redentor de los presos", "guerrero elegido por la gracia de Dios", "vencedor de la muerte", "el que sube las cuestas que es un contento", "clínicamente genial", "enviado de Dios", "padre que ama y vigila", "voz de hierro", "centinela de Occidente", cientos, miles de imágenes de esplendor y gloria.

243

Pero yo me quedo con aquella perla que le dedicara Joaquín Arrarás cuando lo imaginaba conduciendo la nave de la nueva España, la nave de la muerte, la tortura, la expatriación, la desidentificación para tantos de sus compatriotas: "Timonel de la dulce sonrisa".

Literatura o Historia

No ignoro que las teorías dominantes sobre crítica literaria tienden a prescindir de las explicaciones que pueda dar el autor sobre el por qué o para qué o cómo de su obra. La obra debe decirlo todo, pero cuando una novela como *Autobiografía del general Franco* se basa en la falsificación misma de *lo histórico*, creo que el autor merece ser escuchado, sobre todo porque ha suscitado la mirada recelosa de algunos historiadores, sin duda los científicos más celosos de su territorio. Yo había tenido 36 años de cohabitación con Franco y la cultura franquista, desde que nací hasta que Franco murió. Aparte de esta legitimación biológica de mi conocimiento de Franco, a fines de los años 60 recibí el encargo de José Martínez, responsable de *El Ruedo Ibérico*, de redactar un libro de pensamientos de Franco, parodia de *El libro rojo de Mao*. Así nació *El libro pardo del general*, publicado en París sin que yo, naturalmente, lo firmara. Escribirlo significó un vaciado del pensamiento de Franco a partir de sus discursos y escritos, y sobre esta base redacté *Los demonios familiares de Franco*, publicado por Dopesa después de la muerte del dictador. Estaba pues documentalmente preparado cuando me llegó la propuesta de editorial Planeta de escribir un *Yo Franco*, dentro de una colección de supuestas autobiografías, meritorio empeño demasiado ancho para mí, porque jamás me han gustado desafíos literarios que me parezcan algo así como construir la Catedral de Nôtre Dame con mondadientes. Si me enfrentaba al desafío de novelar la vida de Franco, yo sólo podía hacerlo desde la tensión dialéctica del antifranquismo. Tras darle muchas vueltas a la estrategia narrativa, creo que resolví a mi medida los dos problemas previos fundamentales en toda novela: el punto de vista y la verosimilitud lingüística. El punto de vista de una autobiografía de Franco como la mía no es Franco, sino el novelista que ha recibido el encargo, que padecerá a lo largo de todo el libro una escisión entre el mandato profesional y la rebelión personal contra el franquismo. La verosimilitud lingüística pasaba por dotar a Franco de un lenguaje verosímil que no fuera en sí mismo paródico, porque eso hubiera desautorizado al supuesto novelista Marcial Pombo, que le está redactando una autobiografía a su medida

Pero, ¿cómo escribía Franco? Tenemos textos de juventud como *Diario de una bandera*, sus *discursos trascendentales*, los artículos, generalmente sobre masonería, que firmó con el seudónimo Jokin Bor, algunas páginas de lo que iba a ser, ésta sí, su autobiografía, que transcribió su médico el Dr. Pozuelo. A partir de estos referentes construí un lenguaje digno y pulcro, porque Franco lo emplea para autojustificarse y ningún autobiografiado utiliza la autobiografía para autodestruirse. Es una escritura supuesta y verosímil en relación a la estrategia del libro, independientemente de que hubiera sido la escritura real de Franco. Algunos historiadores me reprocharon la excesiva dignidad del código lingüístico del Caudillo, los mismos que se molestaron porque el libro es una inculpación no sólo de Franco sino de los sectores sociales que lo hicieron posible y le ayudaron a sucederse a sí mismo durante casi cuarenta años. Es empeño especial de cierta historiografía española *objetiva* cargar a Franco con todas las cadenas que quitan a los poderes fácticos y a la sociedad cómplice, tal vez porque algunos de esos historiadores provienen de esos sectores y demonizar a Franco significa angelizar a sus propios ancestros

Cuando la novela salió al mercado fue un éxito de ventas sin duda condicionado por la atmósfera que acompaña a todo centenario, y junto a ella aparecieron otros libros apologéticos de Franco, así como la necesaria biografía de Paul Preston. De todas las críticas que se hicieron a mi *Autobiografía del general Franco* la más injusta por lo futil fue una anónima, perdida entre los pliegues de un balance de novedades, publicada en *El País*, en la que se decía que mi visión de Franco era la Coca-Cola y la que había escrito Vizcaíno Casas era la Pepsi-Cola, como si el editor hubiera prefabricado la competencia para cubrir todo el espectro del mercado. Yo desconocía que Vizcaíno Casas fuera a competir conmigo y escribí desde toda clase de angustias la novela más difícil por lo que tenía de condicionantes pretextuales: materia histórica, los hechos ineludibles, documentos, implicación ideológica, voluntad de contribuir a una memoria histórica antifranquista, la única memoria que se merece uno de los criminales de guerra más mediocres del pasado siglo. Al hacer el que supongo último balance por mi parte de aquella novela, descubro que fue ante todo un problema lingüístico: encontrar el código de un sujeto bifronte, franquismo y antifranquismo, puesto que la novela es al mismo tiempo la autobiografía de Franco y de la oposición que él mismo magnificó y la que realmente mantuvo la resistencia desde 1939 hasta el final.

Como siempre ocurre en literatura, la verdad de *Autobiografía del general Franco* no depende de la verdad de los hechos o los datos o de la bondad o maldad de las ideas, sino de la veracidad literaria que se consigue mediante palabras estratégicamente distribuidas para conseguir ofrecer una alternativa a la realidad. Pero Franco aún pertenece a las pesadillas de muchos de los que le sobrevivimos y hasta que no nos muramos todos los verdugos y las víctimas, la literatura hecha a la desmedida de aquella peripecia no obtendrá la prerrogativa de ser leída literariamente.

Contributors

Salvador Cardús is Doctor in Economics by the Universitat Autònoma de Barcelona and Professor of Sociology at the same university. He has held visiting appointments in several other academic institutions, including Cambridge University. Among the books he has authored, *Plegar de viure* (Barcelona: Edicions 62, 1981), *Saber el temps* (Barcelona: Alta Fulla, 1985), *Política de paper. Premsa i poder a Catalunya (1981-1992)* (Barcelona: La Campana, 1995), and *El desconcert de l'educació* (Barcelona: La Campana, 2000) are particularly noteworthy. He has edited *La mirada del sociòleg* (Barcelona: Proa, 1999). In addition to contributing over fifty chapters to collective volumes and numerous articles to specialized journals, he writes regularly for the newspaper *Avui*, of which he was associate editor between 1989 and 1991. He is a founding member of the Catalan Sociological Society, a member of the British Association for the Study of Ethnicity and Nationalism, and a member of the Foundation for the Collective Rights of Peoples. Among other distinctions, he received the National Award for Journalism of Catalonia's Generalitat and the Journalism Prize "Serra i Moret."

Christina Dupláa is Associate Professor at Dartmouth College. She received a Ph.D. in Hispanic and Luso-Brazilian literature from the University of Minnesota, having previously obtained degrees in Journalism and History. She is the author of *La voz testimonial en Montserrat Roig* (Barcelona: Icaria, 1996) and has coedited *Las nacionalidades del Estado español: una problemática cultural* (Minneapolis: University of Minnesota Press, 1986), *Spain Today. Essays on Literature, Culture, Society* (Hanover: Dartmouth College, 1995), and *Breve historia feminista de la literatura catalana, gallega y vasca* (Barcelona: Anthropos, 2000). She has published articles on the representation of women in the culture of Catalan nationalism, on feminism, and on the writing of resistance. She is now at work on a book about memory in the narrative of Josefina R. Aldecoa.

Ofelia Ferrán received a Ph.D. in Romance Studies from Cornell University. An Assistant Professor at the University of Minnesota, she has published articles on contemporary Spanish literature and culture. Her research interests include women's writing, exile, memory, autobiography, and Catalan literature and culture. She is currently working on a book on narrative constructions of memory in contemporary Spanish literature.

David Herzberger is Professor of Spanish and Comparative Literature and Head of the Department of Modern and Classical Languages at the University of Connecticut. He is the author of books on Juan Benet and Jesús Fernández Santos and, more recently, of *Narrating the Past: Fiction and Historiography in Post-War Spain* (Durham, NC: Duke University Press, 1995). He has also co-edited two books on modern Spanish literature. He serves on the editorial board of several journals; his major field of research is the novel and theater of contemporary Spain.

Dieter Ingenschay is Professor of Hispanic Literatures at the Humboldt-University of Berlin. Currently he is the President of the Deutscher Hispanistenverband. His main areas of interest are contemporary hispanic literatures, city literature, Gender and Gay Studies, and the relations between literature and anthropology. He is the author of *Alltagswelt und Selbsterfahrung: Ballade und Testament bei Deschamps und Villon* (Munich: Wilhelm Fink Verlag, 1986) and co-editor of the following books: *Abriendo caminos. La literatura española desde 1975* (Barcelona: Lumen, 1994); *La novela española actual. Autores y tendencias* (Kassel: Reichenberger, 1995); *Werk und Diskurs. K. Stierle zum 60. Geburtstag* (München: Wilhelm Fink Verlag, 1999); *Proust und die Kritik* (Frankfurt am Main: Insel Verlag, 2000); *Die andere Stadt. Großstadtbilder in der Perspektive des peripheren Blicks* (Würzburg: Königshausen & Neumann 2000).

Jo Labanyi is Professor of Modern Spanish Literature and Cultural Studies at Birkbeck College London, and Director of the Institute of Romance Studies, University of London. Her books include *Spanish Cultural Studies: An Introduction* (edited with Helen Graham) (Oxford University Press, 1995), *Culture and Gender in Nineteenth-Century Spain* (edited with Lou Charnon-Deutsch) (Oxford University Press, 1995), *Gender and Modernization in the Spanish Realist Novel* (Oxford University Press, 2000), and the edited

248

volume *Constructing Identity in Twentieth-Century Spain: Theoretical Concepts and Cultural Practice* (Oxford University Press, forthcoming). She is curently writing a book on cinema of the early Franco period, and is co-ordinator of a 5-year AHRB-funded collaborative research project "An oral history of cinema-going in 1940s and 1950s Spain." She is founding editor of the *Journal of Spanish Cultural Studies*.

Joan Ramon Resina is Professor of Romance Studies and Comparative Literature at Cornell University. He is the author of *La búsqueda del Grial* (Barcelona: Anthropos, 1988); *Un sueño de piedra: Ensayos sobre la literatura del modernismo europeo* (Barcelona: Anthropos, 1990); *Los usos del clásico* (Barcelona: Anthropos, 1991); *El cadáver en la cocina. La novela policiaca en la cultura del desencanto* (Barcelona: Anthropos, 1997). He has edited three volumes: *Mythopoesis: Literatura, totalidad, ideología* (Barcelona: Anthropos, 1992); *El aeroplano y la estrella: el movimiento vanguardista en los Países Catalanes (1904-1936)* (Amsterdam: Rodopi, 1997); *Iberian Cities* (New York: Garland, forthcoming). He is the editor of the journal *Diacritics*.

Philip W. Silver, Professor of Spanish Literature at Columbia University, is a scholar and interpreter of Spain's literature and culture, specializing in the areas of poetry, philosophy, and drama. Among his books he considers as especially worthy of note: *Ruin and Restitution: Reinterpreting Romanticism in Spain* (Nashville: Vanderbilt University Press, 1997); *Luis Cernuda: el poeta en su leyenda* (Madrid: Castalia, 1995), *Nacionalismos y transicion: Euskadi, Catalunya, España* (San Sebastian: Txertoa, 1988), and *Ortega as Phenomenologist: The Genesis of «Meditations on Quixote»* (New York: Columbia University Press, 1978).

Maarten Steenmeijer is Associate Professor at the University of Nijmegen. His areas of specialization are modern and contemporary Spanish and Spanish American Literature. In addition to numerous articles and translations (*La Regenta*, the '27 Generation, Sábato, Paz, Onetti, Quiroga, and others), his publications include *Bibliografía de las traducciones de la literatura española e hispanoamericana al holandés* (1946-1990) (Tübingen: Max Niemeyer, 1991), *Spanje is anders* (Amsterdam: Wereldbibliotheek,

1992), *Mythenbouwers van de Nieuwe Wereld* (Amsterdam: Wereldbibliotheek, 1996) and *Moderne Spaanse en Spaans-Amerikaanse literatuur* (Groningen: Martinus Nijhoff, 1996). He has co-edited *La nueva novela histórica hispanoamericana* (Amsterdam: Rodopi, 1991) and *Asimilaciones y rechazos: presencias del romanticismo en el realismo español del siglo XIX* (Amsterdam: Rodopi, 1999).

Manuel Vázquez Montalbán has degrees in Philosophy and Journalism. Essayist, poet, and author of fiction, he has contributed to a number of journals, among which: *Triunfo*, *Por Favor*, *Tele Express*, and *Interviú*. Currently, he is a regular contributor to the newspapers *El País* and *Avui*. Among his many awards are the Grand Prix Littérature Policière Etrangère (1981), the Deutscher Krimi Preis International (1986), Recalmare Prize (1989), Deutscher Kritiker Preis (1989), Premio Nacional de Narrativa (1991), Europe Prize (1992), Premio Nacional de la Crítica (1994), Premio Nacional de las Letras Españolas (1995). He holds the Creu de Sant Jordi, the highest distinction bestowed by the Generalitat de Catalunya for services rendered to Catalonia. Best known as creator of the popular detective Pepe Carvalho, the protagonist of sixteen novels and several short stories, Vázquez Montalbán has also written a number of other highly profiled novels, such as *El pianista* (1985), *Galíndez* (1990), *Autobiografía del general Franco* (1992), *O César o nada* (1998), and extensive essays on social, political, and literary issues.

Lightning Source UK Ltd.
Milton Keynes UK

171125UK00002B/53/A